Chapter 2　Brunei

Chapter 3　Cambodia

Chapter 4　Indonesia

Chapter 5　Laos

Chapter 6　Myanmar

Chapter 7 The Philippines

Chapter 8 Singapore

Chapter 9 Thailand

Chapter 10 Vietnam

Chapter 11 Malaysia

高等院校特色课程英语系列教材

东盟国家社会与文化

第二版

主　编：汤燕瑜　邬跃生　沈燕琼
副主编：唐　晓　沈　斌　班光语　张树德
编　者：(按拼音顺序排列)
　　　　崔　凯　甘　昕　何　兵　刘卫玲
　　　　刘卫平　吕晶晶　宁　波　欧阳海鹏
　　　　沈　斌　唐　晓　汪　婧　闫爱花
　　　　杨　宏　杨　青　袁式亮　张晓梅
　　　　张元芳　钟运生

苏州大学出版社
Soochow University Press

图书在版编目(CIP)数据

东盟国家社会与文化 / 汤燕瑜,邬跃生,沈燕琼主编. —2版. —苏州:苏州大学出版社,2015.11 (2025.1重印)
高等院校特色课程英语系列教材
ISBN 978-7-5672-1574-0

Ⅰ.①东… Ⅱ.①汤… ②邬… ③沈… Ⅲ.①英语－阅读教学－高等学校－教材②东南亚国家联盟－会员国－概况 Ⅳ.①H319.4;K

中国版本图书馆CIP数据核字(2015)第274651号

书　　　名:	东盟国家社会与文化(第二版)
主　　编:	汤燕瑜　邬跃生　沈燕琼
责任编辑:	杨　华
装帧设计:	刘　俊
出版发行:	苏州大学出版社(Soochow University Press)
社　　　址:	苏州市十梓街1号　邮编:215006
印　　　刷:	广东虎彩云印刷有限公司
邮购热线:	0512-67480030
销售热线:	0512-67481020
开　　　本:	787 mm×1 092 mm　印张:17.5　插页:1　字数:423千
版　　　次:	2015年11月第2版
印　　　次:	2025年 1月第3次印刷
书　　　号:	ISBN 978-7-5672-1574-0
定　　　价:	45.00元

凡购本社图书发现印装错误,请与本社联系调换。服务热线:0512-67481020

第二版前言

  高等院校特色课程英语教材《东盟国家社会与文化》是在东盟国家与中国合作关系进入新阶段,经贸合作发展迅速,培养中国—东盟经济发展人才成为社会各界关注的焦点的背景下问世的。教材编写体现了主动适应经济社会发展的人才培养思路,为中国—东盟经济发展人才培养提供有力的支撑。

  教材内容丰富新颖,实用性强,既包含了相关国家的基本概况,又向学习者介绍了中国—东盟自由贸易区、东盟10+3会议、中国—东盟博览会等组织、机构、会展的相关知识,可使学习者了解东盟国家简史,东盟各国的经济、政治、文化发展状况,了解中国—东盟自由贸易区的基本情况与信息,进一步认识建立中国—东盟自由贸易区对我国经济发展的重要意义,从而为服务区域经济发展而做好积极准备。

  该教材是目前国内鲜见的关于东盟国家社会与文化的英文版教材,已在国内高校使用,许多高校图书馆将该书收为馆藏或列为推荐书目。教材的出版不仅使学习者了解东盟各国的社会文化,了解中国—东盟自由贸易区的基本情况,同时对拓展专业相关知识课程,丰富课程体系,对学科专业建设起到积极的作用。我们结合教材研制开发的多媒体网络课件获全国第八届课件大赛二等奖,广西高等教育教学软件大赛一等奖、最佳艺术效果奖。2011年通过广西壮族自治区专家评审获推荐参加全国"十二五"规划教材遴选殊荣。该书出版及投入使用以来,社会反映良好。根据经济、社会的新发展与读者的需求,我们在原有的基础上对全书的一些内容进行更新,主要修订人口、经济总量及时效性信息内容,使之更好地反映东盟各国经济文化的新发展,以及中国—东盟自由贸易区经济合作的新发展。

  在本次修订工作中,汤燕瑜、邬跃生、沈燕琼担任主编,袁式亮、宁波、吕晶晶、甘昕等对教材进行了认真细致的修订,为修订工作的顺利完成付出了心血。

  修订版中还会有不足之处,敬请广大读者提出宝贵意见。

编 者
2015年10月

前　言

东盟国家是中国的友好邻邦,与中国或山水相依,或隔海相望。东盟与中国有着友好往来的传统。进入新世纪以来,双方合作关系进入新阶段,政治互信不断加深,经贸合作发展迅速。2001年东盟和中国10+1领导人会议一致同意建立中国—东盟自由贸易区,2002年正式确立了中国与东盟经济合作框架协议,2004年由广西创办每年一度的中国—东盟博览会国际性会议,促进双方商界合作。新的区域经济格局极大地推进了中国与东盟的经济发展,从而促进亚洲经济发展,引起了国际社会的广泛关注。了解东盟,认识东盟,打造中国—东盟交流合作平台,为中国—东盟经济发展培养专门人才已成为我国社会各界关注的焦点。为此,我们组织有关专家学者编写《东盟国家社会与文化》(英文版)一书,可作为大中专院校有关课程的教材,满足人才培养需求,也可以作为英语爱好者的读物。

《东盟国家社会与文化》聚焦于亚洲的一个区域性组织——东南亚国家联盟。全书共15章,分为两大板块。第一个板块从第1章到第11章,主题是东盟国家概况。该部分借助事实性的描述,从地理、政治、历史、经济、文化等各个视角展示东盟成员国的地貌气候、物产资源、悠久历史和灿烂文化。第二个板块从第12章到第15章,主题是东盟与中国。该板块以历史事件为线索,逐一梳理了东南亚国家联盟、东盟自由贸易区、中国—东盟自由贸易区、东盟10+3会议、中国—东盟博览会等组织、机构、展会的渊源、发展及其成就。读者通过本书,可了解东盟国家简史,东盟各国的经济、政治、文化发展状况,了解中国—东盟自由贸易区的基本情况与信息,进一步认识建立中国—东盟自由贸易区对我国经济发展的重要意义,从而为服务区域经济发展而作积极的准备。

《东盟国家社会与文化》由玉林师范学院汤燕瑜、梧州学院邬跃生担任主编,桂林师范高等专科学校唐晓、广西师范大学沈斌、钦州学院班光语和广西工学院张树德担任副主编,并组织相关院校老师编写。具体编写人员有:玉林师范学院宁波、袁式亮和张元芳,梧州学院刘卫平、何兵和闫爱花,广西工学院欧阳海鹏和杨宏,广西师范大学沈斌、崔凯和汪婧,桂林师范高等专科学校唐晓、杨青和张晓梅,钦州学院钟运生和刘卫玲。

成书之际,我们衷心感谢广西师范大学外国语学院陆巧玲教授帮助审校全部书稿,感谢玉林师范学院外语系外籍专家David Nkhata帮助参与部分英文的译审,以及其他院校外籍专家的审校;感谢苏州大学出版社对此书出版给予的大力支持。

由于编写者水平有限,书中还存在不少瑕疵和谬误,敬请读者和同行指正、批评!

编　者
2009年7月

Contents 目 录

Chapter 1 General Introduction to Southeast Asia

1.1　Brief Introduction ··· 1
1.2　Geographical Features ·· 2
1.3　History ··· 4
1.4　Diverse Political Systems ·· 9
1.5　The Unbalanced Economy Development ····················· 12
1.6　Multiplex Cultures ·· 16

Chapter 2 Brunei

2.1　Country Name ··· 19
2.2　National Symbols ··· 19
2.3　Geography ·· 20
2.4　Brief History ·· 22
2.5　Politics ·· 22
2.6　Economy ··· 25
2.7　Culture ·· 27

Chapter 3 Cambodia

3.1　Country Name ··· 33
3.2　National Symbols ··· 33
3.3　Geography ·· 34
3.4　Brief History ·· 38
3.5　Politics ·· 40

3.6　Economy ……………………………………………………… 42
3.7　Culture ………………………………………………………… 46

Chapter 4　Indonesia

4.1　Country Name ………………………………………………… 52
4.2　National Symbols ……………………………………………… 52
4.3　Geography ……………………………………………………… 53
4.4　Brief History …………………………………………………… 55
4.5　Politics ………………………………………………………… 56
4.6　Economy ……………………………………………………… 57
4.7　Culture ………………………………………………………… 58

Chapter 5　Laos

5.1　Country Name ………………………………………………… 63
5.2　National Symbols ……………………………………………… 63
5.3　Geography ……………………………………………………… 64
5.4　Brief History …………………………………………………… 67
5.5　Politics ………………………………………………………… 68
5.6　Economy ……………………………………………………… 70
5.7　Culture ………………………………………………………… 72

Chapter 6　Myanmar

6.1　Country Name ………………………………………………… 77
6.2　National Symbols ……………………………………………… 77
6.3　Geography ……………………………………………………… 78
6.4　Brief History …………………………………………………… 80
6.5　Politics ………………………………………………………… 81
6.6　Economy ……………………………………………………… 83
6.7　Culture ………………………………………………………… 89

Chapter 7　The Philippines

7.1	Country Name	93
7.2	National Symbols	93
7.3	Geography	94
7.4	Brief History	97
7.5	Politics	98
7.6	Economy	101
7.7	Culture	104

Chapter 8　Singapore

8.1	Country Name	110
8.2	National Symbols	110
8.3	Geography	111
8.4	Brief History	115
8.5	Politics	117
8.6	Economy	119
8.7	Culture	120

Chapter 9　Thailand

9.1	Country Name	124
9.2	National Symbols	124
9.3	Geography	125
9.4	Brief History	127
9.5	Politics	128
9.6	Economy	131
9.7	Culture	132

Chapter 10　Vietnam

10.1	Country Name	137
10.2	National Symbols	137
10.3	Geography	138

10.4	Brief History	141
10.5	Politics	141
10.6	Economy	145
10.7	Culture	148

Chapter 11 Malaysia

11.1	Brief Introduction	151
11.2	National Symbols	151
11.3	Geography	152
11.2	Brief History	154
11.5	Politics	155
11.6	Economy	158
11.7	Culture	160

Chapter 12 ASEAN

12.1	Establishment and Development	164
12.2	Aims and Purposes	165
12.3	Organization	166
12.4	Major Events and Achievements	169
12.5	"10+3" "10+1"	181

Chapter 13 ASEAN Free Trade Area

13.1	Birth of AFTA	195
13.2	The Framework and Contents of AFTA	196
13.3	Characteristics of AFTA	200
13.4	Significance of AFTA	206

Chapter 14 China-ASEAN Free Trade Area

14.1	The Emergence of China-ASEAN Free Trade Area	215
14.2	The Framework and Agreement of China-ASEAN FTA	218
14.3	The Significance of China-ASEAN FTA	221

14.4　Challenges of China-ASEAN FTA ………………………… 225

Chapter 15　China-ASEAN Expo

15.1　Proposal of CAEXPO ……………………………………… 229
15.2　The Contents and Purpose of CAEXPO …………………… 232
15.3　The First China-ASEAN Expo ……………………………… 234

Appendix China-ASEAN Documents ……………………………… 238

参考文献 ………………………………………………………………… 268

Chapter 1 *General Introduction to Southeast Asia*

CHAPTER 1

General Introduction to Southeast Asia

1.1 Brief Introduction

Lying to the south and between oceans far and away from China, Southeast Asia was called "Nanyang" in the past.

Southeast Asia includes 11 countries, Brunei, Cambodia, Indonesia, Laos, Malaysia, Myanmar, the Philippines, Singapore, Thailand, Vietnam and East Timor. East Timor, attaining its independence from Indonesia by referendum in October, 1999, is the youngest nation in Southeast Asia.

Southeast Asia, covering an area of 4,492,837.3 square kilometers, has a total population of about 623,181,539, most of which are oriental race, including several races belonging to the Sino-Tibetan language family, Hindi language family, Austro-Asiatic language family[1] and Malayo-Polynesian language family[2]. Among the above-mentioned races, the Javanese, Kinh (Viet), Thai, Burman, Lao, Khmer[3] and Sulu are the most populous. With an overseas Chinese population of over 20,000,000, Southeast Asia is the largest overseas Chinese community. Overseas Chinese in Singapore account for over 75%, then about 30% in Malaysia. Southeast Asia's population distribution is uneven. It mainly gathers in coastal plains, river-bank plains and estuary deltas with a few in mountainous areas and rainforest.

In Southeast Asia, the largest, also the most populous country is Indonesia, with an area of 1,904,443 square kilometers and a population of 255,500,000 (next only to China, India and the United States). The country with the smallest area (only 714.3 square kilometers) is Singapore; the whole country is just like a city and its area is equal to that of Dongxing, a county-level city in Guangxi of China; 20 kilometers from east to west, 30 kilometers from south to north, you can drive across the country in a day. Though it has the smallest area, Singapore has a population of 5,400,000, much more than that of Brunei, which covers an area of 5,765 square kilometers. As the least populous country in Southeast Asia, Brunei has only 393,000 people, just equal to the population of a small town in China.

Brief Introduction to 11 Countries in Southeast Asia (2015)

Country	Population	Area (sq. km)	Capital
Brunei	393,000	5,765	Bandar Seri Begawan
Cambodia	15,205,539	181,035	Phnum Penh
East Timor	1,178,000	14,874	Dili
Indonesia	255,500,000	1,904,443	Jakarta
Laos	6,646,000	236,800	Vientiane
Malaysia	30,000,000	330,257	Kuala Lumpur
Myanmar	51,419,000	676,578	Nay Pyi Taw
The Philippines	101,000,000	299,700	Manila
Singapore	5,400,000	714.3	Singapore
Thailand	67,200,000	513,115	Bangkok
Vietnam	90,000,000	329,556	Hanoi

Source: http://www.fmprc.gov.cn 来源：中华人民共和国外交部

1.2 Geographical Features

Southeast Asia is named after its location, the southeastern part of Asia. It stands from east longitude 93 degrees to 141.5 degrees, north latitude 25 degrees to south latitude 10 degrees, bestriding the equator. Most are tropical areas. Bordering on China in the north, overlooking Australia in the south, close to the Pacific Ocean in the east, facing the Indian Ocean in the west, and neighboring Bangladesh and India, Southeast Asia has very important geographical position. It links three continents (Asia, Africa and Oceania) and two oceans (the Pacific Ocean and the Indian Ocean). Lying between Malaya and Sumatra Island(苏门答腊岛), the Malacca Strait(马六甲海峡) (total length of about 900 km, the narrowest part is only 37 km) is the shortest and the only sea route from Northeast Asia through Southeast Asia to Europe and Africa, and it has always been a strategic point.

Southeast Asia consists of the Indo-China Peninsula[4] and Malay Islands[5]. With an area of about 2,100,000 square kilometers, the Indo-China Peninsula is named after its location, the southern part of China. Its long and narrow southern part almost reaches down to the equator, where it becomes Malaya. In the Indo-China Peninsula, there are 7 countries, Vietnam, Laos, Myanmar, Cambodia, Thailand, Malaysia and Singapore. Among them, Laos is the only land-locked country without a coastline; Malaysia consists of Malaya in the southern part of the Indo-China Peninsula [Malaya area in southern part ("West Malaysia")], and Sabah(沙巴) and Sarawak(沙捞越) in the northern part of Kalimantan Island(加里曼丹岛) ("East Malaysia"). Located between the southeastern part of the Indo-China Peninsula and the northern part of Australia, between the Pacific Ocean and the Indian Ocean, Malay Islands is made up of over 20,000 islands. 3,500 km from south to north and 6,400 km from east to west, it covers more than 2,300,000 square kilometers in total. Indonesia and the Philippines are island countries in Southeast Asia. Brunei is located on Kalimantan Island. East Timor's territory contains the eastern part of Timor, Oecusse(欧库西) of the north coast in the western part and neighboring Pulau Atauro(阿陶罗岛).

To sum up, Southeast Asia's geography has two outstanding characteristics: one is "heat" and the other is "sea".

"Heat"

"Heat" refers to the tropical areas. Standing in low latitudes, most of Southeast Asia is situated to the south of the Tropic of Cancer[6] and near the equator. It is hot all the year round as if it's only got one season—summer with an annual average temperature between 25℃ and 30℃. There is little difference in temperature between the coldest and the hottest month, less than 2℃ near the equator. However, diurnal temperature difference within 24 hours is greater than the difference between the hottest and coldest month of the year. For example, the Pontianak(坤甸), in Kalimantan Island, has an annual temperature difference of 2℃ while the diurnal temperature difference is 7℃. There is an exception that the northern part close to China has four seasons—spring, summer, autumn and winter. Most areas have just two seasons—dry season(November to May next year) and rainy season(June to October). Frequently exposed to the sun, people here have dark skin color.

Considering the rainfall, there are two climate types: tropical monsoon climate and tropical rainforest climate. The northern parts of the Indo-China Peninsula and the Philippines belong to the tropical monsoon climate type with an annual average rainfall about 1,500 mm. The areas (north latitude 5 degrees to south latitude 5 degrees) near the equator, or the southern part of Malaya and the most of the Malaysian, are of tropical rainforest climate. It rains all the year round with an annual average rainfall over 2,000 mm. The period, from April to May, is the hottest with least rainfall.

"Sea"

Except for Laos, Southeast Asian nations are all coastal countries or island countries. Indonesia, named "the Land of Ten Thousand Islands", has over 17,000 islands. The Philippines, named "the Land of Thousand Islands", has 7,083 islands. Brunei is located in the northwest of Kalimantan Island. In these countries, the common transport between islands is ship. As a result, the high population density puts great pressure on the traffic.

Based on the terrain and geology, Southeast Asia can be divided into "stable" and "unstable" regions. The Indo-China Peninsula and Kalimantan Island belong to the "stable" region while the other islands belong to the "unstable" region. The mountains there were formed during the Himalaya Mountains building in the Tertiary period[7]. Precipitous and coastal, some are even active volcanoes. Volcano eruption and earthquakes frequently occur in Indonesia and the Philippines. Malaysia is one of the areas with the most volcanoes in the world.

The mountains on the Indo-China Peninsula are north-south directional. The Himalayas, go from Tibet towards the east, then turn south at the common boundary of Yunnan Province, China and Myanmar. The main rivers in Southeast Asia all gather in the Indo-China Peninsula, flowing to the seas from north to south following the mountains. The main rivers include the Mekong River, the Red River, the Menam River (湄南河), the Salween River(萨尔温江), and the Irrawaddy River(伊洛瓦底江). The Mekong River, with a total length of 4,400 kilometers, is not only the biggest river in Southeast Asia but also one of the most important international rivers in the world. It sources from Qinghai-Tibet Plateau, crossing Myanmar, Laos, Thailand, Cambodia (the number nations crossed being next only to the Danube River in Europe), and flows to the sea from Vietnam.

History

The 11 Southeast Asian nations have some differences in their economic and social development process, but they all experienced three historical development stages: ancient, modern and present. We mainly talk about the ancient times and modern times in the following.

Chapter 1 General Introduction to Southeast Asia

 **Ancient Times**

(1) The most important ancient country in the Indo-China Peninsula—Cambodia

In the north of the Indo-China Peninsula, there are three countries from east to west boadering China—Vietnam, Laos and Myanmar. There was no real country within Vietnam's borders before the 3rd century AD. Since putting Lingnan down in the Qin Dynasty, China had set up county in the north and the center of Vietnam for over 1,000 years. Until 968 AD Dinh Hoàn founded an independent country. Laos is located to the west of Northern Vietnam. In 1353, King Fa Ngum(法昂) established the first centralized state ruling the whole Laos—Lao Kingdom of Lan Xang(澜沧王国) in Luang Prabang(琅勃拉邦). For 300 years Lan Xang had influence reaching present-day Cambodia and Thailand, as well as all of what is now Laos. Afterwards, Laos was invaded by Vietnam, Myanmar and Thailand. Laos became the French colony in 1893. Myanmar is located to the west of Laos. There were 3 unified kingdoms in ancient Myanmar. The first one is the Pagan Kingdom(蒲甘王朝) established by Anawrahta(阿奴律陀) in 1057; then King Mingyinyo founded the Toungoo Dynasty in the 16th century; the last one is the Konbaung Dynasty established by Alaungpaya in 1752. Myanmar became the British colony in the late 19th century. Myanmar has longstanding grudge with Thailand. Thai chieftains gained independence from the Khmer Empire at Sukhothai(素可泰), which was established as the first sovereign kingdom by Pho Khun Si Indrathit in 1238. The Sukhothai Kingdom covers Luang Prabang in Laos, the northern part of Malaysian Peninsula, Dawei(土瓦), Bago(勃固) and Moktama(马都) in Myanmar. Then Thailand experienced the Kingdom of Ayutthaya(阿育他亚), the Kingdom of Dhonburi/Thon Buri(吞武里) and the Kingdom of Bangkok established in 1782. Although some ancient kingdoms like Kedah and Langkasuka appeared, only the Kingdom of Melaka established by Sumatra Prince Parames(拜里迷) had affected Southeast Asia. Its territory includes the north Sumatra and almost the whole Malaysian Peninsula, laying a strong foundation for present-day Malaysia. Malaysia was invaded by Portugal, the Netherlands and Britain from the 16th century. Malaysia became the French colony in the early 20th century.

Cambodia, located in the south of the Indo-China Peninsula, is an oriental country that has ever created splendid ancient civilization. The archaeologists found from 2000 BC to 1000 BC there lived people along the Lake Tonle Sap(洞里萨湖) and in the lower Mekong River valley and delta regions. As the inhabitants, they mixed with the immigrant Khmer to form Cambodian main ethnic group. The Khmer established the earliest known kingdom in the area, Funan(扶南王国), around the first century AD. The Funan Kingdom had developed marine trade, and become the most powerful country in the

Indo-China Peninsula. The Funan Kingdom began to fall in the second half of the 6th century until it was replaced by Chenla. The Chenla Kingdom lasted 9 centuries, including the early Chenla, Angkor and the late Chenla. During the peak period, Angkor Kingdom reached most of the Indo-China Peninsula, South Vietnam, Laos, Thailand, part of Myanmar and Malaysia. To showcase the powerful kingdom, the empire built the Angkor historical sites which were called the Four Wonders of Ancient East together with the Great Wall in China, the Pyramids in Egypt, and the Borobudur(婆罗浮屠) in Indonesia. The Angkor historical sites were built in 802 AD, made up of the Angkor Thom(吴哥寺), Angkor Wat(吴哥窟) and the Banteay Srei(女王宫). Over 600 architectures spread in the forest of 45 square kilometers. At the centre of the temple stands a quincunx of towers. These towers are believed to represent the five peaks of Mount Meru(麦如神山), the Home of Gods and Center of the Hindu Universe. Angkor Wat features the longest continuous bas-relief(浅浮雕) in the world, which runs along the outer gallery walls, narrating stories from Hindu mythology. The stone-caved relief sculptures(浮雕) in the cloister of Angkor Wat are the art treasure of the world.

(2) **Southeast Asia island country ancient civilization gathered in Indonesia**

Among thousands of islands in Indonesia, some are large, such as Kalimantan (Indonesia part about 540,000 square kilometers), Sumatra (450,000 square kilometers), Irian(伊里安岛)(Indonesia part about 400,000 square kilometers), Sulawesi(苏拉威西岛)(about 190,000 square kilometers), and Java (about 120,000 square kilometers). In the middle of the 7th century, the first powerful kingdom in history, the Sriwijaya / Srivijaya Empire(室利佛逝/三佛齐帝国) was founded in Sumatra. But it fell during the late 13th century and the 14th century, and was replaced by the Majapahit Kingdom. The Majapahit Kingdom reached its peak in the middle of the 14th century, with its territory covering Kalimantan, Sumatra, Irian, Sulawesi, Kepulauan Maluku(马鲁古群岛) and the northern part of the Malaysian Peninsula which laid a strong foundation for present-day Indonesia. The Majapahit Kingdom didn't last long, but left the largest Buddhism sites the Borobudur, marvelous as the Angkor Wat. It is a pyramid-shaped and 9-floor tower, 42 meters high. The Borobudur is full of relief sculptures on cloister on each floor,which brings a name "the Epic on the Stone[8]".

Modern Times

The modern time history of Southeast Asia is all about invasion, governance and colonialism. Except for Thailand, all the Southeast Asian countries were occupied and colonized by European powers. During the 1500s and 1600s the Europeans were able to take control of the international trade of Asia, thereby diverting the profits from this trade to Europe. As a result, the Europeans became stronger while Asian empires and kingdoms

Chapter 1 General Introduction to Southeast Asia

became weaker. By the 1800s the Europeans were in a position to establish their authority over much of Asia, particularly the Indian subcontinent and Southeast Asia. Six countries—Portugal, Spain, the Netherlands, Great Britain, France, and the United States—had colonies in Southeast Asia.

The Portuguese are the first who stepped in Southeast Asia. They captured Malacca (马六甲州) in 1511, holding it until the Dutch seized it in 1641. The Portuguese built up trading spots in Sumatra, Java, Kalimantan and Sulawesi, and seized "the Country of Spice[9]". The 400-year's colonial history of Southeast Asia began at that time.

Following Portugal, Spain began its colonism in the Far East. In 1521, Magellan was ordered by Spain to invade the Philippines. He navigated several times in 30 years. Finally, Spain ruled the Philippines from its conquest of Cebu(宿务) in 1565 and Manila in 1571. Spain colonized the Philippines for over 300 years until its defeat in the Spanish-American War in 1898. The Philippines attained their independence from the US on July 4,1946.

The Dutch came to Indonesia at the end of the 16th century. Japan occupied Indonesia on March 9, 1942, but surrendered on August 15, 1945. At the end of the Second World War, the Dutch had hoped to retain the Netherlands East Indies (东印度) as a colony, but the Indonesians opposed the return of the Dutch, setting up a republic in 1945. In 1949, after four years of fighting, the Indonesians gained their independence with the assistance of the United Nations which served as a mediator between the Indonesians and the Dutch. The Republic of Indonesia was founded on August 15, 1950. Sukarno became the first President of Indonesia.

In the late 18th century, the British continued to expand its colonialism in the Far East to open a new market. The British conquered Burma, fighting three Anglo-Burmese Wars in 1824 – 1826, 1852, and 1885 – 1886. Unlike other colonies which maintained their ethnic identity, Burma was a province of British India. The Burmese, therefore, had two sets of rulers, the British at the top with the Indians in the middle. In 1935 the British agreed to separate Burma from India, putting this agreement into effect in 1937. Burma was able to negotiate its independence from Great Britain in 1948, and became the first country separated from the British Commonwealth. The British navy first occupied Penang (Pinag)(槟榔屿) in 1786, then in order to effectively control the trades in the Malay Peninsula, they sent Raffles to Singapore in 1819. Singapore was almost a desert island with 150 people only. According to a treaty signed by Britain and the Netherlands in 1826, the Netherlands transferred Malacca to Britain in order to balance their relationship in Southeast Asia. Penang, Singapore and Malacca were governed by Britain as the Straits Settlements. The Straits Settlements served as a base for British expansion into the Malay Peninsula between 1874 and 1914. In 1842, Brunei Sultan ceded the Sarawak to Britain. In 1888, Brunei became a British protectorate; it achieved its independence in 1984.

When the Malay States entered into negotiations for their independence—achieved in 1957—Penang and Malacca became part of Malaysia as Singapore did in 1963. However, Singapore was asked to withdraw from the federation in 1965. Singapore has been an independent city state since that date. Sarawak and Sabah which joined Malaysia in 1963 continue to remain members of the federation.

Comparing with Portugal, the Netherlands and Britain, France were late to establish their colonial governance in the Indo-China Peninsula. In the late 18th century and the early 19th century, the French began to land on the Indo-China Peninsula. It invaded Vietnam from attacking Da Nang with French-Spanish fleet in 1858, then captured Saigon (西贡) in 1859. Using the south, then called Cochin China (交趾支那), as a base, the French moved west and north. In 1884, France forced Vietnam to sign the Treaty of Hué (顺化), to accept the French protection. France seized Vietnam and then slavered over China. The French army was defeated, but the Qing Dynasty government signed the humiliating Treaties of Tianjin, admitting the French protection to Vietnam and ending relationship of "suzerainty and vassal (宗藩关系)" between China and Vietnam. Meanwhile, France began to invade neighboring Cambodia. In order to free from Vietnam and Thailand, the Cambodian King placed hopes on France. French army seized Cambodia without much resistance. According to the Franco-Cambodian Treaty, Cambodia accepted French protection in 1863 and it became part of French in the Indo-China Peninsula in 1887. Then Laos was the next target. Laos came under the domination of Siam (暹罗, 泰国旧称) from the late 18th century until the late 19th century. In 1893, France forced Thailand to sign the Franco-Siamese Treaty with two warships to Bangkok. According to the treaty, Thailand agreed to cede the territory of Laos in the east bank of the Mekong River to France, and Laos became the French colony. So, France completed the conquest of the Indo-China Peninsula by 1907 with the governor palace in Hanoi, Vietnam. [Indo-China—the five territories under French authority: Cochin China, Annam (安南山脉), Tongking, Laos, and Cambodia.] The French also wanted to retain their colony after the Second World War. The Vietnamese rejected French rule, and after defeating the French at Dien Bien Phu (奠边府), they obtained their independence at the Geneva Conference in 1954.

Apart from the European invaders, Japan occupied Southeast Asia for a time after the Pearl Harbor Incident and destroying the US Pacific Fleet. However, with Japan's surrender in August 1945, the national liberation movements in Southeast Asian countries broke out. No matter how tough struggles were, all the Southeast Asian nations achieved their independence finally.

Chapter 1 General Introduction to Southeast Asia

The Independent Time Table of Southeast Asian Nations

Country	Independent Time	Colonial Power before Independence
Indonesia	August 17, 1945	The Netherlands
Vietnam	September 2, 1945	France
Laos	October 12, 1945	France
The Philippines	July 4, 1946	The United States
Myanmar	January 4, 1948	Britain
Cambodia	November 9, 1953	France
Malaysia	August 31, 1957	Britain
Singapore	August 9, 1965	Britain
Brunei	January 1, 1984	Britain

1.4 Diverse Political Systems

The political systems in Southeast Asian countries are various, covering all the basic types in the modern world. They can be generally classified into the following five types.

 People's Congress System: Vietnam and Laos

Among the 11 Southeast Asian nations, nine are capitalist countries and the other two—Vietnam and Laos—are socialist countries, both adopting the people's congress system[10] and absolute communist leadership.

After declaring independence in 1945, Vietnam enacted its first constitutional law in 1946. The current one was issued in 1992. The Constitution stipulates as follows: Vietnam is a socialist country, and a democratic country based on workers, farmers and intellectual union; its economy is in socialism-oriented mode, majoring in public ownership and prospering with other economic share; the country adopts the people's congress system, all power belongs to the people; the parliament is the top power organization of people, including the right of legislation, administration, judgment, inspection and so on; under the parliament, the government is responsible for administrative management, the supreme people's court for judgment, the supreme people's procuratorate for supervising the enforcement of the law; the chairman is voted by the parliament; as the representative of the country, the chairman acts independently. Besides, the Communist Party is stipulated as the leader of the country and society. Vietnam now implements a one-party ministerial system—the Communist Party. The other parties did exist for certain period in history but all disappeared in recent years. The Communist Party was founded in 1930, and has more than 3.6 million members.

Parliamentary Republic System: Singapore and East Timor

The Republic of Singapore is one of the two parliamentary republic countries in Southeast Asia. Singapore separated from the Malaysian Federation and became independent in 1965. It enacted the constitutional law in the same year. The constitution stipulates as follows: the president, elected by the parliament, is the chief of the state; the parliament runs a one-house system[11]; there is separation of the executive, legislative and judicial powers; the legislative branch is made up of the parliament and the president; the cabinet is the executive branch, made up of the prime minister, deputy prime ministers and other ministers, and the president appoints the leader of the majority party in the parliament as the prime minister. Nominated by the prime minister, the president appoints the cabinet minister, the chief justice of supreme court, the judges and the attorney general. The prime minister and ministers have to be the parliament members. Singapore is a city-state without local government. Though Singapore has a multi-partied system, the People's Action Party has been the ruling party in Singapore since the foundation of the state. The People's Action Party pronounces views on attracting the talents from industry and business seriously.

Singapore conducts the centralization of the state power, however, it launches strict laws and gathers many honest talents for leadership. As a result, Singapore can keep a rapid economic development and a corruption-free and high-efficient government.

Presidential Cabinet System: Indonesia and the Philippines

Among the 11 countries in Southeast Asia, Indonesia and the Philippines adopted the presidential cabinet system.

Indonesia has promulgated 3 constitutions since its independence, but it still uses the 1945 Constitution of Indonesia. The Constitution confirms the five principles of Indonesia's national philosophy Pancasila(潘查希拉,建国五项原则): first, the sovereign godship; second, the fair and civilized humanitarianism; third, the nationalism of Indonesia's unification; fourth, the democracy guided by consultative and representative system; fifth, the social justice. National organizations include: the People's Consultative Assembly(MPR), the president, the Congress (the People's Representative Council), the Regent House, the Supreme Court, the National Audit Office, etc. The coexistence of the People's Consultative Assembly and the People's Representative Council is the feature of Indonesia's political system.

The Philippines is also a country of the presidential cabinet system. However, unlike

Indonesia, the Philippines elects its president by popular vote for a single six-year term. The legislative body in Philippines is the Congress, made up of the Senate and the House of Commons. Both have legislative power, but the House of Commons has more powers, such as raising important bills like allocating funds and tax.

Monarchy System: Thailand, Cambodia, Malaysia and Brunei

Among the 11 countries in Southeast Asia, there are four countries of monarchy system. Brunei adopts absolute monarchy system. Thailand, Cambodia and Malaysia adopted constitutional monarchy system.

(1) **The constitutional monarchy: Thailand, Cambodia and Malaysia**

The Siamese Revolution of 1932 was a crucial turning point in Thai history in the 20th century. The revolution was a bloodless transition on June 24, 1932, in which the system of government in Siam was changed from an absolute monarchy to a constitutional monarchy. Though several amendments to the constitution, it stipulates as follows: the king is recognized as the head of the state, the head of the armed forces, the upholder of the Buddhist religion, and defender of the faith; the king appoints the cabinet prime minister according to the parliament's nomination, and the ministers according to the prime minister's nomination; the parliament is the legislative body, made up of the Senate and the House of Commons; the cabinet is the administrative body, and the cabinet prime minister has real power but responsible to the parliament; the courts in Thailand independently execute the judicial power on behalf of the king, supervised by the Justice Department and Justice Committee; if the defendant refuses to accept the final judgment made by the Supreme Court, he can submit a written statement to the king for a lesser punishment; the king has no real power, but the tradition, the religion and his own devotional spirit bring the king a prominent position and reputation, especially at the important moment in political life.

Cambodia had been a monarchy country before the 1970 coup by Lon Nol. It began to adopt the presidential republic system. During the Democratic Kampochea (DK) period, Cambodia tried to develop towards an "ultra left socialism". In 1993 Cambodia became known as the Kingdom of Cambodia and Sihanouk became the king once again after ratifying a new constitution which re-established the monarchy.

Malaysia is also a country of the constitutional monarchy system. Unlike Thailand and Cambodia, it is a federate country, consisting of 9 Sultan states and 4 states. As the national top power, the chief of the state is voted by turns among the 9 Sultans. The chief of the state has the legislative, administrative and judical powers, and holds the position of the head of the armed forces, appoints the prime minister according to the parliament's nomination. The Federal Parliament is the top legislative body, the cabinet is the top administrative body and the Supreme Court is the top judical body.

(2) **The absolute monarchy: Brunei**

Different from other 3 monarchy countries, Brunei is a Malay Muslim absolute monarchy country. Its main feature is that the monarch has absolute powers. The constitution in Brunei stipulates the sovereign Sultan is the chief of the state, having the legislative, administrative and judical powers. He is also the prime minister and the defense minister. The finance minister and the diplomatic minister with real powers are taken by the infantes(亲王).

Countries of Military Junta: Myanmar

After achieving its independence in 1948, Myanmar adopted the parliamentary system for a time. The Vice Prime Minister Ne Win started the army coup in 1962, built his "Revolution Council", dissolved the Parliament and stopped the constitution. After Ne Win's resignation in 1988, the State Law and Order Restoration Council (SLORC) took over the political power. In 1992 General Than Shwe became leader of the junta and took the position of the prime minister. In 1997 the ruling junta changed its name to the State Peace and Development Council (SPDC) with 19 members, Than Shwe as the Chairman and the head of the state.

1.5 The Unbalanced Economy Development

Resources and Industry

(1) **Abundant crops especially the tropical crops**

The world's three major barns[12], Siam (Thailand), Yangon (Myanmar), Saigon (Vietnam), are the largest rice producing areas. In 2014, Thailand's rice production reached 20,500,000 tons, and the world's second largest volume of rice exports amounted to 10,800,000 tons; at the same year, Vietnam's rice production reached 45,000,000 tons, and the world's third largest volume of rice exports amounted to 6,500,000 tons. Indonesia, another important rice producing nation in the world, produced about 70,610,000 tons of rice in 2014.

The production of palm oil, rubber, coffee and coconut has played an important even monopolistic role in the world. Malaysia is the second largest palm oil producing country. Indonesia, the second largest one, has a palm planting area of 2,000,000 hectares with the total production of 3,150,000 tons in 2014. Thailand, the largest rubber producing country in the world, planted about 2,000,000 hectares of rubber, and produced about 4,170,000 tons. Indonesia as the second largest producing nation yielded 3,180,000 tons. In 2013, Vietnam's rubber production was 970,000 tons. At the same year, Vietnam's coffee yield amounted to 2,220,000 bags (60 kg each bag), only next to the largest coffee producing nation Brazil.

Indonesia is the country with the second largest number of tropical rainforests in the world (only second to Brazil), also the country with the largest export of plywood and cane. Moreover, with the world's largest production of silk, cotton, pepper and quinine, it is the second largest producing country of tropical crops in the world next only to Brazil.

(2) **Huge potential fishery**

Although Southeast Asian nations own long coastline and vast seas, the fishing, especially the cultivation of marine products, is still in an initial stage. Indonesia's fish production in 2012 was 15,260,000 tons. Thailand produced 4,000,000 tons in 2012. Vietnam's production reached 5,000,000 tons in 2012.

(3) **Abundant reserves of petroleum and tin**

There is huge reserve of petroleum in Southeast Asia. As a member of OPEC, Indonesia is the largest petroleum producing country in Southeast Asia and the largest natural gas export country. Its reserves of about 50 billion barrels petroleum and 73,000 billion cubic meters natural gas, annually yields about 70,000,000 tons of petroleum. As the least populous country in Southeast Asia, Brunei is the second largest petroleum producing country with a daily yield of 200,000 barrels. Brunei's proved reserve of petroleum in 1995 was 1.4 billion barrels, natural gas about 320 billion cubic meters. With an annual petroleum yield of 30,000,000 tons, Malaysia's proved reserve of petroleum was 3.2 billion barrels, natural gas about 0.1 billion cubic meters. Also, Malaysia is the largest tin producing country in the world, accounting for almost half of the world's total production. In recent years, Vietnam has gradually increased its petroleum production, which amounted to 34,000,000 tons in 2015. It has been one of the main petroleum producing countries.

(4) **Rapid industrialization process**

In Southeast Asia, some are rising industrial countries while some are still in the early stage of industrialization and have little important industry in world terms. Except the above-mentioned countries producing petroleum and natural gas, some countries like Singapore and Malaysia have developed rapidly in the production of electronic and office equipment in recent years. Benefiting from the industry shift from Japan, Republic of Korea, China's Taiwan, the manufacture of white electrical appliances industry, e.g. color TV, refrigerators, air conditioners and washing machines, has developed rapidly in Thailand and Malaysia.

(5) Developed tourism

Southeast Asia is rich in the tourism resources. There are numerous famous scenic spots, such as Pattaya Beach(芭堤雅海滩) in Thailand, Angkor Wat in Cambodia and Halong Bay in Vietnam, as well as various folk-customs. Tourism in Thailand, Malaysia and Singapore has enjoyed a high reputation in the world and become the pillar industry for their countries.

The Four Levels of Economic Development

The 11 Southeast Asian nations' economic levels are imbalanced. They can be generally classified into the following four situations.

(1) Developed country Singapore and rich oil country Brunei

Singapore, as a country lacking in natural resources, needs to import almost everything except air. However, under the rule of a group of talents like Lee Kuan Yew, the government succeeds in combining the legal system in developed countries with the eastern fine tradition, and has made great efforts to develop its one-and-only natural resource—human resource. Through tireless efforts over 30 years, Singapore shone in the developing countries and has become the nation with the highest per capita income in Southeast Asia.

Brunei, with the most petroleum and natural gas per capita, has been another rich nation in Southeast Asia through exporting petroleum and natural gas.

(2) Malaysia, Thailand, the Philippines and Indonesia: rising industrial countries

Malaysia is the top among the countries belonging to second level of economic development in Southeast Asia. It not only has abundant resources like petroleum and tropical crops like rubber and palm, but also owns high quality human resources. Since the 1970s, Malaysia's economy kept a rapid developing trend, and in five Five-Year Plans from 1971 to 1995, the average economic growth rate reached 7.1%, 8.6%, 5.1%, 6.8%, and 8.7% respectively. It achieved 8.2% in 1996 and 8.5% in 1997. During the Financial Crisis in Asia, Malaysia's economic development was surely affected, but it recovered quite soon.

The way of Thailand's economic development is worthy of attention for developing countries. Not rich in natural resources, Thailand in its early developing stage made good use of its abundant tropical crops to process farm products, and moved towards agricultural industrialization. Then it gradually attracted foreign capital, drew support from foreign technical and equipment development, and processed foreign raw materials to manufacture household appliances—those high value daily necessities, such as televisions, refrigerators, washing machines and air conditioners, making itself the important household appliances overseas production base for Japan, the Republic of

Korea and China's Taiwan. With its tourism resources, Thailand has endeavored to develop tourism, and as a result, its economy has developed rapidly and people's living standard improved.

The Philippines, whose economic development was splendid during the 1950s – 1960s, used to be the vanguard of Southeast Asian industrialization. In the 1950s, the average production growth rate of processing industry reached 10%, GNP 6%. Whatever the industrialization or the economic development speed or level, the Philippines has been the highest in Southeast Asia and just second to Japan in East Asia. During 1965 – 1980, its industry growth rate achieved 7%, agriculture almost 5%, which made it one of the fastest developing countries in Southeast Asia. The Philippines was listed by the World Bank as a middle-income country in the early 1980s. Recently affected by political and social unrest, the Philippines gave way to Singapore, Malaysia and Thailand in economic growth rate. In 2014, its GDP amounted to 284.6 billion US dollars, 2,849 US dollars per capita, and the volume of export reached 61.8 billion US dollars. Also, a huge labor force export is one feature of the Philippines' economy which earns much foreign exchange each year. In some areas like Hong Kong and other Southeast Asian countries, many maids come from the Philippines.

As a large country, Indonesia has realized that being stable is the key to economic development. Only by keeping stable society can economy develop rapidly. The national economy has attained rapid growth during the past 30 years (1965 – 1998) under the ruling of President Suharto. The annual average economic growth rate was 6.8% during 1969 – 1994, its first Twenty-five-Year Development Plan Period. Afterwards, the democratic movement burst since people were dissatisfied with the long-term high-centralized politics, which caused the fall of the Suharto government. Meanwhile, the long-term lagging of democratic development has restrained greatly the economic growth, even causing social unrest. Suffering from the Asia Financial Crisis in 1997, Indonesia's economy, politics and society haven't yet recovered completely.

(3) **Vietnam under reforming and developing**

As a socialist country, Vietnam's economic mode is similar to that of China but different from that of other Southeast Asian countries. Although rich in resources and fine economic development conditions, Vietnam has a weak economic base and sank into serious economic and social crisis for long time as it experienced long-term wars and implemented the left economic policy. At the end of the 1980s, it adjusted policies at home and abroad, and launched economy-oriented reform and opening to the world policy, breaking away from the crisis finally. Through a series of policies like reforming the land system and state-owned enterprises, bringing in the foreign capital and expanding exports, Vietnam's annual average economic growth rate reached 7.1% in the 1990s. The Asia Financial Crisis in 1997 had little effect on Vietnam. It enjoyed an economic growth rate of 5.4% in 2014.

(4) Cambodia, Laos, Myanmar and East Timor moving in their own conventional ways

Cambodia, Laos, Myanmar and East Timor are the four nations with the lowest economic development levels in Southeast Asia. Cambodia benefits from its fine development condition like rich resources, and much international attention which brings in foreign support and investment.

As to communication with the outside, Laos was restrained a lot by its location—inland without a marine outfall and a convenient railway system. It is not easy to develop commodity export and attract foreign capital. Moreover, the countries around are all developing ones. Although it began to reform and open to the outside in recent years, its economy still went through slow development due to its environment.

As the largest country in the Indo-Chinese Peninsula and the second largest country in Southeast Asia, Myanmar enjoys abundant natural resources like petroleum and gems. It also has long coastline, vast plains, low population and high per capita resources. However, its economic development is still moving at a slow speed due to military supervision and seclusion for years. It is such a big country but the volume of exports in 2014 was only 11.1 billion US dollars.

East Timor, which achieved independence from Indonesia in 1999, is one of the slowest developing countries in the world. Its economy lives on foreign aid and continuing assistances from the local organization of the UN. However, it has rich natural resources especially like petroleum and natural gas. It was reported that the Timor Sea between East Timor and the northern part of Australia is the 23rd largest oilfield in the world with an estimated reserve of 5 billion barrels. Once it explores that, East Timor will be a rich country.

1.6 Multiplex Cultures

Greatly influenced by Indian culture, Arabian Culture, Chinese Culture, and Western religions and cultures, as well as their numerous ethnic groups, Southeast Asian countries have multiplex cultures. Based on religions and cultural traditions, they can be classified into Buddhism, Islam, Catholicism and Eastern Confucianism.

Myanmar, Laos, Thailand and Cambodia, the four countries in the northern part of Southeast Asian mainland, linking together as a unit geographically, believes in Buddhism. In the first half of the 11th century, Buddhism was propagated from India, Sri Lanka to Myanmar, then Thailand, Laos and Cambodia. Then during the 13th and 15th centuries, it was converted into Hinayana completely in the above-mentioned countries.

Situated in Indonesia archipelago and Malaya, the three countries, Indonesia, Malaysia and Brunei, mainly believe in Islam. Indonesia is the country with the largest Islamic population in the world. In the 13th century, Islam expanded its influence into the Southeast Asian islands. Then in the 15th century there came a powerful Islamic kingdom—Malacca. And Islam became the dominant religion in Southeast Asian islands in the 16th century.

The Philippines and East Timor are the countries that mainly believe in Catholicism. European powers like Spain invaded the Philippines, and brought in the Western Catholicism. It gradually developed into the local dominant religion afterwards. About 91% people in East Timor believe in Roman Catholicism.

Over 70% citizens in Singapore are Chinese, whose ancestors emigrated from China in the early years. Bordering on China, Vietnam has long-term association with China. Thus, traditional Confucianism cultures are dominant in these two countries.

Notes

[1] Austro-Asiatic language family:澳斯特罗-亚细亚语系/南亚语系。
[2] Malayo-Polynesian language family:马来-波利尼西亚语系。
[3] Khmer:高棉。
[4] the Indo-China Peninsula:中南半岛。
[5] Malay Islands:马来群岛。
[6] the Tropic of Cancer:回归线。
[7] the Teriary period:第三纪。
[8] the Epic on the Stone:石头上的史诗。
[9] the Country of Spice:香料王园。
[10] the people's congress system:人民代表大会制。
[11] One-house system:一院制。
[12] the world's three major barns:世界三大粮仓。

Exercises

1. Explain the following in English.

(1) referendum
(2) the Indo-China Peninsula

(3) the Malacca Strait

(4) Angkor Wat

(5) protectorate

2. **Fill in the blanks.**

   (1) In Southeast Asia, the largest, also the most populous country is _____.

   (2) The country with the smallest area in Southeast Asia is _____.

   (3) In Southeast Asia, most areas have just two seasons—_____ and _____.

   (4) _____ is not only the biggest river in Southeast Asia but also one of the most important international rivers in the world.

   (5) _____ and _____ adopted the people's congress system and communist leadership.

   (6) The world's three major barns are _____, _____ and _____.

   (7) _____ is the largest petroleum producing country in Southeast Asia and the largest natural gas export country.

   (8) _____ is the only country without coastline in Southeast Asia.

   (9) _____, with the most petroleum and natural gas per capita, has been another rich nation in Southeast Asia.

   (10) _____, _____, _____ and _____, the four countries in Southeast Asia believe in Buddhism.

3. **Answer the following questions.**

   (1) What are the geographical characteristics of Southeast Asia?

   (2) What are the types of political systems in Southeast Asia?

   (3) What are the advantages to develop the industry with the natural resources in Southeast Asia?

   (4) Talk about the four levels of economic development in Southeast Asia.

   (5) From the religions and cultures in some Southeast Asian countries, there is something in common with China. How can we make good use of that to promote economic cooperation?

4. **Discussion.**

   Choose a country in Southeast Asia, and try to give a brief introduction to your desk mate.

CHAPTER 2

Brunei

2.1 Country Name

Full Name: Brunei Darussalam
Short Name: Brunei
Official Name: Negara Brunei Darussalam

2.2 National Symbols

National Flag

The Brunei flag has four colors—a yellow backdrop, with two wide stripes of white and black cutting across from the top left corner to the bottom right, imposed by the state crest in red right in the middle of the standard.[1] The black and white stripes represent Brunei's chief ministers, and the yellow backdrop represents the Sultan of Brunei.

National Emblem

The state crest consists of the royal regalia whose central mast is the emblem of the state with two-pointed flags atop the royal umbrella—followed by the "Wings of Four Feathers" which signify protection of justice, tranquility, prosperity and peace. The upturned hands, the symbol of the

Islamic faith, signify the benevolence of the government and the government's pledge to promote welfare, peace and prosperity. The crescent is the sign of Islam, the national religion of Brunei. The characters inscribed on the crescent are the national slogan, "Always render service with God's guidance". The scroll beneath the crest reads "Brunei Darussalam", meaning "the City of Peace". [2]

2.3 Geography

Location

Brunei is situated on the northern Borneo and the western Pacific Ocean, between 114°0′ and 115°23′ east longitude, 4°0′ and 5°5′ north latitude. It is bounded on the north by the South China Sea and on all the other sides by the Sarawak of Malaysia. It is separated into two unconnected parts of west and east by Lim Bang/Ling Meng(林梦) in Sarawak in the shape of W.[3] The terrain consists of flat coastal plains rising up to mountains in the east and hilly lowlands in the west.[4] Pagon Peak (1,850 m) is the highest point of the country. Brunei consists of 33 islands. Brunei Bay, the biggest one, is the gateway to the outside world.

Area

Brunei covers a total area of 5,765 km² with a coastline of about 161 km along the South China Sea. Much of Brunei is covered by dense tropical rainforests and has very little arable land.

Climate

The climate of Brunei is tropical in general, with a mean annual temperature of around 28℃, March and April being the warmest. Brunei does not have clearly distinguishable wet and dry seasons. It is generally hot, humid and rainy all year round.

Natural Resources

The dominant natural resources of Brunei are oil and natural gas. Brunei is also rich in forest resources and tropical crops. In 1995 Brunei had proven oil reserves of 1.4 billion barrels and natural gas reserves of 320 billion cubic meters. The forest area covers 469,000 hectares accounting for 81% of the country's area.

Tourist Sites

Brunei offers a wide variety of attractive tourist sites.

Bandar Seri Begawan(斯里巴加湾市) is the centre of Brunei's commerce, finance and government. In many ways, it is also the heart of Brunei's cultural landscape, housing some of the nation's most revered landmarks. The city's Sultan Omar Ali Saifuddien Mosque is a stunning tribute to the nation's deep-rooted Islamic faith, while the truly Bruneian Kampong Ayer water village offers a glimpse of the nation's quaint Asian charm.

Beneath Bandar Seri Begawan's lavish adornments, gold towers, sparkling fountains and colorful mosaic tiles, lies a city steeped in quiet respect, grounded in Islamic tradition, and exuding a sense of peace that makes it one of Asia's most distinctive capital cities.

The attractions are the Kampong Ayer, Omar Ali Saifuddien, Jame Asr Hassanil Bolkiah Mosque, Brunei Museum, Jerudong Park, Sudan Palace, the Churchill Museum, and Malay Technology Museum.

Tutong, only a half-hour drive from the urban centre of Bandar Seri Begawan, offers a glimpse of the diverse cultures and unique lifestyles of rural Brunei, making it one of the nation's most distinctive districts. Tutong is graced by abundant natural scenic beauty, which inspires a somewhat mysterious feel. Local color abounds at the cultural village, showcasing the five ethnic Bornean groups that make up the district's diverse population.

Kuala Belait, the district lying behind the glitter of Brunei's legendary wealth, is the birthplace of the nation's wealth, the home of the oil industry and Brunei's economic heartland. It is the base of the country's main export, manufacturing and service (tourism) industries. The real "gold" of Brunei flows deep below the ground in Belait.

Temburong is a living tribute to Brunei's dedication to preserving one of the world's most diverse ecosystems. The Ulu Temburong National Park(乌鲁淡布伦国家公园) offers visitors a peek at a world untouched by man, from above or below the forest canopy. The simple culture of the Bornean longhouse community can also be seen—a complete and unforgettable Borneo experience.

2.4 Brief History

Brunei was called Borneo in ancient China. In the 5th century the Sultanate of Oman established an Islamic Kingdom over Borneo which experienced its golden age at the beginning of the 16th century. From the middle of the 16th century till 1888 Brunei suffered setbacks through invasions by European nations that were competing for territory and spheres of influence in the East Asian region and many other parts of the world. It was therefore occupied at different periods in this era by Portugal, Spain, Holland and finally by Britain which officially made Brunei a British protectorate in 1888. During the Second World War, Brunei was occupied by Japan from 1941 to 1946. It reverted to British protectorate status at the end of the War. A 1959 agreement between Brunei and the UK established a written constitution which gave Brunei internal self-government with the exception of defense, public security. This agreement was amended in 1971 to give Brunei control over all internal affairs excepting some areas of defence. The British government continued to control foreign affairs until 1978 when the Sultan of Brunei concluded negotiations that culminated in the sovereignty of Brunei. Full independence was granted finally on January 1, 1984.

2.5 Politics

Brunei has its own unique political system which rests on the twin pillars of the country's written constitution and the traditional Malay Islamic Monarchy.[5] These two facts dominate both the formal political life of Brunei and its government ethos. An additional and underlying feature is the country's adherence to the rule of law, a system based primarily on the English Common Law System and the independence of the judiciary.

When Brunei achieved its full independence, the Sultan declared Brunei an independent democratic Malay Islamic Monarchy. Since then, the Sultan has consolidated power firmly in the royal family spreading royal benevolence on strictly Islamic doctrines.

Capital

Bandar Seri Begawan is the capital of Brunei.[6] It covers an area of about 16 km² with a population of 393,000 (in 2014). It is located in Brunei-Muara District which is the smallest by size but the most important and most populous of the four districts of Brunei.

Parties

On May 30, 1985 the Sultan allowed the registration of political parties. Since then several political parties have participated in this process notably the Brunei National Democratic Party and the Brunei National Unity Party. At present, however, the National Solidarity Party (the Unity Party) is the only remaining political party of any consequence.

Leaders

The current head of Brunei is His Majesty Sultan Haji Hassanal Bolkiah Mu'izzaddin Waddaulah, the Sultan and Yang Di-Pertuan of Brunei Darussalam.[7] Being the eldest son of the Sultan, he ascended the throne on October 5, 1967. He was born at the palace and received his early education in the form of private tuition at the Istana Darul Hana and attended top institutions in both Brunei and Malaya (Peninsular Malaysia) before furthering his studies in the United Kingdom where he later qualified for admission as an officer cadet at the Sandhurst Royal Military Academy and was commissioned as a captain in 1967. He left Sandhurst in October of the same year to ascend the throne.

Besides being the Sultan and the ruler, His Majesty Sultan Haji Hassanal Bolkiah is concurrently the Prime Minister, Defence Minister, Finance Minister, and head of the religion of Brunei. Being a working monarch, he is involved in the conduct of the state affairs internally and internationally.

His Majesty is married to Her Majesty Raja Isteri Pengiran Anak Hajjah Saleha and has ten children—four princes and six princesses. His Majesty's official residence is the Istana Nurul Iman, which is also the country's seat of administration.

Constitution and Government

Brunei is an independent sovereign Sultanate which is governed on the basis of a written constitution which recognizes the Sultan as the head of the state with supreme executive authority. Brunei began to establish its government on December 1, 1988. Since then, the government went through several reforms. The Sultan is assisted and advised by five councils—the Religious Council, the Privy Council, the Council of Ministers (the Cabinet), the Legislative Council and the Council of Succession.

Brunei's administrative system is centered in the Prime Minister's Office which has provided the thrust behind His Majesty's aim to introduce greater efficiency in the government.

Administration

Brunei is divided into four districts namely Brunei-Muara, Tutong, Belait to the west and Temburong to the east. They have three levels, e.g. district, town and village. The head of the district or town is appointed by the government, but the head of the village is voted by the villagers themselves.

Cabinet

Cabinet members are appointed and presided over by the monarch; it deals with executive matters. The Cabinet has 13 members and each reports to the Sultan.

At present, Cabinet portfolios are: the Prime Minister, Defense Minister, Finance Minister, Senior Minister, Foreign Affairs and Trade Minister, Minister of Education, Religious Affairs Minister, Industry and Primary Resources Minister, Minister of Transportation and Communications, Interior Minister, Minister of Health, Development Minister, Culture, Youth and Sports Minister, Energy Minister, Second Finance Minister, National Economy Development Minister, the Second of Foreign Affairs and Trade Minister, the Attorney-General, the high priest of national Abdul. Cabinet members are appointed on five-year terms.

The Legislature

Members of the legislature are all nominated by the Sultan. There have been no elections since 1984.

The Judiciary

Brunei's judicial system is based on English common law. General criminal cases are heard in the magistrate or the intermediate court. The more serious ones are judged by the High Court. The Supreme Court consists of the Appellate Court and the High Court.

International Relations

Brunei pursues a non-aligned foreign policy. It became a member of the United Nations on February 24,1984. In addition it is a member of ASEAN[8], the Organization of Islamic Conference (now the Organization of Islamic Cooperation) and the World Trade Organization.

Relationship with China

Brunei stands firmly for the One-China policy and established diplomatic relations with China in 1991.

Brunei and China enjoy a long standing friendship as well as long-term friendly interactions. In recent years, the two countries have seen frequent exchanges of high-level visits and the increasing expansion of their cooperation in various fields, including economy, trade, international and regional affairs. In April, 2013, Brunei Sultan Bolkiah paid a state visit to China and the two countries issued a joint communiqué. Chinese Prime Minister Li Keqiang made a state visit to Brunei in October, 2013.

The Brunei government attaches great importance to the relationship with China and regards it as one of the most significant bilateral ties. It is expected that this cooperation will further expand the communication between Brunei and China and strengthen cooperation in the fields of energy, agriculture, infrastructure and tourism. China also regards Brunei as a good neighbor and partner.

2.6 Economy

Brunei was once a small agricultural country, poor and backward. At the beginning of the 20th century, petrol and gas were discovered in Brunei. Since then, they have been explored on a large scale and this has transformed the economic structure of Brunei fundamentally. Brunei is the second largest oil producer in Southeast Asia (next only to Indonesia) and a dominant producer of liquefied natural gas in the world. Oil and gas, which account for about 67% of its GDP, have led to the phenominal economic development of the country. Brunei, with a small population, presently enjoys one of the highest standards of living in the world with a per capita GDP of about Br$53,000 in 2012. The Brunei government provides free medical services, rice subsidies and housing for their people.

However, overdependence on oil and gas exposed Brunei's vulnerability especially after the Asian Financial Crisis of 1997. The government therefore introduced a series of economic reforms aiming at diversification and attracting foreign investment.

The first are those concerning petrol and natural gas, such as oil refining, natural gas liquefaction, chemical fertilizer, plastics, and chemical raw materials. The second are agriculture, forestry and fishery industries including the expansion of rice growing and vegetable planting, breeding of cows, sheep, chicken, shrimp and fish, and the production of eggs and milk so as to reduce the level of imports and raise food self-sufficiency. Thirdly, the government hopes to invigorate foreign investment by offering attractive incentives aiming at development and investment in small- and medium-sized enterprises and other commercial ventures. For example, the government allows foreign investors to own 100% shares in the high tech fields and the import-export oriented industries. The government also intends to privatize the government-run sectors, i. e. telecommunications, postal service, water and electricity utilities and transportation with the twin objectives of improving service delivery and efficiency and reducing the fiscal burden of the government. At present, 95% of small- and medium-sized enterprises are private. In recent years, the construction industry has expanded rapidly; the garment industry has also made a great progress and now has become the second-largest source of export earnings to oil and gas.

Other areas of diversification and expansion are in tourism and information technology. The government allocated some Br $900,000,000 to this sector alone to redress the imbalances in the communication industry. In 2012, 20% of the households have fixed phone installations, mobile phone users reached 480,000, and more than 60,000 people (15% of the population) are using the Internet.

There is no doubt that the 1997 Asian Financial Crisis impacted adversely on the Brunei economy. The country suffered severe losses in the state-run companies, and the Brunei currency had to be devalued as the effects of the depression spread to all sectors of the economy.

The government responded to this by setting up the National Economic Council to oversee the privatization and diversification process. The input of this body has resulted in the rapid expansion of the construction and textile industries. There are 12 huge textile industries that have been set up.

Following these measures, the economy of Brunei has recovered sufficiently. Brunei has the second-highest Human Development Index among the Southeast Asia nations, after Singapore, and is classified as a "developed country". According to the International Monetary Fund(IMF), Brunei is ranked fifth in the world by gross domestic product per capita at purchasing power parity and is one of two countries (the other being Libya) with a public debt at 0% of the national GDP. *Forbes* also ranks Brunei as the fifth-richest nation out of 182, based on its petroleum and natural gas fields.

Agriculture

Agricultural output accounts for 20% of the gross domestic product. The sector (including forestry and fishery) employs about 5% of the total labor force. There are small areas of rice and other tropical crops like rubber, pepper, coconut, etc. 80% of the food is imported. 25% of the rice consumed is grown locally while the remainder is imported. Vegetables, beef, chickens, poultry, etc., have achieved near self-sufficiency levels.

Industry

Industrial output accounts for 50% of the gross domestic product. The sector employs about 33% of the total labor force. Oil and natural gas exploitation and refining are the main industries and construction is the second largest emerging industry. Other significant sectors are food processing, furniture manufacturing, ceramics, cement, textile, construction materials and so on. The government has made a series of projects to promote industrial development ranging from hi-tech production of semi-conductors to labor intensive industries.

Services

The service industry accounts for 30% of the gross domestic product and employs about 60% of the total labor force. The services sector is relatively underdeveloped compared with other sectors. But in recent years, it has made great progress under the government's encouragement of developing services industries.

Trade and Investment

Important and substantial adjustments have been made to the tax and investment regime in order to attract foreign investment and address the growing international trade competition and globalization.

Some significant incentives for foreign investors include no personal income tax, no export tax, no sales tax, no payroll tax, no business tax, etc.

One significant incentive is that foreign investors now enjoy a 20-year preferential tax free rebate.

2.7 Culture

Brunei's culture is mainly derived from the Old Malay World, which encompassed the Malay Archipelago and from this stemmed the Malay Civilization. Based on historical facts, various cultural elements and foreign civilizations have had some influence on the culture of the country. The main cultural influences can be traced to four dominating periods and developments namely animism, Hinduism, Islam and occupation by Western countries. However, it is Islam that has had the greatest impact on the culture and way of life of the Brunei people. It is the basis of state ideology, government and societal management.

A visit to the Brunei Arts and Handicraft Centre built in 1975 is a living testimony of the diversity of Brunei's rich cultural history. There one can see artifacts of renowned Brunei boat making, silver-smithing, bronze tooling, cloth as well as mat and basket weaving. Other relics and works of art include artistic Malay weaponry, wood carvings, traditional games, traditional musical instruments, "silat" (the traditional art of self-defense) and decorative items for women. Some of these are kept in the Brunei Museum and the Malay Technology Museum. They have been ingrained as part of the richest traditional cultures in the Malay world.

Languages

The official language of Brunei is Malay. English is popular, and Chinese is widely understood.

Population and Ethnicity

The population of Brunei was about 393,000 in 2013. Brunei has a mixture of Southeast Asian ethnic groups: about two-thirds are Malay, one-tenth Chinese, and the remainder indigenous peoples and Indians.

Religion

Islam is the official religion of Brunei which is enshrined in the Brunei Constitution, with His Majesty the Sultan and Yang Di-Pertuan as the head of the Islamic faith in the country. Thus Islam plays a central role in the life of every Muslim in Brunei. Other faiths practiced in the state include Christianity and Buddhism.

Education

At present there are about 250 government schools and 60 private schools throughout the country. The formal school system has adopted a 6-3-2-2 pattern. This pattern represents primary, lower secondary, upper secondary and pre-tertiary levels respectively.

The literacy rate of males and females are 93.7% and 84.7% respectively.

The government of Brunei is well aware that the growing population of Brunei needs to be given a high level of education. Thus, millions of dollars have been allocated for this purpose.

Free education is provided to all citizens from pre-school onwards. The government has a school feeding scheme whereby full meals are given to rural schools and light meals to those in the urban areas. Students who are not eligible for hostels accommodation get free transport to and from school.

The establishment of the University Brunei Darussalam (UBD) enables the locals to pursue degree courses in the state. Amongst the English-medium first degrees which can be obtained from the University of Brunei Darussalam are Education, Mathematics &

Computer Science, Electronics & Electrical Engineering, Geography/Economics, Management Studies and Public Policy & Administration. The Malay-Medium degrees offered by UBD are Education and Islamic Studies. The government, however, continues to award scholarship to qualified Brunei citizens for courses not available at UBD. At the moment more than 2,000 Bruneians including government scholarship holders are studying in Britain, the USA, New Zealand, Australia, Canada, Egypt, Malaysia, Singapore and other countries.

Malay is the national language and is promoted as a medium of instruction in non-technical subjects. English remains the language of business and education in Brunei. Brunei's bilingual policy has been beneficial to the country as it produces a pool of educated workers who are able to communicate in both English and Malay.

Media

Brunei's media are not diverse. The private press is either owned or controlled by the royal family, or exercises self-censorship on political and religious matters. In Brunei a press law provides prison terms of up to three years for reporting "false news". The only local broadcast media are operated by the government-controlled Radio Television Brunei. Foreign TV is available via cable. Radio Television Brunei, state-controlled, broadcasts in Malay and English. Radio Station Brunei, state-controlled, broadcasts in Malay, English, Mandarin Chinese and Gurkhali. *Borneo Bulletin*—English-language daily, *Media Permata*—Malay-language newspaper are the main press and newspapers.

Brunei's Main Festivals

New Year's Day (January 1)

National Day (February 23)

Royal Brunei Armed Forces Day (May 31) (文莱皇家武装部队庆祝日)
His Majesty the Sultan's Birthday (July 15) (苏丹陛下华诞)
Fasting Month (September of the Muslim calendar) (斋戒月 回历每年9月)
Hari Raya Aidiladha (In the early October of the Muslim calendar) (开斋节 回历每年10月初)
Birthday of the Prophet Muhammad (June 15) (穆罕默德先知诞辰日)
Awal New Year (April 6) (回历新年)
Chinese New Year, Christmas, and so on (华人春节、圣诞节等)

Notes

[1] The Brunei flag ... in the middle of the standard.

文莱国旗由黄、白、黑、红四色组成,黄色的旗面上横斜着黑、白宽条,中央绘有红色的国徽。

[2] The characters inscribed on the crescent ... meaning "the City of Peace".

在新月中央写着国家箴言"永远在真主的指引下",底部的饰带上写着"和平之城——文莱"。

[3] It is bounded on the north ... as the shape of W.

文莱北面濒临南海,东、南、西三面与马来西亚的沙捞越州接壤,并被沙捞越州的林梦分隔为不相连的东、西两部分,形成W状。

[4] The terrain consists of flat costal plains ... in the west.

地形为由沿海平原向东部山区崛起,西部为低地丘陵。

[5] Brunei has its own unique political system ... of Malay Islamic Monarchy.

文莱有着它独有的政治制度:文莱国体是伊斯兰君主国;同时宪法规定,苏丹为国家元首,拥有行政、立法、司法全部权力,并且也是宗教领袖。

[6] Bandar Seri Begawan is the capital of Brunei.
Brunei Town was the capital of Brunei Darussalam in the 17th century, but since October 4,1970, it has been changed to Bandar Seri Begawan.

文莱首都是斯里巴加湾市。原称文莱市,17世纪被定为文莱首都,1970年10月4日改为现名。

[7] The current head of Brunei is His Majesty Sultan Haji Hassanal Bolkiah Mu'izzaddin Waddaulah, the Sultan and Yang Di-Pertuan of Brunei Darussalam.

苏丹·哈吉·哈桑纳尔·博尔基亚·穆伊扎丁·瓦达乌拉,现任国家元首、首相兼国防大臣、财政大臣。

[8] ASEAN:the Association of Southeast Asian Nations,东南亚国家联盟。

Exercises

1. **Explain the following in English.**
   (1) Bandar Seri Begawan
   (2) Brunei's political system
   (3) ASEAN
   (4) APEC
   (5) Brunei's bilingual policy

2. **Fill in the blanks.**
   (1) The _____ name of Brunei is _____ Brunei Darussalam.
   (2) The Brunei flag has _____ colors—a _____ backdrop, with two wide stripes of _____ and _____ cutting across from the top left corner to the bottom right, and imposed by the state crest in _____ right in the middle of the standard.
   (3) The "Wings of Four Feathers" in the Brunei's National Crest signifies _____, _____, _____, and _____.
   (4) The characters inscribed on the crescent are _____, "Always render _____ with God's guidance". The scroll beneath the crest reads "Brunei Darussalam", meaning _____.
   (5) Brunei Darussalam is situated on _____ Borneo, _____ Pacific Ocean, between 114°4′ and 115°23′ east _____, 4°0′ and 5°05′ north _____.
   (6) The climate of Brunei is _____ in general. Brunei does not have clearly distinguishable _____ and _____ seasons, hot, humid and rainy _____.
   (7) The dominant natural resources of Brunei are _____ and _____. Brunei is also rich in _____, _____.
   (8) Brunei was called _____ in ancient China. The Sultanate of Oman Kingdom was established as _____. It was introduced in _____ century, and came to _____ in the early 16th century.
   (9) Brunei has its own _____ political system which rests on the twin pillars of the country's _____ and the tradition of _____.
   (10) Brunei is divided into _____ districts namely Brunei-Muara, Tutong, Belait and Temburong, which have _____ levels, e. g. _____, _____, _____. The head of the district and town are _____, but the head of the village is _____.

3. **Answer the following questions.**
   (1) What are the two main export products in Brunei's economies? What contributions do

they make to Brunei citizens?

(2) What preferential policies has the Brunei government issued in order to face the economic globalization and the fierce international competition?

(3) What is the climate in Brunei? What are the major differences between Brunei and China in terms of the climate?

(4) What are the structural components of Brunei's population? In what way are they related to Brunei's history?

(5) What are some of the features in the education system that is special in Brunei?

4. **Discussion.**

(1) It's said that Brunei lives on petrol and gas. Is it right by saying that? Is it true in Malaysia and China?

(2) Brunei is a typical wealthy oil-rich country in Southeast Asia. However, with the development of the oil industry, what problem has been exposed? What measures should the government take to develop its economy? What do you think we can learn from it?

(3) Brunei is rich in natural scenic and cultural resourses. How should Brunei develop its tourism and protect its environments at the same time?

CHAPTER 3

Cambodia

3.1 Country Name

Full Name: Kingdom of Cambodia
Short Name: Cambodia
Local Full Name: Preahreacheanacha of Kampuchea (phonetic pronunciation)
Local Short Name: Kampuchea
Former Names: Kingdom of Cambodia, Khmer Republic, Democratic Kampuchea, People's Republic of Kampuchea, State of Cambodia

3.2 National Symbols

National Flag

The flag is composed of three colors—red, blue and white, with a palace in the middle which is named Angkor Wat or Angkor Vat but was once named as Vrah Vishnulok. The red color stands for the nation, white for Buddhism and blue for the royal family, coinciding with the national aphorism "Nation, Religion, King". This flag was put again into use in 1993 when monarchism was restored.

National Emblem

It is a yellow design of Angkor Wat, with an eight-square windmill on the top. In the center is a king sword, as the symbol of the king's sovereign power, with elephants and lions guarding on both sides as well as five layers of imperial carriage canopies, the number of which in Cambodian customs means "perfect and lucky". On both top sides are palm leaves symbolizing victory. The bottom ribbon carries a line in Cambodian "King of the Kingdom of Cambodia". The national emblem stands for a unified, integrated, united and blest country under the King's leadership.

3.3 Geography

Location and Population

The Kingdom of Cambodia, whose capital is Phnom Penh, is located in the south of the Indo-China Peninsula, Southeast Asia, and is bordered to the west and northwest by Thailand, to the northeast by Laos, to the east and southeast by Vietnam, and to the southwest by the Gulf of Thailand.

By 2014, it has the population of 15,205,539, including over 20 peoples with Khmer as the majority (over 80%). Most Cambodians are Theravada Buddhists of Khmer extraction, but the country also has a substantial number of predominantly Muslim Cham, as well as ethnic Chinese and Vietnamese.

Area

Cambodia has the territory of 181,035 squared kilometers. Its border length is 2,572 km, border length with Laos 541 km, with Thailand 803 km and with Vietnam 1,228 km. Its coastline is 460 km. It is divided into 20 provinces and 4 municipalities.

Cambodia falls within several well-defined geographic regions. The largest part of the country, about 75 percent, consists of the Great Lake Tonle Sap Basin and the Mekong Lowlands. To the southeast of the plain lies the delta of the Mekong River, which extends through Vietnam to the South China Sea. The basin and delta regions are rimmed with mountain ranges to the southwest by the Cardamom Mountains(豆蔻山脉) and the

Elephant Range and to the north by the Dangrek Mountains, which separates Cambodia from Thailand.

Climate

Cambodia's climate is governed by the monsoon winds, which define two major seasons. From mid-May to early October, the strong prevailing winds of the southwest monsoon bring heavy rains and high humidity. From early November to mid-March, the lighter and drier winds of the northeast monsoon bring variable cloudiness, infrequent precipitation, and lower humidity. The weather between these seasons is transitional. December and January are the coolest months, while March and April are the hottest. Maximum temperatures are high throughout the year, ranging from about 82℉(28℃) in January, to about 95℉(35℃) in April. Annual precipitation varies considerably throughout the country, from more than 200 inches (5,000 mm) on the seaward slopes of the southwestern highlands to about 50 – 55 inches (1,270 – 1,400 mm) in the central lowland region. Three-fourths of the annual rainfall occurs during the months of the southwest monsoon.

Resources

Of Cambodia's total land area, only 21 percent is cultivated. Areas surrounding the Mekong and the Tonle Sap are the most fertile regions. The country's once-ample timber resources have been poorly managed and are being rapidly depleted by local and foreign entrepreneurs. Although Cambodia is not rich in mineral resources, Batdambang[1] province in northwestern Cambodia contains limited quantities of zircons, sapphires, and rubies. The central part of the country contains commercial deposits of salt, manganese, and phosphate. The Gulf of Thailand is thought to contain petroleum deposits, but the extent and accessibility of the reserves have yet to be determined.

Rivers and Lakes

Cambodia's most important river is the Mekong River, the longest river in Southeast Asia and the tenth largest in the world. The Mekong River flows from north to south through Cambodia and is navigable for much of its course. Other rivers in the country include the Tonle Srepok and the Tonle Sab.

Cambodia's principal lake, the Tonle Sap (Great Lake), is the largest freshwater lake in Southeast Asia. From the northwest, the Tonle Sap drains into the Mekong River via the Tonle Sab River, entering the Mekong River at Phnom Penh. Each year during the monsoon season (approximately May to October), the waters of the Mekong River increase and reverse the flow of the Tonle Sab, which begins to drain into the lake. The lake then expands dramatically, flooding the provinces along its banks. When dry weather returns, the river reverses its course again and flows back into the Mekong River, draining the northwestern provinces. At the height of the flooding, the Tonle Sap reaches more than 10,000 sq km, or about four times its size in the dry season. The lake is one of the richest sources of freshwater fish in the world.

Tourism

(1) Angkor Archaeological Park

Angkor Archaeological Park, located in northern Cambodia, is one of the most important archaeological sites in Southeast Asia. Stretching over some 400 sq km, including forested area, Angkor contains the magnificent remains of several capitals of the Khmer Empire, from the 9th to the 15th century. These include the famous Temple of Angkor Wat and, at Angkor Thom, the Bayon Temple with its countless sculptural decorations. Angkor was declared a UNESCO World Heritage site in 1992—the same year it was also placed on the List of World Heritage in Danger. UNESCO has now set up a wide-ranging programme to safeguard this symbolic site and its surroundings.

Angkor Lake

Angkor Wat Temple

The temples of Angkor, built by the Khmer civilization between 802 and 1220 AD, represent one of mankind's most astonishing and enduring architectural achievements.

Angkor Wat combines two basic plans of Khmer temple architecture: the temple mountain and the later galleried temple. It is designed to represent Mount Meru[2], home of the devas in Hindu mythology. Within a moat and an outer wall 3.6 kilometers long are three rectangular galleries, each raised above the next. At the centre of the temple stands a quincunx of towers.

Angkor Wat consists of five central shrines, encircled by a moat and three galleries. The five central shrines have three levels, connected by numerous exterior staircases and decreasing in dimensions as they go up. The temple culminates in the sanctuary, a great central tower pyramidal in form. Towers also surmount the angles of the terraces of the two upper stages.

Three galleries with vaulting supported on columns lead from the three western portals to the second stage. They are connected by a transverse gallery, thus forming four square basins.

The western exterior forecourt of the main temple contains two "libraries", or smaller temple structures. As of 2004, the library on the left was under renovation by a Japanese archeological team. The area surrounding the exterior moat is a lawned park, incongruous in Cambodia.

Khmer decoration, profuse but harmonious, consists chiefly in the representation of gods, men and animals, which are displayed on every flat surface. Combats and legendary episodes are often depicted; floral decoration is reserved chiefly for borders, mouldings and capitals.

Sandstone of various colours was the chief material employed by the Khmers; limonite was also used. The stone was cut into huge blocks which are fitted together with great accuracy without the use of cement.

(2) **Banteay Chhmar**

This enormous complex, which was a temple city, is one of the most intriguing in the Khmer empire, both for its scale and its remote location. Never excavated, Banteay Chhmar fits the picture of a lost Khmer city with its ruined face-towers, carvings, forest surroundings and bird life flying through the temple. It has a romantic and discovery feel to it. Banteay Chhmar dates from the late 12th to the early 13th century and it means Narrow Fortress. It is thought to have been built by Jayavarman II. It was later rebuilt by Jayarvarman VII as a funerary temple for his sons and four generals who had been killed in a battle repelling a Cham invasion in 1177.

Like Preah Khan, Angkor Wat and Angkor Thom, Banteay Chhmar originally enclosed a city with the temple at the heart. No traces of the city that surrounded the temple remain. The temple area covers 2 km by 2.5 km. It contains the main temple complex and a number of other religious structures and a baray to its east. A moat filled with water and a huge wall inside of that enclose the center of the temple. This moat is still used to

Banteay Chhmar

present day by locals for fishing and daily chores. A bustling small market and village bounds the east and southeast and perhaps there has been continuous habitation there since the founding of the temple.

Inside the moat, a stone rest house and chapel can be seen. The highlight of Banteay Chhmar is the bas-reliefs, which are comparable with the Bayon. They depict battle against the Chams, religious scenes and a host of daily activities. In parts, the outer wall has collapsed. On the west side a spectacular multi-armed Lekesvara can be seen. The temples central complex is a jumble of towers, galleries, vegetation and fallen stones. Beautiful carvings can be seen throughout.

(3) **Phnom Penh**

Phnom Penh is the capital and largest city of Cambodia, located at the confluence of the Mekong and the Tonle Sap rivers. Despite its reputation as a "rough" city, Phnom Penh is easy to get around and is a great introduction to Cambodia.

For western visitors, even those who have visited other Asian cities, Phnom Penh can be a bit of a shock. It can be very hot and dusty, its infrastructure is lacking, and it is very poor—much poorer than, for example, Ho Chi Minh City (Saigon).

But things are changing, and Phnom Penh is becoming more pleasant and relaxing, especially over the past four years or so. It is striving to architecturally become more of a "developed capital", including high rise buildings, while still retaining much of the beauty that made it a Paris of the East before 1970. The city's French colonial buildings are beautiful, so its streetscapes make for a pleasant walk.

3.4 Brief History

Little is known of the early history of Cambodia, although there is evidence of habitation in parts of the country as far back as 4000 BC. It is also known that Chinese and Indian traders exchanged goods with people living on the coasts of present-day Cambodia and Vietnam in the early AD centuries. According to Chinese chroniclers, a kingdom known as "Funan" flourished between AD 300−600. A dynasty founded by the prince Jayavarman—possibly descended from the rulers of Funan—ruled from settlements in the eastern part of the country between around AD 790 and the 11th century. Cambodian power spread westwards during this period into parts of Thailand.

The succeeding dynasty, which ruled throughout the 12th and early 13th centuries, was based at the famous temple complex of Angkor Wat. Under King Suryavarman, the Cambodians extended their influence still further into southern Vietnam and northern Thailand. By the end of the 15th century, Angkor had been abandoned and fell into ruin. It has remained unoccupied ever since, with the exception of a brief period during the early 16th century. From then until the establishment of the French protectorate, Cambodia was in thrall to its more powerful Thai and Vietnamese neighbours.

French involvement in Cambodia came about through its colonial engagement in

Vietnam, and was largely intended to forestall possible British or Thai incursions along the Mekong River. The unstable ruling family in Cambodia at the time, headed by King Norodom, needed little persuasion to accept French protection and control over its foreign and security policies. A brief attempt to reassert Cambodia's independence in the 1880s was put down by the French, who then absorbed Cambodia into what became French Indo-China. It became an Associated State of the French Union in 1949, and achieved full independence in 1953.

In 1955, King Norodom Sihanouk abdicated in favor of his father, Norodom Suramarit, to allow himself to enter politics. Using the title Prince Sihanouk, he founded a mass movement, the Popular Socialist Community, which held power between 1955-1966. Prince Sihanouk became Head of State in 1960, following the death of his father. In March 1970, two years after the bombing began, Prince Sihanouk was overthrown by a right-wing coup, which proclaimed a Khmer Republic under the rule of General Lon Nol. Khmer Rouge Communist guerrillas, allied with their Vietnamese counterparts, stepped up their military campaign against the government. In 1975, they took control.

At the end of 1978, the Vietnamese army invaded Cambodia and overthrew the Khmers. A new constitution was declared in 1981. By 1982, Phnom Penh was repopulated by the return of up to 600,000 inhabitants from the countryside. The Vietnamese-controlled government experienced continuing armed opposition from an unlikely coalition of supporters of Prince Sihanouk, the KPNLF (Khmer Peoples' National Liberation Front) and the Khmer Rouge.

A UN-led effort began to stabilize the country and in 1991, a political settlement was reached. Under the terms of the 1991 settlement, the UN provided a 16,000-strong peacekeeping force and extensive administrative support. The operation was widely perceived as a success and sufficient political stability was created to allow a general election in 1993. This produced a narrow victory for Funcinpec, the party led by Prince Sihanouk, who had returned to the country from exile to assume the presidency. Funcinpec entered into a government of national unity with its main opponent, the Cambodian People's Party (CPP), the political descendant of the government that took over following the Vietnamese intervention in 1978, led by Hun Sen.

In 1998, the CPP gained a small overall majority at National Assembly elections, however, mindful of international reaction, the CPP chose to form a coalition government with Funcinpec. More importantly, Cambodia finally had a government which enjoyed undisputed international recognition.

3.5 Politics

The politics of Cambodia formally takes place according to the nation's constitution (enacted in 1993) in a framework of a parliamentary representative democratic monarchy, whereby the Prime Minister of Cambodia is the head of government, and of a multi-party system. Executive power is exercised by the government. Legislative power is vested in both the government and the two chambers of parliament, the National Assembly of Cambodia and the Senate.

Executive Branch

The prime minister of Cambodia is a representative from the ruling party of the National Assembly. He or she is appointed by the king on the recommendation of the president and vice presidents of the National Assembly. For one person to become the Prime Minister, he or she must first be given a vote of confidence by the National Assembly.

The prime minister is officially the head of government in Cambodia. Upon entry into office, he or she appoints a Council of Ministers who are responsible to the prime minister. Officially, the prime minister's duties include chairing meetings of the Council of Ministers (Cambodia's version of a cabinet), appointing and leading a government. The prime minister and his government make up Cambodia's executive branch of government.

The current Cambodian prime minister, Samdech Hun Sen, is a member of Cambodian's People Party (CPP).

Legislative Branch

The legislative branch of the Cambodian government is made up of a bicameral parliament: the Senate and the National Assembly of Cambodia.

The official duty of the Parliament is to legislate and make laws. Bills passed by the Parliament are given to the king who gives the proposed bills Royal Assent. The king does not have veto power over bills passed by the National Assembly (the lower house) and, thus, cannot withhold Royal Assent. The National Assembly also has the power to dismiss the prime minister and his government by a two-thirds vote of no confidence.

Political Parties

Major political parties in Cambodia are Cambodian's People Party (CPP), Human

Rights Party, Sam Rainsy Party, Norodom Ranarridh Party, Funcinpec, League for Democracy Party. Among them, CCP, Funcinpec and Sam Rainsy Party are Parliamentary parties who have dominated Cambodian politics over the last decade. Besides, there are still many minor parties.

Judicial Branch

The judicial branch is independent from the rest of the government, as specified by the Cambodian Constitution. The highest court of judicial branch is the Supreme Council of the Magistracy. Other, lower courts also exist. Until 1997, Cambodia didn't have a judicial branch of government despite the nation's Constitution requiring one.

Monarchy

Cambodia is a constitutional monarchy, i. e. the king reigns but does not rule, in similar fashion to Queen Elizabeth Ⅱ of the United Kingdom. The king is officially the Head of State and is the symbol of unity and "eternity" of the nation, as defined by Cambodia's constitution.

From September 24, 1993 to October 7, 2004, Norodom Sihanouk(October 31,1922—October 15,2012) reigned as King. After the abdication of King Norodom Sihanouk in 2004, he was succeeded by his son Norodom Sihamoni.

Succession to the Throne

Unlike most monarchies, Cambodia's monarchy isn't necessarily hereditary and the king is not allowed to select his own heir. Instead, a new King is chosen by a Royal Council of the Throne, consisting of the President of the National Assembly, the Prime Minister, the Chiefs of the Orders of Mohanikay and Thammayut, and the First and Second Vice-President of the Assembly. The Royal Council meets within a week of the King's death or abdication and selects a new king from a pool of candidates with royal blood.

Provincial and Local Governments

Below the central government are 24 provincial and municipal administrations. (In rural areas, first-level administrative divisions are called provinces; in urban areas, they are called municipalities.) The administrations are part of the Ministry of the Interior and their members are appointed by the central government. Provincial and municipal administrations participate in the creation of nation budget; they also issue land titles and license businesses.

Since 2002, commune-level governments (commune councils) have been composed of members directly elected by commune residents every five years.

In practice, the allocation of responsibilities between various levels of government is uncertain. This uncertainty has created additional opportunities for corruption and increased costs for investors.

3.6 Economy

The economy of Cambodia has seen rapid progress in the last decade. Its growth rate increased annually from 4% in both 2000 and 2001 to 7% in 2014. Per capita income, although rapidly increasing, is low compared with most neighbouring countries. The main domestic activity on which most rural households depend is agriculture and its related sub-sectors. Manufacturing output is varied but is not very extensive and is mostly conducted on a small-scale and informal basis. The service sector is heavily concentrated in trading activities and catering-related services. Reuters has reported that oil and natural gas reserves have been found off-shore. Production of oil could potentially have a great effect on the future of the economy.

During 1995, the government implemented firm stabilization policies under difficult circumstances. After four years of solid macroeconomic performance, Cambodia's economy slowed dramatically in 1997–1998 due to the regional economic crisis, civil violence, and political infighting. Foreign investment and tourism fell off. In 1999, the first full year of peace in 30 years, progress was made on economic reforms. Growth resumed and had remained about 5.0% during 2000–2003. Tourism was Cambodia's fastest growing industry, with arrivals up 34% in 2000 and up another 40% in 2001 before the September 11, 2001 terrorist attacks in the US. More than 4.5 million foreign tourists visited Cambodia in 2014. Economic growth has been largely driven by expansion in the clothing sector and tourism. Clothing exports were fostered by the US-Cambodian Bilateral Textile Agreement signed in 1999. Even given Cambodia's recent growth, the long-term development of the economy after decades of war remains a daunting challenge. The major economic challenge for Cambodia over the next decade will be fashioning an economic environment in which the private sector can create enough jobs to handle Cambodia's demographic imbalance. About 60% of the population is 20 years or younger; most of these citizens will seek to enter the workforce over the course of the next 10 years.

The overall recent economic performance has been characterized by balanced contributions from agriculture, manufacturing, construction, tourism and services. Despite the global downturn, the Cambodia economy remains in good shape underpinned by a continuous increase in investment in agriculture, broad base development of non-agriculture sectors, political stability, active private sector participation, reform efforts, increased official development aids and sustained foreign direct investment. According to the Circular on the Preparation of Budget Strategic Plan 2010 of the Royal Government of Cambodia, the economy still manages to grow around two percent and three percent in 2009 and 2010 respectively. With the development of the economy, the total of GDP reaches $16.27 billion, per capita $1,122 in 2014.

Agriculture, Forestry, and Fishing

Even before being plunged into civil conflict in the 1970s, Cambodia lacked significant industrial development, with most of the labor force engaged in agriculture. In 2001, agriculture accounted for 50% of GDP and engaged 80% of the economically active population. The tillable land area of the country is 670 hectares but the cultivated land area is only 2.5 million hectares.

Rice is Cambodia's major crop, its principal food, and, in times of peace, its most important export commodity. Rice is grown on most of the country's total cultivated land area. The cultivated rice land can be divided into three areas. The first and richest (producing more than one ton of rice per hectare) covers the area of the Tonle Sap Basin and the provinces of Batdambang, Kampong Thum, Kampong Cham, Kandal, Prey Veng, and Svay Rieng. The second area, which yields an average of four-fifths of a ton of rice per hectare, consists of Kampot and Kaoh Kong provinces along the Gulf of Thailand, and some less fertile areas of the central provinces. The third area, with rice yields of less than three-fifths of a ton per hectare, is comprised of the highlands and the mountainous provinces of Preah Vihear, Stoeng Treng, Rotanokiri (Ratanakiri), and Mondol Kiri.

In addition to rice, other food products include cassava, corn (maize), sugarcane, soybeans, and coconuts. The principal fruit crops, all of which are consumed locally, include bananas, oranges, and mangoes, and are supplemented by a variety of other tropical fruits, including breadfruits, mangosteens, and papayas.

Rubber production is considered a key area for development for Cambodia's agricultural sector, which employs around 4.75 million of Cambodia's 8 million-strong labour force, yet provides just 32% of the country's GDP. Dry rubber production in this country was only 1,300 tons in 1980 but up to 96,700 tons in 2014.

As far as livestock is concerned, animal husbandry has been an essential part of Cambodian economic life. From 1980 to 2004, the numbers of cattle, buffalo, pig and poultry increased a lot:

Year	Cattle	Buffalo	Pig	Poultry
1980	772,000	375,000	131,000	2,442,000
2004	3,035,400	680,500	2,484,250	16,033,700

Cambodia's preferred source of protein is freshwater fish, caught mainly from the Tonle Sap, which is the biggest freshwater fishery in Southeast Asia, and from the Tonle Sab, the Mekong, and the Basak rivers. Cambodia also has good conditions of saltwater fishing and fisheries owing to its coastline. From 1980 to 2004 the country's fisheries developed a lot:

Year	Inland Caught Fish (T)	Marine Caught Fish (T)	Aquaculture Fish (T)
1980	18,400	1,200	0
2004	250,000	42,000	33,500

Cambodia has another natural resources—forests, which covered approximately 70% of the country in the 1960s but only 53% in 2000 and which potentially constitute a second pillar of the economy. Forestry has been limited because of transportation difficulties and damage from war. The main products of the forest industry are timber, resins, wood oil, fuel, and charcoal.

 Industry

Industry accounted for only 5 percent of Cambodia's GDP in 1985, down from 19 percent in 1969. Industrial activity continued to be concentrated in the processing of agricultural commodities, mostly rice, fish, wood, and rubber. Manufacturing plants were small, and they employed an average of fewer than 200 hundred workers. These plants aimed to produce enough consumer goods (soft drinks, cigarettes, and food items) and household products (soap, paper, and utensils) to satisfy local demand.

Until the mid-1990s, Cambodia's industry was dominated by rice mills (of which there were approximately 1,500) and 80 to 100 state-owned enterprises. The latter half of the 1990s see the rapid development of Cambodia's garment industry, facilitated by the achievement of political stability, an abundant supply of cheap labor, good road access to Cambodia's major seaport, and having GSP (Generalized System of Preferences) and Most Favored Nation trading status since 1992 for exports to 28 European and American countries. Industrial production growth rate of 5.5% (2003 est.), 12% (2007 est.) and 9.56% (in 2014) shows the rapid development of Cambodia's industry.

In late 1969, the Cambodian government granted a permit to a French company to explore for petroleum in the Gulf of Thailand. By 1972 none had been located, and exploration ceased when the Khmer Republic fell in 1975. Subsequent oil and gas discoveries in the Gulf of Thailand and the South China Sea, however, could spark renewed interest in Cambodia's offshore area, especially because the country is on the same continental shelf as its Southeast Asian oil-producing neighbors.

Tertiary Industry

Recently the services industry develops rapidly, with banks, restaurants, hotels, transportation, travel agencies, trading gradually restored or developed. Tourism was Cambodia's fastest growing industry, with arrivals up 34% in 2000 and up another 40% in 2001 before September 11, 2001 terrorist attacks in the US. Cambodia received 1.42 million foreign tourists in 2005 and 2.13 million in 2008, 3 million in 2010, 4.5 million in 2014. And it will reach 5 million in 2015. Tourism has become one of Cambodia's triple pillar industries.

Postal, telegraph, and telegram services under the Ministry of Communications, Transport, and Posts were restored throughout most of the country in the early 1980s. Government telecommunications network (Camintel) runs telecommunication services especially calls at post offices or telecom offices in most towns while the Australian firm Telstra, also runs public call boxes in Phnom Penh. Internet services started in 1997. Internet shops or cafes can be easily found in Phnom Penh or Siem Reap. Users of the Internet reached 2,500,000 in 2014.

Trade and Investment

Since the new government got in office in 1993, free market economy and open policies were carried out so that the import and export trading began rising, resulting in the first peak of 1.38 billion US dollars in 1995. After the falling in 1996 and 1997, the total of import and export went up again and kept the steady growing, amounting to 1.47 billion US dollars of export and 1.61 billion US dollars of import in 2002. The export commodities mainly include clothing, timber, rubber, rice, fish, tobacco, footwear and the import ones mainly include industrial products and oil products. Oil products account for 22.6% of the import in 2001 and more in the following years. In September 2003 Cambodia joined the WTO and promised to limit the export amount of such products as rice, round logs and forestry products.

In order to attract foreign direct investment (FDI), the government has strengthened the country's legal framework, bolstered its institutions and liberalized the relevant regulations, in ways that are conducive to private sector investment and business activities in Cambodia. The 1994 Law on Investment, which was revised for the third time in 2002, provides similar treatment to foreign and domestic investors alike, with the exception of the issue of land ownership, as set forth in Cambodia's constitution. Even in this area, the regulations are generous, with foreign investors able to lease land for a period of up to 70 years (90 years according to the 2002 version), and with the possibility of renewal thereafter. In 2002, Cambodia also expressed its welcoming attitude towards BOT (build-operate-transfer) investment and the revised Law on Investment granted generous incentives to investors, especially those concerned in investment projects geared towards exports.

3.7 Culture

Languages

The official Cambodian language known in English as Khmer is a subdivision of the larger Austro-Asiatic language group with three dialects in the west, the central, and the east. The language spoken in Phnom Penh, the central part of Cambodia, is considered as the capital dialect and standard language. In the process of language development, Khmer has extensively absorbed vocabulary in foreign countries and other ethnics. The Khmer script, created by a combination of Sanskrit, Pali and native language, is an alphabetic writing with many clusters and 66 letters in total, containing 21 vowels, 12 independent vowels, and 33 consonants.

Ethnics

Cambodia, in contrast to its Southeast Asian neighbors, has a fairly homogeneous population. Ninety percent of its 14 million people are ethnic Khmers. The remaining population consists of more than twenty distinct ethnic groups, most of which are small indigenous people groups, known collectively as Khmer Loeu, living in isolated mountain areas. Minority groups living in the lowlands, often among or adjacent to Khmers, include Chinese, Vietnamese and Cham. Due to its status as a developing nation and the relatively recent peace, many other ethnic groups can be found, particularly in Phnom Penh, in statistically insignificant numbers. These investors, opportunity seekers, and Non-Governmental Organization (NGO) employees include Europeans, Americans, Koreans, Japanese, Thai, Lao and Russians.

Religion

Religion in Cambodia is predominantly Buddhist with 95% of the population being Theravada[3] Buddhist. Most of the remaining population adheres to Islam, Christianity, Animism and Hinduism. Buddhism plays an important role in Cambodian social life. Buddhist temples (wats) become a center for their religious activities and the preservation of culture and the provision of local education.

Cambodia was first influenced by Hinduism during the beginning of the Funan Kingdom. Hinduism was one of the Khmer Empire's official religions. Cambodia is the home to one of the only two temples dedicated to Brahma in the world. Angkor Wat of Cambodia is the largest Hindu temple of the world. Christianity, introduced into Cambodia by Roman Catholic missionaries in 1660, made little headway, at least among the Buddhists. Islam is the religion of a majority of the Cham (also called Khmer Islam) and Malay minorities in Cambodia. Highland tribal groups, most with their own local religious systems, probably number fewer than 100,000 persons. Among the Khmer Loeu, the Rhade and Jarai groups have a well developed hierarchy of spirits with a supreme ruler at its head.

Customs

(1) **Meeting and greeting**

Greetings between Cambodians are dependent on the relationship, hierarchy or age between the people. The traditional greeting is a bow combined with a bringing of the hands together at chest level (similar to bringing hands together for prayers). If one intends to show greater respect, the bow is lower and the hands brought higher. With foreigners Cambodians have adopted the western practice of shaking hands. Women may still use the traditional Cambodian greeting. The simple rule is to respond with the greeting you are given. In Cambodia people are addressed with the honorific title "Lok" for a man and "Lok Srey" for a woman followed with the first name or both the first and surname.

(2) **Gift giving etiquette**

Gifts are usually given at Cambodian New Year (Chaul Chnam). Unlike most other cultures, Cambodians do not celebrate birthdays. In fact, many older people may not know the exact date of their birth. If one is invited to a home, you should take nicely presented fruit, sweets, pastries or flowers. Knives as gifts are forbidden. Gifts are usually wrapped in colorful paper. Do not use white wrapping paper, as it is the color of mourning. When giving gifts, one should use both hands. Gifts are not opened when received.

(3) **Dining etiquette**

Table manners are fairly formal. If unconfident with the dos and don'ts, simply follow what others do. When invited to the dining table, one waits to be told where to sit as one would not want to upset any hierarchical arrangements. The oldest person is usually seated first. Similarly the eldest person should start eating before others. One has never to discuss business in such social settings.

(4) **Others**

In Khmer culture a person's head is believed to contain the person's soul, so it's a taboo to touch or point your feet at it. It is also considered to be extremely disrespectful to point or sleep with your feet pointing at a person, as the feet are the lowest part of the body and are considered to be impure.

Customary Cambodian teachings include the following: if a person does not wake up before sunrise, he is lazy; you have to tell your parents or elders where you are going and what time you are coming back home; close doors gently, otherwise you have a bad temper; sit with your legs straight down and not crossed (crossing your legs shows that you are an impolite person); and always let other people talk more than you.

(5) **Festivals**

Several festivals are held annually which are of interest to both international and domestic tourists. The major festivals are as follows:

Bonn Chaul Chhnam (April) is the traditional New Year's festival when Khmers clean and decorate their houses, make offerings and play traditional games.

Bonn Chroat Preah Nongkoal (May) is the Royal Ploughing Ceremony which inaugurates the planting season and involves symbolic ploughing and sowing of seed.

Bonn Dak Ben and Bonn Pchoum Ben (September) is the festival held for commemoration of the spirits of the dead; 15 days later offerings are made in the temples.

Bonn Kathen (October) is a 29-day religious festival when people march in procession to the temples where the monks change from their old robes to new ones.

His Majesty the King's Birthday (13 May – 15 May) is celebrated in regal fashion and the Royal Palace is sometimes open to the public.

Independence Day (November 9) celebrates the date when Cambodia achieved independence from France in 1953.

Bonn Om Took (November) is the water festival which ushers in the fishing season and marks the reversing of the current in the Tonle Sap River. This very popular festival attracts many people to watch the longboat races on the Tonle Sap in Phnom Penh, fireworks and a lighted flotilla of boats.

 Education

An estimated 76 percent of Cambodia's adult population is literate. Public education is free and compulsory for the first 9 years. Primary school attendance increased rapidly in the 1990s, and by 2006 virtually all children were enrolled, as well as many older people who were unable to attend school in their earlier years. Secondary education was more limited, with only 25% of eligible children enrolled. Seven institutions of higher learning, including the University of Phnom Penh, the University of Fine Arts, and the University of Agricultural Sciences, operate in the country. Only 5.3% of Cambodians of usual university age were enrolled in these schools in 2007.

Perennially handicapped by insufficient funding, Cambodia's educational system was devastated in the late 1970s when the Khmer Rouge regime closed schools and executed thousands of teachers. The regime viewed intellectuals, among others, as potential sources of opposition to its attempt to create an ideal socialist, agrarian society. In the 1980s thousands more teachers fled the country or sought better-paying work. Ever since then, efforts to revive the education system have been hampered by a shortage of funds and trained personnel.

However, during the past years, there have been significant improvements, expecially in terms of primary net enrollment gains and the development of a policy framework. The government has invested in vocational education in order to tackle poverty and unemployment. In 2014, there're 2,772 kindergartens, 6,476 primary schools, 1,321 middle schools and 63 universities.

Notes

[1] Batdambang is the main town which lies in western Cambodia. It is the second largest urban area in Cambodia and lies along the Sangke River northwest of Phnom Penh, the national capital. Among its industries are a textile mills and rice mills; there is also a rice research station. Cultural assets include the Buddhist temple Wat Poveal and 10th-century ruins of the Khmer empire, including several temples.

[2] Mount Meru is a sacred mountain in Hindu, Buddhism and considered to be the center of all physical and spiritual universes. Many Hindu temples, including Angkor Wat, have been built as symbolic representations of the mountain.

[3] Theravada literally is the oldest surviving Buddhist school. Founded in India, it is relatively conservative, and generally closest to early Buddhism, and for many centuries has been the predominant religion of Sri Lanka (about 70% of the population) and most of continental Southeast Asia (Cambodia, Laos, Myanmar, Thailand). Today Theravada Buddhists number over 100 million worldwide, and in recent decades Theravada has begun to take root in the West and in the Buddhist revival in India.

Exercises

1. **Explain the following items in English.**

    (1) the Kingdom of Cambodia

    (2) Khmer Empire

    (3) the Tonle Sap

    (4) Angkor Archaeological Park

    (5) National Assembly

2. **Fill in the blanks.**

    (1) The Kingdom of Cambodia is a country in _____ with a population of over _____ people. The kingdom's capital and largest city is _____.

    (2) Cambodia is bordered to the west and northwest by _____, to the northeast by _____, to the east and southeast by _____, and to the southwest by the _____.

    (3) Except the smaller rivers in the southeast, most of the major rivers and river systems in Cambodia drain into the _____ or into the _____.

    (4) Angkor was declared a _____ in 1992—the same year it was also placed on the List of World Heritage in Danger.

    (5) The _____ of Cambodia is a representative from the ruling party of the National Assembly. He or she is appointed by the _____ on the recommendation of the President and Vice Presidents of the National Assembly.

    (6) The _____ is officially the head of government in Cambodia.

    (7) The legislative branch of the Cambodian government is made up of a bicameral parliament: the _____ and the _____.

    (8) The upper house of the Cambodian legislature is called the _____. It consists of _____. Two of these members are appointed by the king, two are elected by the lower house of the government, and the remaining fifty-seven are elected popularly by _____.

    (9) The three most important political parties in Cambodia are the _____ (CPP), the _____, and the _____.

    (10) Cambodia is a _____, i.e. the king reigns but does not rule, in similar fashion to Queen Elizabeth II of the United Kingdom. The king is officially the Head of State and is the symbol of unity and "eternity" of the nation, as defined by Cambodian Constitution.

3. Answer the following questions.

(1) What is the political system of Cambodia? Explain it in detail.

(2) Give a brief introduction to the Kingdom of Cambodia.

(3) Which river is the most important one in Cambodia? Describe it in brief.

(4) Does Cambodia have a long and rich history? If yes, give a brief introduction.

(5) Who is the present monarch of Cambodia and what roles does he or she play in Cambodian political and social life?

(6) What customs in Cambodia are really prevailing?

(7) What are the religious beliefs for most Cambodians?

4. Discussion.

(1) The civilization of Khmer Empire used to be dominant and definitely influential in ancient Southeast Asia with the construction of Angkor Wat as its maximum. You are supposed to find further detailed information about the civilization and the Angkor Wat and discuss the impact of Khmer Civilization to other countries in Southeast Asia in the past and even today.

(2) Red Khmer used to be a very important political and military force in Cambodia. Discuss the historical significance of Red Khmer based on the materials you have found.

(3) Cambodia is a Buddhist kingdom with many customs based on the teachings of Buddhism. Discuss the differences of customs between Cambodia and other Southeast Asian countries.

CHAPTER 4

Indonesia

4.1 Country Name

Full Name: The Republic of Indonesia
Short Name: Indonesia
Local Full Name: Republik Indonesia
Local Short Name: Indonesia

4.2 National Symbols

National Flag

The flag is divided into two horizontal bands of red (top) and white (bottom) with an overall ratio of 2∶3. Red stands for courage while white represents purity of intent. The flag's colours represent blood (red) and spirit (white).

National Emblem

The coat of arms[1] of Indonesia is called Garuda Pancasila. The main part of the coat of arms is the golden mythical bird Garuda with a shield on its chest and a scroll gripped by its leg bears the national motto: "Bhinneka Tunggal Ika", roughly means "Unity in Diversity". The shield's five emblems represent Pancasila, the five principles of Indonesia's national philosophy. Garuda Pancasila was designed by Sultan Hamid Ⅱ of Pontianak, and was adopted as national coat of arms on February 1,1950.

Chapter 4 Indonesia

4.3 Geography

Indonesia is an archipelago[2] in Southeast Asia consisting of 17,508 islands (6,000 inhabited) and straddling the equator. The largest islands are Sumatra, Java (the most populous), Bali(巴厘), Kalimantan [Indonesia's part of Borneo(婆罗洲)], Sulawesi(苏拉威西岛), the Nusa Tenggara Islands(努沙登加拉群岛), the Moluccas Islands(马鲁古群岛), and Irian (伊里安岛) (the western part of New Guinea). Its neighbor to the north is Malaysia, to the east is Papua New Guinea and to the south is Australia.

Indonesia, part of the "ring of fire", has the largest number of active volcanoes in the world. Earthquakes are frequent. Wallace's line, a zoological demarcation between Asian and Australian flora and fauna[3], divides Indonesia.

Indonesia shares land borders with Malaysia on the island of Kalimantan(巴蒂克岛), Papua New Guinea on the island of New Guinea, and East Timor on the island of Timor. Indonesia also shares borders with Singapore, Malaysia, and the Philippines to the north and Australia to the south across narrow straits of water. The capital, Jakarta, is on Java and is the nation's largest city, followed by Surabaya(泗水), Bandung(万隆), Medan(棉兰), and Semarang(三宝垄).

With a territory of 1,904,443 square kilometers, Indonesia is the world's 16th largest country in terms of land area. Its average population density is 134 people per square kilometer, 79th in the world, although Java, the world's most populous island, has a population density of 940 people per square kilometer.

Lying along the equator, Indonesia has a tropical climate, with two distinct monsoonal wet and dry seasons. Average annual rainfall in the lowlands varies from 1,780 – 3,175 millimeters (about 70 – 125 in), and up to 6,100 millimeters (about 240 in) in mountainous regions. Mountainous areas—particularly in the west coast of Sumatra, West Java, Kalimantan, Sulawesi, and Papua—receive the most rainfall. Humidity is generally high, averaging about 80%. Temperatures vary little throughout the year; the average daily temperature range of Jakarta is 26℃ – 30℃ (78.8°F – 86°F).

 Natural Resources

Indonesia's size, tropical climate, and archipelagic geography, support the world's second highest level of biodiversity(after Brazil), and its flora and fauna is a mixture of Asian and Australian species. Once linked to the Asian mainland, the islands of the Sunda Shelf(Sumatra, Java, Borneo, and Bali) have a wealth of Asian fauna. Large species such as the tiger, rhinoceros, orangutan, elephant, and leopard, were once abundant as far east as Bali, but numbers and distribution have dwindled drastically. Forests cover approximately 60% of the country. In Sumatra and Kalimantan, these are predominantly of Asian species. However, the forests of the smaller, and more densely populated Java, have largely been removed for human habitation and agriculture. Sulawesi, Nusa Tenggara, and Maluku, having been long separated from the continental landmasses, have developed their own unique flora and fauna. Papua was part of the Australian landmass, and is home to a unique flora and fauna closely related to that of Australia, including over 600 bird species.

The country has extensive natural resources, including crude oil, natural gas, tin, copper, and gold.

Mount Semeru and Mount Bromo in East Java

The critically endangered Sumatran Orangutan

Tourist Sites

Bali's landscape of rugged coastlines, sandy beaches and barren volcanic hillsides provide a picturesque backdrop to this "Island of the Gods".

Located just east of Bali, Lombok (龙目) is "an unspoiled Bali" with beautiful beaches and the large, looming volcano of Mount Rinjani.

Jakarta is the fourth largest city in the world, and the capital of Indonesia. This bustling city is located on the island of Java.

Yogyakarta(日惹) is the most popular tourist destination on the island of Java, thanks to its proximity to the temples of Borobudur[4] and Prambanan[5].

4.4 Brief History

The early history of Indonesia is the story of dozens of kingdoms and civilizations flourishing and fading in different parts of the archipelago. Some notable kingdoms include Srivijaya (7th – 14th century) on Sumatra and Majapahit (1293 – c. 1500), based in eastern Java but the first to unite the main islands of Sumatra, Java, Bali and Borneo (now Kalimantan) as well as parts of the Malay Peninsula.

The first Europeans to arrive (after Marco Polo who passed through in the late 1200s) were the Portuguese, who were given permission to erect a godown near present-day Jakarta in 1522. By the end of the 16th century, however, the Dutch had pretty much taken over and the razing of a competing English fort in 1619 secured their hold on Java, leading to 350 years of colonization.

Various nationalist groups developed in the early 20th century, and there were several disturbances, quickly put down by the Dutch. Leaders were arrested and exiled. Then during World War II, the Japanese conquered most of the islands. After the War, the founding fathers of Indonesia, Sukarno (Soekarno) and Hatta declared the independence of the Republic of Indonesia. After four years of fighting, the Dutch accepted this on December 27, 1949. The 1950 Constitution was an attempt to set up a liberal democracy system with 2 chambers of the parliament. Indonesia held its first free election in 1955.

Under Suharto from 1966 to 1997, Indonesia enjoyed stability and economic growth, but much of the wealth was concentrated in the hands of a small corrupt elite and dissent was brutally crushed. During the Asian Financial Crisis of 1997 the value of the Indonesian rupiah plummeted, halving the purchasing power of ordinary Indonesians, and in the ensuing violent upheaval, now known as Réformasi(改革,改良), a more democratic government installed.

From the declaration of their independence Indonesia claimed West Papua as part of their nation, but the Dutch held onto it into the 1960s, and in the early sixties there was armed conflict over it. After a UN-brokered peace deal and a referendum, West Papua became part of Indonesia and was renamed as Irian Jaya(伊里安加亚), which apocryphally stands for Ikut(追随;参加) (part of) Republic of Indonesia, against the Netherlands.

The former Portuguese colony of East Timor was annexed by Indonesia in 1975, but there was armed resistance to this. After decades of civil war, in October, 1999, a provincial referendum for independence was overwhelmingly approved by the people of East Timor, and East Timor gained its independence.

4.5 Politics

With Jakarta as the country's special capital region, Indonesia is a republic with a presidential system. As a unitary state, power is concentrated in the national government. Following the resignation of President Suharto in 1998, Indonesian political and governmental structures have undergone major reforms. Four amendments to the 1945 Constitution of Indonesia have revamped the executive, judicial, and legislative branches. The president of Indonesia is the head of state, commander-in-chief of the Indonesian Armed Forces, and the director of domestic governance, policy-making, and foreign affairs. The president appoints the council ministers, who are not required to be elected members of the legislature. The 2004 presidential election was the first in which the people directly elected the president and vice president. The president may serve a maximum of two consecutive five-year terms.

The highest representative body at the national level is the People's Consultative Assembly (MPR). Its main functions are supporting and amending the constitution, inaugurating the president, and formalizing broad outlines of state policy. It has the power to impeach the president. The MPR comprises two houses: the People's Representative Council (DPR), with 550 members, and the Regional Representatives Council (DPD), with 128 members. The DPR passes legislation and monitors the executive branch; party-aligned members are elected for five-year terms by proportional representation. Reforms since 1998 have markedly increased the DPR's role in national governance. The DPD is a new chamber for matters of regional management.

Most civil disputes appear before the State Court; appeals are heard before the High Court. The Supreme Court is the country's highest court, and hears final cassation appeals and conducts case reviews. Other courts include the Commercial Court, which handles bankruptcy and insolvency; the State Administrative Court to hear administrative law cases against the government; the Constitutional Court to hear disputes concerning legality of law, general elections, dissolution of political parties, and the scope of authority of state institutions; and the Religious Court to deal with specific religious cases.

In contrast to Western powers and tensions with Malaysia, Indonesia's foreign relations since the Suharto "New Order" have been based on economic and political cooperation with Western nations. Indonesia maintains close relationships with its neighbors in Asia, and is a founding member of ASEAN and the East Asia Summit. The nation restored relations with the People's Republic of China in 1990.

4.6 Economy

Indonesia's estimated GDP for 2014 is US $783 billion. In 2014, estimated nominal per capita GDP is US $3,402. The industry sector is the economy's largest one and accounts for 46.4% of GDP. This is followed by services (38.6%) and agriculture (14.4%). However, since 2012, the services sector has employed more people than other sectors, accounting for 48.9% of the total labor force. This is followed by agriculture agriculture (38.6%) and industry (22.2%). Major industries include petroleum and natural gas, textiles, apparel, and mining. Major agriculture products include palm oil, rice, tea, coffee, and spices.

Indonesia's main export markets are China, Japan, Singapore, and the United States. The major suppliers of imports to Indonesia are Japan, China, and Singapore. In 2014, Indonesia ran a trade deficit with export revenues of US $176 billion and import expenditure of US $178.2 billion. The country has extensive natural resources, including crude oil, natural gas, tin, copper, and gold. Indonesia's major imports include machinery and equipment, chemicals, fuels and foodstuffs. The country's major export commodities include oil and gas, electrical appliances, plywood, rubber, and textiles.

Jakarta, the capital of Indonesia and the country's largest commercial center

Using water buffalo to plough rice fields in Java

In the 1960s, the economy deteriorated drastically as a result of political instability, a young and inexperienced government, and ill-disciplined economic nationalism, which resulted in severe poverty and hunger. Following President Sukarno's resignation in the mid-1960s, the New Order administration brought a degree of discipline to economic policy that quickly brought inflation down, stabilized the currency, rescheduled foreign debt, and attracted foreign aid and investment. Indonesia is only member of OPEC (Organization of Petroleum Exporting Countries) in Southeast Asia, and the 1970s oil price increase provided an export revenue windfall that contributed to sustained high economic growth rates. Following further reforms in the late 1980s, foreign investment flowed into Indonesia, particularly into the rapidly developing export-oriented manufacturing sector, and from 1989 to 1997, the Indonesian economy grew by an average of over 7%.

Indonesia was the country hardest hit by the Asian Financial Crisis of 1997. Against the US dollar, the currency dropped from about Rp. 2,000 to Rp. 18,000, and the economy shrunk by 13.7%. The rupiah has since stabilized at around Rp. 10,000, and there has been a slow but significant economic recovery. GDP growth exceeded 5% in 2014, and is forecast to increase further. This growth rate, however, is not enough to make a significant impact on unemployment, and stagnant wages growth. Increases in fuel and rice prices have worsened poverty levels. As of 2014, an estimated 11% of the population lived below the poverty line, and unemployment rate reached 5.9%.

4.7 Culture

Population and Ethnicity

The national population is 255 million. 130 million people live on the island of Java, the world's most populous island. Despite a fairly effective family planning program that has been in place since the 1960s, the population is expected to grow to around 315 million by 2035, based on the current estimated annual growth rate of 1.25%.

Most Indonesians are descendants from Austronesian-speaking peoples who originated from China's Taiwan. The other major groupings are Melanesians, who inhabit eastern Indonesia. There are around 300 distinct native ethnicities in Indonesia, and 742 different languages and dialects. The largest is the Javanese, who comprise 42% of the population, and are politically and culturally dominant. The Sundanese, ethnic Malays, and Madurese are the largest non-Javanese groups. A sense of Indonesian nationhood exists alongside strongly maintained regional identities. Society is largely harmonious, although social, religious and ethnic tensions have triggered horrendous violence. Chinese-Indonesians are an influential ethnic minority comprising less than 3% – 4% of the population. Much of the country's privately-owned commerce and wealth is Chinese-Indonesian-controlled.

Languages

The official national language, Indonesian, is universally taught in schools, and is spoken by nearly every Indonesian. It is the language of business, politics, national media, education, and academia. It was originally a lingua franca for most of the region, including present-day Malaysia, and is thus closely related to Malay. Indonesian was first promoted by nationalists in the 1920s, and declared the official language on the proclamation of independence in 1945. Most Indonesians speak at least one of the several hundred local languages (bahasa daerah), often as their first language. Of these, Javanese is the most widely-spoken as the language of the largest ethnic group. On the other hand, Papua has over 270 indigenous Papuan and Austronesian languages(澳斯特罗尼西亚语系，即马来-波利尼西亚语系的另一术语), in a region of just 2.7 million people. Much of the older population can still speak a level of Dutch.

Religion

Although religious freedom is stipulated in the Indonesian constitution, the government officially recognizes only six religions: Islam, Protestantism, Roman Catholicism, Hinduism, Buddhism, and Confucianism. Although it is not an Islamic state, Indonesia is the world's most populous Islam-majority nation, with almost 87.2% of Indonesians declared Muslim according to the 2010 census. 10% of the population is Christian, 1.7% Hindu, and 0.9% Buddhist or others. Most Indonesian Hindus are Balinese, and most Buddhists in modern-day Indonesia are ethnic Chinese. Though now minority religions, Hinduism and Buddhism remain defining influences in Indonesian culture. Islam was first adopted by Indonesians in northern Sumatra in the 13th century, through the influence of traders, and became the country's dominant religion by the 16th century. Roman Catholicism was brought to Indonesia by early Portuguese colonialists and missionaries, and the Protestant denominations are largely a result of Dutch Calvinist and Lutheran missionary efforts during the country's colonial period. A large proportion of Indonesians practice a less orthodox, syncretic form of their religion, which draws on local customs and beliefs.

Arts and Sports

Indonesia has around 300 ethnic groups, each with cultural differences developed over centuries, and influenced by Indian, Arabic, Chinese, Malay, and European sources. Traditional Javanese and Balinese dances, for example, contain aspects of Hindu culture and mythology, as do wayang kulit (shadow puppet) performances. Textiles such as batik, ikat and songket are created across Indonesia in styles that vary by region. The most dominant influences on Indonesian architecture have traditionally been Indian; however, Chinese, Arab, and European architectural influences have been significant. The most popular sports in Indonesia are badminton and football. Liga Indonesia is the country's premier football club league. Traditional sports include sepak takraw, and bull racing in Madura. In areas with a history of tribal warfare, mock fighting contests are held, such as, caci in Flores, and pasola in Sumba. Pencak Silat is an Indonesian martial art. Sports in Indonesia are generally male-orientated and spectator sports are often associated with illegal gambling.

Cuisine and Music

Indonesian cuisine varies by region and is based on Chinese, European, Middle Eastern, and Indian precedents. Rice is the main staple food and is served with side dishes of meat and vegetables. Spices (notably chili), coconut milk, fish and chicken are fundamental ingredients. Traditional Indonesian music includes gamelan(以打击乐器为主的大型民族音乐——加美兰音乐) and keroncong(一种四弦弹奏乐器,格朗章音乐). Dangdut(现代流行歌曲化了的马来西亚民间歌曲) is a popular contemporary genre of pop music that draws influence from Arabic, Indian, and Malay folk music. The Indonesian film industry's popularity peaked in the 1980s and dominated cinemas in Indonesia, although it declined significantly in the early 1990s. Between 2000 and 2005, the number of Indonesian films released each year has steadily increased.

Literature and Media

The oldest evidence of writing in Indonesia is a series of Sanskrit inscriptions dated to the 5th century. Important figures in modern Indonesian literature include: Dutch author Multatuli, who criticized treatment of the Indonesians under Dutch colonial rule; Sumatrans Muhammad Yamin and Hamka, who were influential pre-independence nationalist writers and politicians; and proletarian writer Pramoedya Ananta Toer, Indonesia's most famous novelist. Many of Indonesia's peoples have strongly-rooted oral traditions, which help to define and preserve their cultural identities. Media freedom in Indonesia increased considerably after the end of President Suharto's rule, during which the now-defunct Ministry of Information monitored and controlled domestic media, and restricted foreign media. The TV market includes ten national commercial networks, and provincial networks that compete with public TVRI. Private radio stations carry their own news bulletins and foreign broadcasters supply programs. At a reported 63 million users in 2012, Internet usage is limited to a minority of the population, approximately 24%.

 Notes

[1] coat of arms: a design or a shield that is a symbol of a family, city or other orgnization, 盾形纹章, 盾徽。
[2] archipelago: a large group of islands, 群岛。
[3] flora and fauna: plant and wildlife, 植物和野生动物。

Chapter 4 Indonesia

> [4] Borobudur: a ninth-century Mahayana Buddhist monument in Magelang, central Java, Indonesia, 婆罗浮屠, 世界上最大的古老佛塔, 位于爪哇岛中部马吉冷婆罗村。
>
> [5] Prambanan: the largest Hindu temple compound in central Java in Indonesia, located approximately 18 km east of Yogyakarta, 普兰巴南, 巨大的印度教神庙群, 位于爪哇岛中部, 距日惹市东部约18公里。

 **Exercises**

1. **Explain the following in English.**
   (1) People's Consultative Assembly
   (2) poverty line
   (3) Austronesian
   (4) Chinese Indonesians
   (5) Indonesian
   (6) wayang kulit
   (7) Indonesian cuisine

2. **Fill in the blanks.**
   (1) The national flag of Indonesia is divided into _____ horizontal _____ of red (top) and white (bottom).
   (2) The coat of arms of Indonesia is called _____.
   (3) Indonesia is an _____ in Southeast Asia consisting of _____ islands (6,000 inhabited) and straddling the _____.
   (4) The country has extensive _____, including crude oil, _____, _____, _____, and _____.
   (5) With a territory of _____ square kilometers, Indonesia is the world's 16th largest country in terms of _____.
   (6) Indonesia is a _____ with a presidential system. As a unitary state, power is concentrated in the _____.
   (7) Indonesia maintains close relationships with its neighbors in Asia, and is a founding member of _____ and the _____. The nation restored relations with _____ in 1990.
   (8) The _____ of Indonesia is the economy's largest and accounts for 46.4% of GDP (2012), which is followed by _____ (38.6%) and _____ (14.4%).

(9) There are around _____ distinct native ethnicities in Indonesia, and _____ different languages and dialects.

(10) Indonesian cuisine varies by region and is based on _____, _____, _____, and Indian precedents.

3. **Answer the following questions.**

(1) What is the Indonesia's national motto?

(2) What is the interesting point of Indonesia?

(3) What is the most populated island in Indonesia?

(4) How is the Indonesia's political system structured?

(5) What religions does the Indonesian government officially recognize?

4. **Discussion.**

(1) What mostly makes Indonesia a unique country?

(2) What destinations will you choose when you travel in Indonesia?

(3) What kind of investment is most likely to deliver more returns in Indonesia?

Chapter 5
Laos

5.1 Country Name

Full Name: The Lao People's Democratic Republic
Short Name: Laos

5.2 National Symbols

National Flag

The national flag of the Lao People's Democratic Republic is dark blue with red edges and a white circle. The width of the flag is two-thirds of its length. The area of the red edges on each side is one-half of the dark blue area. The area of the white circle is equal to four-fifths of the dark blue area. The blue color symbolizes prosperity, the red for revolution and the white circle for full moon. This flag used to be the banner of Lao Patriotic Front.

National Emblem

The national emblem of the Lao People's Democratic Republic is a circle depicting in the bottom part, one-half of a cog wheel and red ribbon with the inscription "Lao People's Democratic Republic", and decorated with crescent-shaped ears of rice on the two sides and red ribbon stretched between the middle of the rice ears with the inscription "Peace, Independence, Democracy, Unity and Prosperity". A picture of That Luang

Pagoda is located between the tips of the rice ears. A road, a paddy field, a forest, and a hydroelectric dam are depicted in the middle of the circle. The pagoda is the symbol of Laos. The cog wheel, the hydroelectric dam, the forest and the field represent Laos' industry, water conservation and forestry respectively, and rice for agriculture.

5.3 Geography

Location

Laos is located in the north of the Indo-China Peninsula, between 13°52′ and 22°05′ north latitude, 100°10′ and 107°30′ east longitude. A mountainous and landlocked country, Laos shares borders with Vietnam to the east, Cambodia to the southeast, Thailand to the southwest, Myanmar to the northwest and China to the north.

Area

Laos has an area of about 236,800 square kilometers. Its land shape is long from north to south and narrow from east to west with high north and low south, leaning from the northwest to the southeast. The country consists of three parts: Upland Lao, Midland Lao and Lowland Lao. Laos is a mountainous and landlocked country with about 80% mountainous areas and highlands. And it has been the "Roof of Indo-China" all through the ages. Phou Bia[1] is the highest mountain at 2,818 m. The Mekong River, originated from China, is the longest river with 1,846.8 km throughout the country.

Climate

The climate is tropical-subtropical and monsoonal. There is a distinct rainy season from May to November, followed by a dry season from December to April. Local tradition holds that there are three seasons: rainy (September—November), cold (November—March) and hot (March—July). The average temperature is 20℃–30℃. The rain water is abundant with annual amount of 1,250 cm – 3,750 cm. The best time to visit is November—February, when the temperatures are in 27℃– 36℃ with high humidity. The worst time to visit is March—May, when the temperatures and humidity climb even higher and the temperatures in April—May usually exceed 40℃.

Natural Resources

Laos is rich in natural resources. Among its mineral reserves are substantial deposits of tin, plumbum, potassium, copper, iron, gold, gypsum, coal, salt and other valuable metals. Its abundant water resources are probably the most important natural resources of the country. There are more than 20 rivers of over 200 km in the country. Among them, the Mekong River is the longest one, and its part in Laos covers 40% of the whole length of the Mekong River. According to an investigation, the installed capacity of the Mekong River is 4,200 megawatts, and Laos occupies 30% of it and reaches an annual generation capacity of 40 billion kilowatt-hours. Throughout the country more than 60 places with good water resource can be set up as hydropower stations. The forests area in Laos is 1.7 million hectares, accounting for 50% of the nation's total land area. There are a number of rare wood forest products, such as cypress, teak, rosewood, deal, benzoin, turpentine and lac.

A small boat crosses the Mekong River

Tourist Sites

(1) Vientiane

Vientiane is the capital city and the largest city of Laos, situated in the Mekong Valley. It is about 3,920 square kilometers in the area with a population of nearly 850,000. Since the 14th century, it has been the capital city many times. It is not only a historical city and a Buddhist holy land, but also the center of politics, economy and culture of the country. "Vientiane" means "Walled City of Scandal Wood" in local language. Compared with the hectic and bustling capitals in other Southeast Asian countries, Vientiane's deliciously relaxing atmosphere makes it look like a small town. It is small, charming and picturesque. It contains some wide boulevards, colorful and sacred pagodas and fascinating museums. All the colleges and universities of Laos are here.

Quiet and charming city

A quiet and wide street with shaded trees

The Buddhist College of Laos

(2) That Luang

Situated on the top of a hill in the northeast of Vientiane, That Luang (Great Stupa) was built in 1566 by King Setthathirat of Lang Xang. Urns with the ashes of kings and royal members are kept here. The most solemn traditional religious festival, That Luang Festival, is held here in November of each year. That Luang's building structure has a unique style which the Lao people are proud of. It is the most important national monument in Laos, a symbol of both the Buddhist religion and Lao sovereignty.

That Luang, symbol of Laos

(3) Patuxai

The Patuxai (literally Victory Gate or Gate of Triumph), is a monument in the center of Vientiane, built in the 1960s as a memorial for Lao's independence struggle. It is called "Anusavadi" by local people. Although bearing a general resemblance to the the Arc de Triomphe in Paris(巴黎凯旋门), it is typically Laotian, condensing the essence of Lao's typical construction. Today it is a "must-see" attraction for foreigners. On the top of the arch, people can have an overlook of Vientiane.

Patuxai

(4) Wat Prakeo (Wat Haw Pha Kaew)

Wat Prakeo, also a must for tourists, is located at Setthathirath Street of Vientiane. It was built as royal temple in 1565 by the great King Xaisethathirath, for the containment of the precious Emerald Buddha[2] only. The Emerald Buddha was removed from the temple to Bankok in 1778 during the invasion. The Buddha is still kept in Bankok now, and the Lao temple was later destroyed and rebuilt in 1936. In 1987 the temple was made national museum of cultural relics and now it houses a large collection of ancient materials.

Wat Prakeo

The Emerald Buddha

5.4 Brief History

Laos has a long history. From the 1st century to the mid-14th century AD, three ancient states—Ko Tamong, Vinang Chan (or Land Chenla), and Lan Xang (meaning million elephants), successively appeared in present-day Laos. In 1352, Fa Ngum, the ruler of Muang Swa (now Luang Prabang, political center of Lan Xang) unified most of what is now Laos in the kingdom of Lan Xang, which was the first feudal state of many nationalities in the history of Laos. And this period is the important time when Laos's economics, culture and arts developed independently.

In the early 18th century, four separate kingdoms of Luang Prabang, Vientiane, Xiang Khouang and Champasak were formed after the the kingdom of Lan Xang disintegrated. From the end of the 18th century to the middle of the 19th century, these kingdoms were gradually dominated by the Siamese and were replaced by the French in 1893. After Laos became a French protectorate, the Franco-Siamese Treaty defined the boundaries of Laos in 1907. In September, 1940, Laos was occupied by the Japanese. When the Japanese surrendered in 1945, an independence movement known as Lao Issara set up a government under Prince Phetsa-rath. In 1946 France invaded Laos again. In 1950 the Lao Issara (later called Lao Patriotic Front) was rebuilt and formed a Resistance Government of the Pathet Lao, by Prince Souphanouvong.

In 1954 France was compelled to sign Geneva Agreements on Indo-Chinese Problems, and French forces withdrew from Laos. Afterwards, the US replaced the

French. In 1962, the US was compelled to sign Geneva Agreements on Laos Problems, and Laos founded the Laotian National Union Government with Prince Phouma as Prime Minister and Prince Souphanouvong as Vice Prime Minister. In 1964, the US supported pro-American forces that disrupted the Laotian National Union Government and attacked the liberated area. In February 1973, the Agreement of Resorting Peace and Reconciliation in Laos was signed. In April 1974, the Provisional National Union Government was set up with Prince Phouma as Prime Minister, and the National Coalition Political Council was formed with Prince Souphanouvong as President. In December 1975, the first National Congress of People's Representatives was held in Vientiane, in which the monarchy was abolished and the Lao People's Democratic Republic was proclaimed.

5.5 Politics

Capital

Vientiane is the capital of Laos, with an area of 3,920 square kilometers and a population of nearly 850,000. Vientiane is the political, economic and cultural center of the country.

Parties

Laos is led by the Lao People's Revolutionary Party with 192,000 members at present. Its objective is to lead Lao people to carry out innovation, build and develop the people's democratic system, to build Laos into a country of peace, independence, democracy, unity and prosperity, and pave the way for the system of socialism. The current Central Committee was elected on March, 2011, including 61 members, and 11 Standing Committee, Choummaly Sayasone as the president.

Leaders

The president of the country is elected by a two-thirds vote of the National Assembly for a term of five years. The president appoints and dismisses the prime minister and members of the government, with the approval of the National Assembly. He also presides over meetings of the government. In addition, the president receives and appoints ambassadors and declares states of emergency or war. The present president is Choummaly Sayasone, and Prime Minister Thongsing Thammavong.

Government

The Laos government is the administrative organization of the state, consisting of the prime minister, deputy prime ministers, ministers and chairmen of the ministry-equivalent committees. The prime minister is appointed by the president with the approval of the National Assembly. The government serves a five-year term. The central government subordinates 21 ministries and commissions: the Bureau of Premier House, Ministry of National Defense, Ministry of Public Security, Ministry of the Interior, Ministry of Foreign Affairs, Ministry of Justice, Planning Commission, Ministry of Finance, Ministry of Forests and Agriculture, Ministry of Transport and PT, Ministry of Industry and Commerce, Ministry of Trade, State Bank, Ministry of Press, Culture and Tourism, Ministry of Labor and Welfare Community, Ministry of Education and Sports, Ministry of Public Health, ect.

Administration

Laos is divided into 16 provinces, 1 municipality and 1 special zone.

16 provinces: Vientiane, Phôngsali, Louang Namtha, Oudomsay, Bokeo, Louangphrabang, Xam Nua, Xaignabouri, Xiangkhoang, Bolikhamxay, Khammouan, Savannakhet, Saravan, Xekong, Champasak, Attapu

1 municipality: Vientiane

1 special zone: Xaixmboun

Constitution

Laos adopted its Constitution in August, 1991 after the Sixth Session of the Second People's Supreme Assembly, amending it most recently in 2003. The Constitution prescribes that the state of the Lao People's Democratic Republic is a people's democratic state. All powers are of the people, and by the people. The rights of the multi-ethnic people to be the masters of the country are exercised and ensured through the functioning of the political system with the Lao People's Revolutionary Party as its leading nucleus.

Cabinet

The Supreme People's Assembly of Laos was renamed as the National Assembly in August, 1992. The National Assembly is the highest authority and the legislative branch in the country for approving all new constitutions and laws. The session is held twice a year, and the members are elected from district and serve five-year terms. The sixth National Assembly was elected in May, 2011 with members of 132, Pany Yathotu as the chairman.

Legislation and Justice

The People's Courts are the judiciary organizations of the state comprising the People's Supreme Court, People's Provincial and Municipal Courts, People's District Courts and Military Courts. The People's Supreme Court is the highest judiciary organization of the state.

Diplomacy

Laos consistently carries out an independent and neutral foreign policy of peace, which claims to develop friendly relations with other countries based on the Five Principles and to attach great importance to cooperating with its regional neighbors, and transforms relations with Western countries to create good exterior surrounding for domestic development. In 2006, the Eighth Congress empathizes that Laos will consistently adhere to dealing with foreign countries by multi-level and multi-form, strengthening the strategic cooperation with socialist countries, maintaining a special relationship with Vietnam, increasing cooperation with China, enhancing good neighborliness with Southeast Asian nations and actively pursuing international economic and technological assistance. Laos was admitted into the Association of Southeast Asian Nations (ASEAN) in July 1997, applied to join the World Trade Organization (WTO) in 1998 and was granted full membership on February 2, 2013. By the end of 2012, Laos has established diplomatic relations with 135 countries.

5.6　Economy

Laos is an agricultural country, with agriculture dominating the economy, while industry foundation and services are weak. The New Economic Mechanism has been pushed since 1988. In the past 20 years, a range of effective reforms led to increased economic growth that has continued since the early 1990's, with GDP at an average annual rate of 6.2%, per capita income from US$200 in 1985 to US$1,490 in 2013, rice production doubled, and industrial output rising by 6.8 times. But Laos is still one of the poorest and undeveloped countries, bearing a difficult mission of development. The report in the 8th Congress of the LPRP (Lao People's Revolutionary Party) states all forces must be mobilized to promote the sustainable development of national economy, and the economy expanded by 7.9% each year from 2006–2010.

Agriculture

Subsistence agriculture used to account for nearly half of GDP and provides 80% of total employment. The land is vast with little population, 800,000 hectares suitable for cultivation. But in fact, only 80,000 hectares are cultivated with about 80% used for growing rice, mainly located in Vientiane area, Savannakhét, Saravan, and Champasak. Besides rice, other main crops are corn, sweet potatoes, coffee, tobacco, peanuts, cotton. Laos has plenty of tropical-subtropical fruits, such as coconuts, pineapples, oranges, chrysocarp(黄色果), mangos, grapefruits and papayas. Since the 1990s, animal husbandry has also been developing rapidly, especially industry farm. In the sixth Five-Year Plan, since the Lao government accelerated the industrial growth and modernization, the agricultural contribution to GDP descended to 25.2% in 2013 resulting from the development of manufacturing and services.

Industry

The primary types of industry of Laos are electricity production, wood, mining, garment, clothes, food, beer, manufacturing and so on, including small repair shops, weaving, wood and bamboo processing. In 2013 industrial value accounts for 28% of the national total GDP, and the number of employed people is over 0.1 million.

Services

The services sector in Laos has a weak foundation and started late. However, since the adoption of the innovation and opening policy, it has developed rapidly. The Lao government encourages investment in banking, insurance, transportation, communication and hospitality industry.

Tourism

After the enforcement of Laos' innovation and opening policy, tourist industry became a rising economy. In recent years, Laos has signed cooperation agreements with over 500 foreign tourism companies and has opened 15 international tour ports. Meanwhile many measures have been taken, including increasing the investment to tourist infrastructure, reducing visa fee, and relaxing border tour registration. As a result the tourist industry has achieved a sustainable development. In 2001 the Lao National Tourism Administration set up the Mekong Tourism Information Center. In 2012 Laos had 3.3 million foreign tourists, and the annual tourism revenues were about 514 million US dollars. By 2014 the Lao National Tourism Administration aims to attract 3.58 million visitors each year. The city of Luang Prabang and the Wat Phou[3] in Champasak have been classified as two UNESCO World Heritage Sites. And there are a number of tourist attractions, such as the Patuxai, the Wat Prakeo, the M. Khong Fall, the Khouang Xi and so on.

Energy Development

It is estimated that Laos owns over 18,000 megawatts available potential water power, but only a small part of it has been developed. Surrounded by energy hungry neighbors, the country is deemed to be the "Kuwait(发电机,比喻)" of Southeast Asia. The Lao government has established hydropower development as one of its major subjects for national economy and tries to increase exchange revenue by selling electricity to regional countries (Thailand, Vietnam and so on). Each year the exchange revenue by selling electricity accounts for a quarter of the total. The Nam Theun 2 in Khammouan(甘蒙) is the biggest hydropower station in Laos, and it began to operate in 2009, expected to generate profits of 1.9 billion dollars in 25 years of contract period since 2009.

Trade and Investment

The first law on the promotion of foreign investment was enacted in 1988 soon after the country started the New Economic Mechanism. Its subsequent amendment took place in 1994 and most recently in 2004. On the basis of mutual benefit, the law encourages foreign involvement in every field. After more than ten years, by 2007 Laos had attracted over one thousand foreign invested projects, and the value of the agreements is over 100 million dollars. The FDI is mainly distributed in the fields of hydropower, handicraft, hotel, tourism, wood processing, agriculture, bank, insurance, etc. The major contributors are Thailand, the US, the Republic of Korea, Malaysia, France and China. Some organizations (UN, ADB and EU) and Japan and other countries offer Laos 200 – 300 million dollars of grants and loans each year to build highways, bridges, ports, hydropower stations, communication and hydraulic facilities and other infrastructures. At present Chinese major investment fields in Laos are mining, hydropower and farming, including garment, motorcycle accessory assembling, etc.

5.7 Culture

Languages

Lao is the official language of government, education, and mass communications.

Lao belongs to the Tai language family. There are variations in pronunciation and vocabulary from north to south. Lao has many borrowings from Pali and Sanskrit (Sanscrit)[4], particularly in its literary forms. Most Lao people can understand and speak Thai. For some historical reasons, Lao has also been influenced by Cambodian language, Chinese, French and English.

Ethnics

The population of Laos is 6.6million (in 2014), and the annual growth rate is 2.3%. Laos is a multi-national country, with over 40 ethnic groups in all, including many branches and sublines. The number of population differs greatly from the kind of ethnic groups, some 0.5 million, some about one thousand, some even only five or six hundred. The dominant ethnic group just accounts for a little more than 60%. It is usually said that there are three main nationalities in Laos: Lao Lum (the dominant one, about 62.82% of the population), Lao Theung (about 26.10%) and Lao Soung (about 11.08%). Each tribe has its own distinctive customs, dialects and clothes.

Religion

Generally the Buddhists in Laos are about 60% of the population, Animists and others 40%. The faith of Buddhism was introduced in the eighth century by Meng Buddhist monks. Buddhism became the state religion of the Kingdom of Laos in the 14th century. A number of Laotian kings were important patrons of Buddhism. Laos was the center of the Buddhist faith of Southeast Asia in the 16th and 17th centuries. The Buddhism of Laos was greatly destroyed by foreign invasion in the 19th century. In the early 1990s increased prosperity and a relaxation of political control stimulated a revival of popular Buddhist practices, and at that time all lowland Lao were Buddhists.

Traditionally, even today, all males are expected to spend a period as a monk or novice prior to marriage and possibly in old age. Being ordained also brings great merit to one's family. The period of ordination need not be long; it could last from only 3 –5 days or a couple of months, but many men choose to spend years gaining both religious and secular knowledge.

Customs

(1) **Common courtesy**

Lao people are frank, open and friendly, and they possess a strongly developed sense of courtesy and respect. Everyone who adheres to the latter will receive a warm welcome. The generally accepted form of greeting among Lao people is the nop. It is performed by placing one's palm together in a position of praying at chest level, but not touching the body or clothes. The higher the hands are, the greater the sign of respect is. Nonetheless, the hands should not be held above the level of the nose. The nop is accompanied by a slight bow to show respect to persons of higher status and age. It is also used as an expression of thanks, regret or saying good-bye.

A Lao Girl

(2) **In temple**

Religion is the major part of daily life. When visiting a temple, especially Buddhist temples, one should be discreet and show respect to the people's beliefs. One should always show respect to clerics who allow you to visit their place of worship.

Dress neatly and comfortably and always take your shoes off before entering the pagoda lounge or foyer. Show respect in temples and shrines. For women or ladies, please don't touch the Buddha, or turn your back on the Buddha. If women touch a monk, he'll have to spend days ritually cleansing disgrace away. Never point your feet at any object when talking to anybody. Feet are considered the lowest part of the human body. Never point your feet at anyone. On the other hand, never touch someone's head because head is the highest part of the body. It shall always be respected.

Buddha statues, images, or religious relics are considered sacred objects. Therefore, standing up in front of Buddha statute is a sign of disrespect. Never make an attempt to climb or sit on them. When sitting in front of such relics, never point your feet towards them. Should you wish to speak to a monk, please try to keep your head lower than his. For a woman to hand in an object to a monk, she should just leave the object on the table.

Generally speaking, there is no admission charge when people would want to visit pagodas. However, some temples around larger cities do impose collect levies. Donations can be made in boxes.

(3) **Being guest**

Presents are necessary if you visit a family. Usually, the presents should be wrapped beautifully, and flowers basket, fruits basket, food basket and crafts are suitable. Guests should go through the front door, and take off their shoes before going into the house. Pay attention not to pointing your feet to anyone.

Wedding Ceremony

One of the most important of Lao customs is the marriage ceremony, a tradition that characterizes the uniqueness of the Lao culture. Most couples live together and are accepted and acknowledged by their families and society as "husband and wife" once they have gone through the ritual of marriage ceremony, despite the fact many of them may or may not be married under law.

It is believed in a traditional Lao marriage ceremony that customs and traditions must be adhered to ensure a happy and long lasting marriage. The length of the wedding festivities is determined by the financial means of the families of the bride and groom; however, most last about one day. Groom should give bride-price to the bride; the amount is up to the bride's appearance and her family background.

A Lao Bride

Wedding is first held at the bride's home. On the wedding day, the bride's family will invite a *Mor Phon*[5] to chant scriptures and a community elder to conduct the *Sou Khouan* (well-wishing ceremonies). Before the groom is allowed to enter, the bride's younger female relative cleans his feet with water. In front of the *Mor Phon* there are two bowls of rice, gifts and congratulation from two families. Following the chants, the *Mor Phon* ties the wrists of the groom and the bride with a white cotton string. This is called *phouk khene*[6]. As he ties the string, he gives blessings to the couple. Next, the guests join in the *phouk khene* to offer good wishes to the couple. After the *Sou Khouan*, guests are invited to dine.

Notes

[1] Phou Bia：普比亚山。
[2] Emerald Buddha：碧玉佛像。
[3] Wat Phou：瓦普寺。
[4] Pali and Sanskrit(Sanscrit)：巴利文和梵文。
[5] Mor Phon：僧侣。
[6] phouk khene：拴线。

Exercises

1. **Explain the following in English.**

   (1) Roof of Indo-China

(2) Patuxai

(3) The Plain of Jars

(4) nop

(5) phouk khene

2. **Fill in the blanks.**

(1) The Lao national flag consists of three colours, and its blue color symbolizes _____, the red for _____ and the white circle for _____.

(2) The _____ and the _____ in Laos have been classified as two UNESCO World Heritage Sites.

(3) In _____, the monarchy was abolished and the Lao People's Democratic Republic was proclaimed.

(4) When being a guest of Lao people, pay attention not to pointing your _____ to anyone.

(5) In Laos, the highest mountain is _____ and the longest river is _____.

(6) Laos consistently carries out an independent and neutral foreign policy of peace, and Laos has established diplomatic relations with _____ countries by the end of 2012.

3. **Answer the following questions.**

(1) What pictures can you find in the Lao national emblem? What do they represent?

(2) When are the best and the worst time to visit Laos for traveling?

(3) List some main tourist sites in Laos.

(4) How many main nationalities are there in Laos? What are they?

(5) What should women pay attention to in temples?

4. **Discussion.**

(1) Discuss the similarities between Lao politics and Chinese politics.

(2) Give a brief introduction to Lao agriculture.

(3) Suppose you have an opportunity to invest in Laos. Talk about your investment plan.

CHAPTER 6

Myanmar

6.1 Country Name

Full Name: Republic of the Union of Myanmar
Short Name: Myanmar
Used Full Name: the Union of Burma
Used Short Name: Burma

6.2 National Symbols

National Flag

Myanmar adopted a new flag on October 21, 2010. The design of the flag has three stripes of yellow, green and red with a five-pointed white star in the middle. The three colours of the stripes are meant to stands for solidarity, peace and tranquilty, and courage and decisiveness.

National Emblem

The new national emblem of Myanmar was adopted on October 21, 2010. It is surrounded by traditional Burmese flower design and a star with five vertices at its top. It uses the colours red and gold/yellow, and has two chinthe (mythical lions) facing

opposite one another. At its center is a map of Myanmar surrounded by laurel or olive branches. The words on the central portion of the scroll is "The Republic of the Union of Myanmar".

6.3 Geography

Location

Myanmar is the largest country in mainland Southeast Asia, situated in the western Indo-China, between the Tibetan Plateau and the Malay Peninsula. It is located between Bangladesh and India to the northwest. It shares its longest borders with Tibet and Yunnan of China to the northeast and is bounded by Laos and Thailand to the southeast. Myanmar has contiguous coastline along the Bay of Bengal and the Andaman Sea to the southwest and the south. The country has 3,200 km coastline. In the north, the Hengduan Shan Mountains form the border with China. Three mountain ranges, namely the Rakhine Yoma, the Bago Yoma, and the Shan Plateau(掸邦高原) exist within Myanmar, all of which run north-to-south from the Himalayas. The mountain chains divide Myanmar's three river systems, which are the Ayeyarwady (Irrawaddy) River(伊洛瓦底江), the Salween (Thanlwin) River(萨尔温江), and the Sittang River(锡当河). The Ayeyarwady River, Myanmar's longest river, nearly 2,170 kilometers long, flows through the country's middle flat plain, the Burmese wealthiest area, into the Gulf of Martaban(马达班湾). Its river territory area occupies over 60% of the land area.

Area

Myanmar has a total area of 676,578 square kilometers.

Climate

Much of the country lies between the Tropic of Cancer and the equator. It is of the tropical monsoon climate, with its coastal regions receiving over 5,000 mm of rainfall annually and approximately 2,500 mm in the delta region, while average annual rainfall in the Dry Zone, which is located in central Myanmar, is less than 1,000 mm. Northern regions of the country are the coolest, with average temperatures of 21℃ (69.8℉). Coastal and delta regions have mean temperatures of 32℃ (89.6℉). On May 3, 2008, Cyclone Nargis hit the densely populated cities in Irrawaddy delta such as Yangon. More than half of the country's population was affected and over 120,000 people were killed. It was the worst natural disaster in Burmese history.

Chapter 6 Myanmar

Natural Resources

Myanmar has superior natural conditions with abundant forests, fisheries, water and rich underground mineral resources deposits. The country has 34.12 million hectares forest land, covering over 50% of the land area. It gets the name of "forest country". There are many kinds of plants and animals in the forest. Myanmar's teak production ranks the first place in the world. The large reserves of oil and gas exist in the inland and coastal area. Mineral resources, mainly tin, tungsten, zinc, aluminum, antimony, manganese, gold and silver, are rich. Myanmar gets the high status of jewelry in the world, among which, ruby is the most valuable, so the stone of Myanmar is also designated as ruby. In addition, high-quality spinel, tourmaline, peridot are also produced in Myanmar. The species of fish and water resource are rich. The three major rivers, the Irrawaddy River, the Chindwin River(钦敦江,亲敦江), the Salween River that run through the north to the south, due to the lack of water conservancy facilities, have not yet been fully exploited.

Tourist Sites

Myanmar has many scenic spots and historical sites. Yangon (Rangoon), the former capital city of Myanmar on the Yangon River, known for name of "Oriental Garden" and "Capital of Gem", and has many tourist spots such as the famous gold-plated Shwedagon Paya (pagoda), the tallest pagoda in the world; the reclining Buddha in Chaukhtatgyi Paya, 75 meters long, 30 meters high, the largest in the world; and the

Shwedagon Pagoda

exquisite Karaweik Palace and the beautiful Inya Lakes. Mandalay, the second-largest city, is known as "the Capital of Gold". In the country features Mandalay Hill, a well-known Buddhist resort, there are eight pagodas, such as Mahamuni Paya and Shwenandaw Kyaung. Bagan, an ancient city, is known as "city of pagodas", with a number of pagodas packed and temples located on the charming banks of the Ayeyarwady River. The Bagan Museum has a large number of ancient relics not only reflecting the splendid culture of ancient Myanmar, but also providing valuable historical information for study of the formation and development of the history of Myanmar, Buddhism and ethnic languages. The Inle Lake(因莱湖) is in the south of Taunggyi(东枝), nestled in the hills of capital of Shan State(掸邦). Popular tourist attractions are lakeside floating markets, villages on the lake's floating islands and footrowers—fishermen who row with their legs. The Inle Lake is the hometown of the famous long-necked tribe (kajaani tribe), where the long-necked women can be seen.

6.4 Brief History

Myanmar is an ancient civilized country with a long history. Myanmar was unified in 1044 AD, and then went through the three feudal dynasties: the Bagan (Pagan) Dynasty, the Taungoo Dynasty and the Konbaung Dynasty. The British began their conquest of Myanmar in the 19th century, expanding their holdings after each of the three wars. In 1886, the British gained complete control of Myanmar, annexing it to India. Myanmar was administered as a province of British India until 1937 when it became a separate, self-governing colony. Since 1920, Burma started off the national liberation movement. In 1942, Myanmar was under Japanese occupation. The people of Myanmar carried out the heroic struggle against Japanese aggression. After Japanese surrender in 1945, the United Kingdom recontrolled Myanmar. After the War, the Burmese, with General Aung San at the helm, fought for complete political and economic independence from Britain. The country became independent from the United Kingdom on January 4, 1948, as the "Union of Burma". In 1962, General Ne Win led a military coup, abolishing the government headed by U Nu and establishing a military government with socialist economic policies. It became the "Socialist Republic of the Union of Burma" on January 4, 1974. In 1988, national demonstrations broke out due to the deteriorating economic situation. On August 8, the military opened fire on demonstrators. On September 18, the army led by Defense Minister General Saw Maung staged a coup d'état, took the power, formed the SLORC. In 1997, SLORC was renamed the State Peace and Development Council (SPDC). The military government announced the abolition of the Constitution, the dissolution of the People's Assembly and the National Authority. On September 23, "Socialist Republic of the Union of Burma" was changed into "Union of Burma". On June 18, 1989, the SLORC adopted the name "Union of Myanmar" for English transliteration. In mid-August 2007, broke out in Yangon the largest demonstration in two decades in Myanmar. It was put down by the military government. In May 2008, a new constitution was passed in the referendum, and the country was renamed "the Republic of the Union of Myanmar".

6.5 Politics

Capital

Nay Pyi Taw is the capital of Myanmar. Nay Pyi Taw means "Royal City". It has a population of about 11,580,000(2014). Nay Pyi Taw is approximately 390 kilometers north of Yangon, about 300 kilometers from Mandalay, the second largest city in northern Myanmar, which is located in a small basin in Sittang Valley in the central Myanmar, surrounded by mountainous jungles, and is a place that easy to hold but hard to attack. On November 6, 2005, departments of the government began to move to Nay Pyi Taw in batches. Nay Pyi Taw was officially announced as the new administrative capital of Myanmar in March 2006.

Yangon is the largest city and a former capital of Myanmar, located on the left bank of the Yangon River, one of the branches of the Irrawaddy River. Yangon, with the population of more than 5 million, continues to be the country's political, economic and cultural center.

Parties

National League for Democracy (NLD) is the largest political party and most influential opposition party. National Unity Party (NUP) is the primary pro-regime party and the second largest political party. Shan National League for Democracy (SNLD) is the ethnic party of Shan State. The Union Solidarity Development Association (USDA) is a pro-regime socio-political organization. There are also other smaller ethnic parties: Union Paoh National Organization, Shan State Kokang Democratic Party, Mro or Khami National Solidarity Organization, Lahu National Development Party, Union Karen League, Kokang Democracy and Unity Party, and Wa National Development Party.

Leaders

General Thein Sein has been President of Myanmar since March, 2011. He was the Prime Minister from 2007 until 2011. On October 16, 2012, General Thein Sein was re-elected as the chairman of the Union Solidarity and Development Party. Aung San Suu Kyi serves as General Secretary of the National League for Democracy.

Government

According to the 2008 Constitution, Myanmar is governed as a presidential republic.

The current government was established in the 2011 elections. The 2015 general elections has began and a new government will be formed in February, 2016.

Administration

The country is divided into seven states and seven regions (formally called divisions). They are: Ayeyarwady Region, Bago Region, Magway Region, Mandalay Region, Yangon Region, Sagaing Region, Tanintharyi Region, Chin State, Kachin State, Kayin State, Kayah State, Mon State, Rakhaine State, and Shan State. Regions are habituated by Burmans while states are home to ethnic minorities.

Constitution

"Burma Socialist Federal Constitution" was formulated on January 3, 1974 and suspended since September 18, 1988, when the junta "the State Peace and Development Council" (SPDC) took power. In 1993, National Convention was held to formulate a new constitution. In April 1996, the National Convention was suspended till May 17, 2004. The new constitution draft was completed by the drafting committee of constitution on February 19, 2008 and was approved in the referendum in May.

Legislation

According to the newly approved constitution (2008), the Assembly of the Union is composed of the House of Nationalities (the upper house) and the House of Representatives (the lower house). The legislative power of the Federal Union shall be vested in the Federal Congress. The National Assembly will have no more than 224 members and the People's Assembly no more than 440 members.

Justice

In Myanmar, the court and procuratorate is divided into four grades: the Supreme Court and the Supreme Procuratorate, three courts and prosecutors under the division of state, county and town. The Supreme Court is the country's highest judiciary and the Supreme Procuratorate is the country's highest prosecution.

Diplomacy

Myanmar carries out a peaceful, neutral and non-aligned foreign policy. It pursues an independent and active foreign policy, not attached to any countries and major powers. The United States and some Western countries have applied long-term economic sanctions and a policy of diplomatic isolation on Myanmar for the reason of the military regime's violation of human rights. Since the reforms following the 2010 elections, foreign relations with western nations have thawed.

Advocating the Five Principles of Peaceful Coexistence with all countries, Myanmar develops its good-neighborly relations between the neighboring countries. Now it is a member of the Association of South East Asian Nations (ASEAN), Bay of Bengal Initiative for Multi-Sectoral Technical and Economic Cooperation (BIMSTEC), and several other regional organizations and initiatives. By the end of May, 2013, Burma had established the foreign relationships with 111 countries. Developing the relationship between member countries of ASEAN is the focus of Myanmar's diplomacy.

China and Myanmar are friendly neighbors linked by common mountains and rivers and the two peoples enjoy long-standing friendship, towards which the Myanmar people affectionately call the Chinese people "Pauk-Phaw" (meaning full brothers). On June 8, 1950, the two countries formally established diplomatic relationship and mutually sent ambassadors. In 1954, China and Myanmar together with India jointly advocated the Five Principles of Peaceful Coexistence. China began to provide financial assistance to Myanmar. For long there has been the tradition of maintaining frequent exchange of visits between leaders of China and Myanmar. In 1960, the two governments signed "Sino-Burmese Border Agreement", and "Sino-Burmese Friendship and Mutual Non-aggression Treaty", smoothly settling the issue of demarcation of boundary left behind by history in the spirit of mutual respect, understanding and friendly consultation. Henceforth, the people of the two countries live together in peace and harmony. The late Chinese Marshal Chen Yi had composed more than a dozen poems describing his visits to Myanmar (by that time called Burmese), among which "To Burmese Friends" presented a vivid portrayal of the Sino-Myanmar "Pauk-Phaw" friendship. In the poem the lines of "At the top of a river lies the home of me/ At the other end, that of thee/ Infinite feeling we harbor for each other/As from the same river we fetch drinking water" are still widely recited by the peoples of the two countries. Since 1988 when the current Myanmar government took the national responsibilities, the Chinese Government has adhered to its principle of non-interference into other countries' internal affairs and has maintained normal contacts with Myanmar. The two nations have had good cooperation in international and regional affairs, and the bilateral relations have developed steadily.

6.6 Economy

Myanmar has superior natural condition and rich resources, but the economic development has been slow for many years. It is one of the least developed countries in the world. Since 1988, Myanmar has moved from a centrally planned economy to a market-oriented economy and has liberalized domestic and external trade, promoting the development of the private sector and the introduction of foreign investment. In the 2013 - 2014 fiscal year, the gross domestic product approximately is US$56,400, which grows by 7.5%, and per capita gross domestic product is about US$1,095.

Agriculture

The major agricultural product is rice, which covers about 60% of the country's total cultivated land area. Rice accounts for 97% of total food grain production by weight. Through collaboration with the International Rice Research Institute, 52 modern rice varieties were released in the country between 1966 and 1997, helping increase national rice production to 14 million tons in 1987 and to 19 million tons in 1996. By 1988, modern varieties were planted on half of the country's ricelands, including 98 percent of the irrigated areas. In 2008 rice production was estimated at 50 million tons.

Agriculture, which includes crop production, livestock, fishery, and forestry, is the mainstay of the Myanmar economy. This sector is responsible for much of the income and employment in the country. About 50% of the GDP comes from agriculture, and as much as 65% of the labor force is employed in this sector alone. Myanmar produces enough food to feed its entire population. In the absence of purchasing power, however, some people go hungry. Further, about a third of the rural households do not have any land or livestock. Only half of the arable land is under cultivation. Rice accounts for about half of the agricultural output. Other main crops are wheat, corn, peanuts, sesame, cotton, pulses, sugarcane, oil palm, tobacco and linen.

Livestock, fishery and forestry are mainly operated by private sectors. Livestock is mainly all kinds of poultry the farmers raise. Fishery refers to ocean fishery and fresh-water fishery in some big interior lakes. The government allows the foreign corporations to fish in the defined sea area and impose charges on them. Myanmar is rich in forests and woodland. Myanmar's forests, which are government-owned, are the source of teak and other hardwoods, such as padauk, door frame, ebony, ironwood, etc. and splint, bamboo and so on.

Industry

Primarily an agricultural country, Myanmar has always lagged behind in industrial production. Since the 1970s, there has been a steady growth in industrial production. In 1988, the government liberalized the economy, abandoned government-planned economy, and encouraged foreign investment. Much of the industrial sector, especially heavy industries, is controlled by the government, although the share of private enterprise in this area is steadily growing. Industry accounts for only about 20 percent of the GDP and employs only 10 percent of the total labor force. Most of the industries center around agricultural processing, textiles, footwear, wood and wood products, copper, tin, tungsten, iron, construction materials, petroleum and natural gas, pharmaceuticals, and fertilizers. In addition, the government has opened 18 special industrial zones all over the country, 5 of which are in the Rangoon area. Foreign investment is encouraged in 2 of the zones. While these zones are not fully developed, several factories and plants manufacturing clothing, consumer goods, and iron and steel materials are already operating there.

Tourism

Myanmar, the land of Buddhist pagodas, is a fascinating country and has great tourism potentials. Rangoon, Mandalay, Pagan, Pegu, and Tawnggyi, with their palaces and shrines and pagodas, are the centers of tourism. Both the government and private enterprises are heavily engaged in the tourism industry. In order to attract tourists, the country has improved roads, built international standard hotels, and other better facilities. Tourism, so far, makes up only a small percentage of the GDP. According to the traveling statistical data of Myanmar indicated that in 2012 roughly 1,060,000 foreigners visited the country, and the tourist income is US$534 million.

Since 1992, the government has encouraged tourism in the country; however, fewer than 270,000 tourists entered the country in 2006 according to the Myanmar Tourism Promotion Board. Myanmar's Minister of Hotels and Tourism Saw Lwin has stated that the government receives a significant percentage of the income of private sector tourism services.

The most common way for travellers to enter the country seems to be by air. According to the website *Lonely Planet*, getting into Myanmar is problematic: "No bus or train service connects Myanmar with another country, nor can you travel by car or motorcycle across the border—you must walk across. It is not possible for foreigners to go to/from Myanmar by sea or river." There are a small number of border crossings that allow the passage of private vehicles, such as the border between Ruili (China) to Muse, the border between Htee Kee (Myanmar) and Ban Phu Nam Ron (Thailand) (the most direct border between Dawei and Kanchanaburi), and the border between Myawaddy (Myanmar) and Mae Sot (Thailand). At least one tourist company has successfully run commercial overland routes through these borders since 2013. "From Mae Sai (Thailand) you can cross to Tachileik, but can only go as far as Kengtung. Those in Thailand on a visa run can cross to Kawthaung but cannot venture farther into Myanmar."

Flights are available from most countries, though direct flights are limited to mainly

Thai and other ASEAN airlines. According to *Eleven* magazine, "In the past, there were only 15 international airlines and increasing numbers of airlines have begun launching direct flights from Japan, Qatar, China's Taiwan, Republic of Korea, Germany and Singapore." Expansions were expected in September 2013, but yet again are mainly Thai and other Asian-based airlines, "Thailand-based Nok Air and Business Airlines and Singapore-based Tiger Airline", according to Eleven Media Group's *Eleven*.

Infrastructure

In Myanmar, inadequate infrastructure—roads, bridges, canals, railways, ports and communication facilities—impedes economic growth. Myanmar's long coastline is home to many excellent natural harbors such as Bassein port, Bhamo port, Mandalay port, Rangoon port, Tavoy port and Moulmein port. The Rangoon port is the biggest harbor in Myanmar. "Myanmar Five-star Steamship Company" is the only enterprise that engages in ocean shipping. A salient geographic feature of Myanmar is its many rivers, especially the Irrawaddy. The country's waterways remain the most important traditional mode of transportation to many remote areas of the country. Of more than 12,800 kilometers of waterways, 3,200 kilometers are navigable by large commercial vessels. In recent years, the government constructs the road and the railroad vigorously; the overland transportation has developed greatly. Myanmar has a total of 113,800 kilometers of roads. Myanmar has numerous rivers, therefore the present government takes it as one of the three big national causes to build bridges. These bridges connect the roads divided by the rivers to form the network.

Myanmar has a total of 5,000 kilometers of railways, over 320 locomotives, and more than 4,000 rail cars. Rail services remain poor despite attempts to renovate the existing lines, add new ones, and upgrade railway services on the main routes.

Myanmar has 80 airports. Both the private sector and the state sector are active in air transportation. The Department of Civil Aviation is responsible for the airports and the state-run airlines. Myanmar Airways International, Rangoon Airways, Air Mandalay and Air Bagan are the chief airlines of the country. Myanmar's chief airports are at Rangoon, Mandalay, Nay Pyi Taw, Heho and Pagan. The Rangoon Airport and the Mandalay Airport are the international ones.

At present, it has already established direct route with 13 countries and areas, the main international airways being Bangkok, Beijing, Singapore, China's Hong Kong, Kuala Lumpur, London, China's Taipei and so on. There are altogether 18 domestic services; the big cities and the main scenic sites have been connected by air.

Communication

Telecommunication in Myanmar has developed in recent years, but is still very poor.

Myanmar now has 416,000 fixed line phones with a density of 8 phones per one thousand people. Every region and the cities have the microwave transmission telephone apparatus and porous telephone input via the satellite. Auto telephone exchanges are available only in some towns. Many towns in Myanmar still don't have auto telephone exchange and still have to rely on manual exchange. International direct dialling (IDD) is available to the main cities. Mobile phones were first introduced about 15 years ago. A few years later, government started selling CDMA (Code Division Mutliple Access) mobile phones to the general public. Then come the GSM (Group Special Mobile). It is faster, newer with better voice quality. As usual, it was available only to government officers and those with connections in the government telecoms office. The fees are high and coverage limited.

Myanmar's information industries develop rapidly. At present the number of Burmese personal computing users is 380,000, only accounts for 0.7% of the total population. The number of Internet users is only 120,000, hence the market just started. The Internet has become part of the daily life of some of the Burmese living in the large cities. However, the speed of the Internet in Myanmar is usually quite slow, individual access is also quite expensive and mostly available to major cities. To fill this gap, Internet cafés have sprung up all over Myanmar.

Economic Liberalisation, Post-2011

In March 2012, a draft foreign investment law emerged, the first in more than 2 decades. Foreigners will no longer require a local partner to start a business in the country, and will be able to legally lease but not own property. The draft law also stipulates that Burmese citizens must constitute at least 25% of the firm's skilled workforce, and with subsequent training, up to 50%~75%.

In 2012, the Asian Development Bank formally began re-engaging with the country, to finance infrastructure and development projects in the country. The United States, Japan, and the European Union countries have also begun to reduce or eliminate economic sanctions to allow foreign direct investment which will provide the Burmese government with additional tax revenue.

In December, 2014, Myanmar signed an agreement to set up its first stock exchange. The Yangon Stock Exchange Joint Venture Co. Ltd will be set up with Myanma Economic Bank sharing 51 percent, Japan's Daiwa Institute of Research Ltd 30.25% and Japan Exchange Group 18.75%.

Trade and Investment

The government relaxes restrictions on foreign trade, allowing private foreign trade business, and opening the border trade with neighboring countries. Main exports are natural gas, rice, corn, a variety of beans, marine products, rubber, leather, minerals, timber, pearls and precious stones. Imports are fuel oil, industrial raw materials, chemical products, mechanical equipment, spare parts, hardware products and consumer goods etc. In the 2013−2014 fiscal year, the Burmese total volume of import-export trade accounts for US$248.7 billion, with exports amounting to US$11.11 billion, imports US$13.766 billion, US$48.616 billion in surplus. Most of Myanmar's export-import trade are with Asian countries, accounting for 90% of the total volume of trade, including about 51.3% with ASEAN countries. Japan, Singapore, Thailand, Malaysia, and China are its major trading partners. Singapore is the single most important partner both in terms of imports and exports, providing 31% of imports and taking 10% of exports. There has been a decline in trade with Europe and the United States since 1988. The Western countries headed by the US apply the economic sanctions to Myanmar. Myanmar's import-export trade with the United States constitutes about 5% of the total foreign trade. From January to September in the 2014−2015 fiscal year, the total volume of foreign trade surpassed US$24.83 billion, which grew by 37.8% compared to the same period.

Myanmar mainly exports the agricultural product, the aquatic product, the forest product to China. It mainly imports the construction and the electrical product, the chemicals and the compound, the haulage device and spare parts, personal and the household goods from China. Myanmar with the giant market, the numerous varieties' import demands, the advantaged geography convenience, product with better quality and reasonable price, has extremely good commercial opportunities to develop the bilateral trade and the processing industry with China. The marine traffic line between Guangxi and Myanmar is as far as more than 4,000 kilometers, and Guangxi's product may be transported through Nanning-Kunming Railway to Kunming, then to the Sino-Myanmar boundary. It is advantageous in the bilateral trade.

Myanmar has adopted the market-oriented economic system since the year 1988. Substantial stabilization and reform measures had been taken to be in line with the new economic system. The initial step taken towards a more liberalized economy is to allow foreign direct investment and to encourage the private sector development. In the area of legal framework, one of the first laws on investment issued by the State Law and Order Restoration Council is "the Union of Myanmar Foreign Investment Law", issued on November 30, 1988 to induce foreign investment and to boost investment particularly in the private sector.

Up to March 31, 2014, the total foreign investment in Myanmar is approximately US $46.4 billion, and it has 422 enterprises from 30 nations. Among them the first 4 countries are: China, Singapore, Republic of Korea, and Thailand. The main invested fields are: hydroelectric power, petroleum and natural gas, manufacturing, mining industry, real estate, hotel and tourism, traffic and communication, agriculture, etc. The biggest investment is in the area of hydroelectric power, second is petroleum and natural gas. In December, 2008, the biggest project of hydroelectric power BOT (build-operate-transfer) that China invests in Myanmar is Shweli first-level hydroelectric power station. It symbolizes that the Chinese hydroelectric development enterprises make a steady step in the field of cooperation and exploitation in the exploration of hydroelectric energy resources overseas.

In September, 2008, the amounts of investment came up to US$1.3 billion in Myanmar from China's 28 enterprises, accounting for 84% of the total foreign investment. The country's abundance of hydroelectric potential stands at the forefront of investment opportunities. Although 41% of current electricity originates from hydroelectric plants, only 1% of hydroelectric potential is being utilized. Myanmar's natural gas deposits constitute other potentially successful investment opportunities. In order to meet the demands and qualifications of increased economic growth and attract foreign investment, its infrastructure needs tremendous expansion and further development. Under the current economic plan, roads, bridges, and rail systems have been given priority. Investment opportunities in infrastructure have bright prospects. Myanmar is a developing country based on agriculture with rich land and water resources as well as the cheap workforce. Myanmar's agriculture and the telecommunications industry are worth Chinese investors' more attention. In Myanmar, the cooperative demands on the light farm machinery and the small farm tools are enhancing unceasingly, thus the joint-venture factories are profitable. The forestry, mining and the food processing also have the potential market of investment. Tourism in Myanmar has a bright future, so it will be a good choice to invest guesthouse or to open the Chinese restaurant in Myanmar. Myanmar will become a hot place for Chinese to invest and exploit.

6.7 Culture

Languages

The official language and primary medium of instruction of Myanmar is Burmese. A substantial number of people understand English and Chinese. Each national minority has its own language, and some have their written languages such as Kachin(克钦语), Karen(克伦语), Shan(掸语) and Mon(孟语). The Indian and Chinese residents speak various languages and dialects of their homelands. English is also spoken, particularly by the educated urban elite, and is the secondary language learnt in government schools.

 Ethnics

Myanmar has a population of about 51 million (2014). A majority of Myanmar's people are ethnic Burmans (65%). The major ethnic minorities are Kachin(克钦族), Kayah(克耶族), Kayin(克伦族), Chin(钦族), Mon(孟族), Rakhine(若开族), and Shan(掸族). Indians and Chinese are the largest non-indigenous groups.

Mon, who form 2% of the population, are ethno-linguistically related to the Khmer. Overseas Indians are 2%. The remainder are Kachin, Chin, Rohingya, Anglo-Indians, Gurkha, Nepali and other ethnic minorities. Included in this group are the Anglo-Burmese. Once forming a large and influential community, the Anglo-Burmese left the country in steady streams from 1958 onwards, principally to Australia and the UK. It is estimated that 52,000 Anglo-Burmese remain in Myanmar.

 Religion

Buddhism is Burma's national religion. About ninety percent of the population embraces Buddhism (mostly Theravada), but other religions can be practiced freely. Other religions—Christian (7%), Muslim (4%), Hinduism (2%), and animistic beliefs (1%)—are less prevalent.

Myanmar's Buddhism is mainly the Hinayana Buddhism (Theravada). Buddhism is not only religious belief of Burmese people, but also the fountainhead of their moral education. Buddhism's scriptures, "Mangala Sutta" particularly, are the philosophy in Burmese people's life, which root deeply in everybody's mind. In daily life, paying tribute to Buddha is a routine matter; moreover, Buddhists are requested to walk on barefoot, rather than in shoes or the socks. In Burma, All boys of Buddhist family need to be a monk in the temple for a period of time to live a chakra life(自净心灵的生活) before marriages. Monks are venerated and supported by the lay people. So long as the monks come to beg alms, people won't hesitate to take out the best belongings to them. The Burmese worship the Buddha sincerely, so that the people are simple, honest and genial, and the social crime rate is quite low.

 Customs

Despite modern changes and globalized cultural blending, Myanmar people have been able to preserve their own lifestyles and activities that have existed since time immemorial. The people of Myanmar communicate in their own language, wear their own style of clothing including the longyi, relish their own style of food, pray in their

Chapter 6 Myanmar

own way, play their own games, celebrate their own festivals, receive treatment with their own traditional medicines, and perform their own rituals in every aspect. Although some of Myanmar's beliefs, superstitions, customs and lifestyles have gradually disappeared, many still remain and are cherished and highly valued by the majority of the people.

There are no surnames in Myanmar people's names. However, an appellation should be put before a firstname to distinguish different genders, ages and social positions. For the elder or men of high social positions, their names should be called with a prefix of U (which means uncle); for peers prefixed with a Ko (which means elder brother); for juniors prefixed with a Mao (younger brother). Similarly, a Du should come before the name of women who are elder or of higher social positions than you are (it means aunt); and a Ma for peers or juniors (it means sister or girl).

Myanmar people usually eat rice noodles, wheat flour noodles or fried rice at breakfast. The lunch and supper are more formal at which they usually eat rice as staple food. The nonstaple food includes chicken, fish, shrimp, egg, pork as well as the onion, the water spinach and so on. The Burmese do not eat beef. They like fruits and tea. The features of Myanmar food are fatty, sour, spicy and heavy-flavoured.

For clothing, it is extremely characteristic in Myanmar. Both men and women, except the armyman, wear "skirts" (sarong) which are made out of longyi in the Myanmar's hot climate. They don't like to wear shoes, but sandals. An item used year-round is an umbrella.

Many of the life styles and activities are unique to Myanmar people. For example, the Shin Pyu or novitiate ceremony, which allows a young boy to experience temporary monastic life, is a religious practice virtually nonexistent in other parts of the world. In Myanmar, when one enters a pagoda or a temple, he must take off shoes, the head of state being no exception, otherwise he would be regarded disrespectful to Buddha, and would get into troubles sometimes.

Exercises

1. **Explain the following in English.**
    (1) The State Peace and Development Council
    (2) The national flag of Myanmar
    (3) Aung San Suu Kyi
    (4) The Myanmar Constitution
2. **Fill in the blanks.**
    (1) _____ is not only religious belief Burmese people, but also the fountainhead of

their _____ education.

(2) Myanmar has a total area of _____ square kilometers. _____ is the capital of Myanmar.

(3) There are no _____ in Myanmar people's names. However, an _____ should be put before a firstname to distinguish different genders, ages and social positions.

(4) In Myanmar, when enters the pagoda or the _____, anybody must take off _____, no exception even the head of state.

(5) The president, the current head of Myanmar is General _____.

(6) _____, which includes crop production, livestock, fishery, and forestry, is the mainstay of the Myanmar economy.

(7) The new national emblem of Myanmar is surrounded by traditional Burmese _____ and a star with _____ at its top.

(8) On May 3, 2008, _____ hit the densely populated cities in Irrawaddy delta such as Yangon.

(9) Myanmar has adopted the _____ economic system since the year _____.

(10) Myanmar became independent from _____ on January 4, _____, as the "Union of Burma".

3. Answer the following questions.

(1) What are the mineral resources of Myanmar?

(2) What are the main tourist sites of Myanmar?

(3) How was the history of colonization in history?

(4) Why do we say Myanmar has great tourism potential?

(5) What's the relationship between China and Myanmar?

4. Discussion.

(1) How does the location and climate affect the plantation in Myanmar?

(2) How many recognized seasons in a year in Myanmar? How is it different from your own country?

(3) What's the opportunity of trade and investment in Myanmar?

(4) What are the features of the culture in Myanmar as a whole? How is it influenced by other nations?

CHAPTER 7

The Philippines

7.1 Country Name

Full Name: Republic of the Philippines
Short Name: Philippines

7.2 National Symbols

National Flag

The flag[1] is horizontally divided into two fundamental colors, royal blue and scarlet red, with a white equilateral triangle based at the hoist side. At the center of the triangle is a golden-yellow sun with eight primary rays, each containing three individual rays, and  at each corner of the triangle is a five-pointed golden-yellow star. The flag is displayed with the blue field on top in time of peace, and with the red field on top in time of war.

National Emblem

On the top of the emblem, the three five-pointed stars have the same symbolism as the national flag. In the center, it is a golden-yellow sun with eight primary rays. In the blue field on the left side is the eagle of the United States and in the red field on the right is the Lion-Rampant of Spain, both representing colonial history. Beneath is the scroll with the words "Republic of the Philippines" inscribed thereon.

7.3 Geography

Location

The Philippines, which is located in Southeast Asia, constitutes an archipelago of 7,107 islands. It generally lies between 116°40′ and 126°34′east longitude, and 4°40′ and 21°10′ north latitude, and borders the Pacific Ocean on the east, the South China Sea on the west, and the Celebes Sea or Sulawesi Sea(西里伯斯海,苏拉威西海的旧称) on the south. This position accounts for much of the variations in geographic, climatic and vegetation conditions in the country.

The islands are commonly divided into three island groups: Luzon(吕宋岛), Visayas (米沙鄢群岛), and Mindanao(棉兰老岛). The busy port of Manila, on Luzon, is the national capital and second largest city after its suburb Quezon(奎松) City.

Area

The Philippines covers a total land area of approximately 299,700 square kilometers.

Climate

The local climate is hot, humid, and tropical. The average yearly temperature is around 26.5°C (79.7°F). There are three recognized seasons: "Tag-init" or "Tag-araw" (the hot season or summer from March to May), "Tag-ulan" (the rainy season from June to November), and "Tag-lamig" (the cold season from December to February). The southwest monsoon (from May to October) is known as the "Habagat" and the dry winds of the northeast monsoon (from November to April) as the "Amihan".

Natural Resources

An archipelago like the Philippines offers diverse natural resources, from land to marine to mineral resources. It is also the biggest copper producer in Southeast Asia and among the top ten producers of gold in the world. Other natural resources like iron ore (main producer in SE Asia), chrome, copper, nickel, cobalt, silver are also abundant. It is home of 2,145 fish species, four times more than those found in the Bahamas. Palay (Rice) and corn are the main crops, together with other cash crops like coconuts, sugarcane, bananas, mangos, pineapple products, vegetables, egg, tobacco, coffee, and so on. The 7,107 islands boast beautiful beeches and sceneries offering soothing leisure and relaxation spots for vacationers and tourists.

Mount Apo, the highest mountain in the Philippines

Mayon Volcano, the most active volcano in the Philippines

Most of the mountainous islands used to be covered in tropical rainforest and are volcanic in origin. There are many active volcanos such as Mayon Volcano(马荣火山), Mount Pinatubo, and Taal Volcano(塔阿尔火山), which attract many tourists every year. The highest mountain is Mount Apo located in Mindanao measuring at 2,954 meters (about 9,691 ft) above sea level. The longest river is the Cagayan River(卡加延河) in northern Luzon.

Tourist Sites

The Philippines is an exotic tourist destination in Southeast Asia boasting several fascinating tourist destinations of the world. Sprawling across 300,000 square kilometers, the beautiful archipelago is home to 7,107 enchanting islands. Luzon, Visayas, and Mindanao constitute the main island groups in the country. The country is renowned for its beautiful islands, golden beaches, astonishing volcanoes, numerous diving spots and exotic wildlife. Nature lovers, wildlife enthusiasts, honeymooners and adventure seekers are all lured by the major Philippines tourist attractions.

Today, a trip to the Philippines usually begins in the capital city of Manila, where visitors head straight for Rizal Park(黎刹公园), surrounded by sophisticated shops and restaurants, bustling and colorful markets, and historic museums. Manila, which was named after a white-flowered mangrove plant called Nilad, was a tiny Malay settlement along the Pasig River(帕西格河) ruled by Rajah Sulayman in the 16th century. The Spanish colonizers moved the capital of the Philippines from Cebu to Manila in 1571. They built the walled city of Intramuros, which for the next 300 years, became the nerve center of the Spanish rule. The Intramuros, or old town, is another must-see for a trip back to the city's colonial past. For outdoor adventure, Mindoro Island(民都洛岛) lies just south of Manila, offering crystal clear waters and white sandy beaches, as well as a colorful coral reef on the northern coast, perhaps bested only by the famed diving and snorkeling spots found on Palawan Island(巴拉望岛).

Cebu Island, as one of the most popular overall tourist destination in the Philippines, also offers world-class diving place as well as wonderful history (here is where Spanish explorer Ferdinand Magellan first landed in the 16th century), and the nearby attractions include the Chocolate Hills(巧克力山), so named for their chocolate drop shape and color.

The Chocolate Hills in Bohol

Of course, a visit to the Philippines would not be complete without a trip up north to Luzon where the chiseled, centuries-old rice terrace of Banaue lies. The Banaue Rice Terraces are part of the Rice Terraces of the Philippine Cordilleras, ancient sprawling man-made structures from 2,000 to 6,000 years old, which is a UNESCO World Heritage Site.

The Banaue Rice Terraces
Beach in Cebu Province

Mindanao is the second-largest and most southerly island, with a very different feel from the rest of the country. A variety of Muslim ethnic groups live here. Mindanao's many natural attractions, rich flora and fauna, cultural diversity, and colorful ethnic festivals make Mindanao one of the most exciting tourist destinations in Southeast Asia. In the southwestern tip of Mindanao is Zamboanga(三宝颜) City, considered by some as the most romantic place in the Philippines and a favorite resort amongst tourists. The city is noted for its seashells, unspoiled tropical scenery and magnificent flowers.

Zamboanga was founded by the Spanish, and the 17th-century walls of Fort Pilar(皮拉尔堡), built to protect the Spanish and Christian Filipinos from Muslim onslaughts, are still standing. The city has a number of hotels, cars for hire, good public transport and vintas (small boats), often with colorful sails, available to take visitors round the city bay. The flea market sells Muslim pottery, clothes and brassware. About 2 km (about 1.2 miles) from Fort Pilar are the houses of the Badjaos, which are stilted constructions on the water. Water gypsies live in boats in this area, moving to wherever the fishing is best. Plaza Pershing and Pasonanca Park are worth visiting. Santa Cruz Island(圣克鲁斯岛) has a sand beach which turns pink when the corals from the sea are washed ashore, and is ideal for bathing, snorkeling and scuba diving. There is also an old Muslim burial ground here.

Apart from its scenic surroundings, the Philippines is also blessed with major cultural and historic sites. You can unwind the past with architectural marvels of Vigan[维甘(美

岸）] in Ilocos(伊罗戈) and the remains of the Second World War. The colorful festivals are celebrated with much gusto and make for major Philippines tourist attractions.

7.4 Brief History

Archaeological and paleontological discoveries show that humans existed in Palawan around 50000 BC. The aboriginal people of the Philippine Islands, the Negritos, are an Australo-Melanesian people who arrived in the Philippines at least 30,000 years ago. The Austronesian (Malayo-Polynesian) people originated from populations of Taiwanese aborigines that migrated from mainland Asia approximately 6,000 years ago, who settled in the islands, and eventually migrated to Indonesia, Malaysia, and soon after, to the Polynesian islands, and Madagascar.

The Philippine Islands had cultural ties with Malaysia, Indonesia, and India during ancient times, as proven by the extent of Tantric, and Hindu-Buddhist influence in the area, and trade relations with southern China, and other neighboring countries as early as the 5th century.

The beginnings of colonization started to take form when Philip II of Spain ordered successive expeditions. Miguel López de Legazpi arrived from Mexico in 1565, and formed the first Spanish settlements in Cebu. In 1571 he established Manila as the capital of the Spanish East Indies.

Spanish rule brought political unification to an archipelago of previously independent islands and communities which later became the Philippines, and introduced elements of Western civilization such as the code of law, printing and the Gregorian calendar. The Philippines was ruled as a territory of the Viceroyalty of New Spain from 1565 to 1821, and administered as a province of Spain from 1821 to 1898.[2]

The Spanish-American War began in Cuba(古巴) in 1898, and soon reached the Philippines when Commodore George Dewey defeated the Spanish squadron at the Manila Bay. As a result of its defeat, Spain ceded the Philippines, together with Cuba, Puerto Rico(波多黎各), and Guam(关岛) to the United States as ratified in the Treaty of Paris in 1898. The country's status as a territory changed when it became the Commonwealth of the Philippines in 1935, which provided self-governance. Plans for independence over the next decade were interrupted during the Second World War when Japan invaded, and occupied the islands. After the Japanese were defeated in 1945, and control returned to the Philippines and American forces in the Liberation of the Philippine Islands from 1944 to 1945. The Philippines was granted independence from the United States on July 4,1946.

Since 1946, the newly independent Philippine state has faced political instability. The late 1960s and early 1970s saw economic development that was second in Asia, next to Japan. Ferdinand Marcos was, then, the elected president. Barred from seeking a third term, Marcos declared martial law on September 21, 1972, and ruled the country by decree.

The return of democracy, and government reforms after the events of 1986 were hampered by national debt, government corruption. The Philippines economy improved during the administration of Fidel V. Ramos, who was elected in 1992. However, the economic improvements were negated at the onset of the Asian Financial Crisis of 1997. Gloria Macapagal-Arroyo took Philippine leadership in 2001 following the impeachment of the Estrada government. Benigo Aquino Ⅲ won the 2010 national elections and served as the president.

7.5 Politics

Capital: Manila

The city of Manila, or simply Manila, is the capital of the Philippines and one of the 17 cities and municipalities that make up Metro Manila[3]. Covering a total land area of 38.3 square kilometers, Manila is the second most populous city in the Philippines, with more than 1.6 million inhabitants. The metropolitan area is the second most populous in Southeast Asia.

Manila lies about 950 kilometers southeast of China's Hong Kong and 2,400 kilometers northeast of Singapore. The river bisects the city in the middle. Almost all of the city sits on top of centuries of prehistoric alluvial deposits built by the waters of the Pasig River and on some land reclaimed from the Manila Bay. The layout of the city was haphazardly planned during Spanish Era as a set of communities surrounding the original Spanish Era walled city of Manila, called intramuros.

As the capital city, Manila is the economic, political and cultural center of the country, with several functional places like Cultural Center, International Conference Center, Trade and Business Exposition Center, etc. It is also a culturally interesting city with a long history, for it was influenced by Indian and Chinese civilization, as well as Spanish and American culture, which attracts numbers of visitors every year.

Parties

There're more than 100 parties in the Philippines. Major parties include Liberal Party, Lakas-Christian Muslim Democrates, National People's Coalition, Moro National Liberation Front, Moro Islamic Liberation Front and Communist Party of the Philippines.

Liberal Party is the current ruling party.

Leaders

Benigno Aquino Ⅲ (born February 8,1960) is the 15th president of the Philippines since June, 2010. He now is the chairman of the Liberal Party.

Government

The Philippines has a presidential, unitary form of government (with some modification; there is one autonomous region largely free from the national government). The president functions as both head of state and head of government, and is commander-in-chief of the armed forces. The president is elected by popular vote for a single six-year term, during which time she or he appoints and presides over the cabinet.

The cabinet is appointed by the president with the consent of the Commission of Appointments' elections; president and vice-president are elected on separate tickets by popular vote for six-year terms. Last election was held on June, 2010. Next election will be held in May, 2016.

Administration

The Philippines is divided into three island groups: Luzon, Visayas, and Mindanao. These are divided into 18 regions, 2 autonomous regions(Autonomous Region in Muslim Mindanao and Cordillera Administrative Region) and National Capital Region, with 81 provinces, 144 cities, 1,490 municipalities and 42,029 barangays under its jurisdiction.

Constitution

The Philippine Constitution has been rewritten seven times starting from the Biak-na-Bato Constitution to the 1987 Constitution. It was ratified in early 1987, signaling the country's return to democracy. The political evolution and every significant event in the Philippine history resulted in a change in the constitution. To date, the 1987 Constitution still stands, although some sectors have started to lobby for change in certain provisions as well as the change of the whole constitution.

Legislation

The bicameral Congress is composed of the Senate(24 seats; one-half elected every three years; members elected by popular vote to serve six-year terms), serving as the upper house whose members are elected nationally to a six-year term, and the House of Representatives(214 seats; members elected by popular vote to serve three-year terms.

Additional members may be appointed by the president but the Constitution prohibits the House of Representatives from having more than 250 members), serving as the lower house whose members are elected to a three-year term, and are elected from both legislative districts and through sectoral representation. Last election of Senate was held in July, 2013; next election to be held in July, 2016. Last election of House of Representatives was held on May 16, 2013; next election to be held in May, 2019.

 Justice

The judicial power is vested in the Supreme Court, composed of a Chief Justice as its presiding officer and fourteen associate justices, all appointed by the president from nominations submitted by the Judicial and Bar Council. Attempts to amend the constitution to either a federal, unicameral or parliamentary form of government have been satisfactory since the Ramos administration.

 Diplomacy

In its foreign policy, under the principle of equality, mutual benefit and respect, the Philippines cultivates constructive relations with its Asian neighbors, with whom it is linked through membership in ASEAN, the ASEAN Regional Forum (ARF), and the Asia-Pacific Economic Cooperation (APEC) forum. The Philippines chaired ASEAN from 2006 to 2007, hosting the ASEAN Heads of State Summit and the ASEAN Regional Forum. The Philippines is a member of the UN and some of its specialized agencies, and served a two-year term as a member of the UN Security Council from January 2004 to 2006, acting as UNSC President in September, 2005. Since 1992, the Philippines has been a member of the Non-Aligned Movement. The government is seeking observer status in the Organization of the Islamic Conference (OIC).

The Philippines also values its relations with the countries of the Middle East, in no small part because hundreds of thousands of Filipinos are employed in that region. The welfare of the some four to five million overseas Filipino contract workers is considered to be a pillar of Philippine foreign policy. Foreign exchange remittances from these workers exceed 11 percent of the country's gross domestic product.

The fundamental Philippine attachment to democracy and human rights is also reflected in its foreign policy. Philippine soldiers and police have participated in a number of multilateral civilian police and peacekeeping operations, and a Philippine Army general served as the first commander of the UN Peacekeeping Operation in East Timor. The Philippines presently has peacekeepers deployed in eight UN Peacekeeping Operations worldwide.

US-Philippine relations are based on shared history and commitment to democratic principles, as well as on economic ties. The historical and cultural links between the Philippines and the United States remain strong. The Philippines modeled its governmental institutions on those of the United States and continues to share a commitment to democracy and human rights. At the most fundamental level of bilateral relations, human links continue to form a strong bridge between the two countries. There are an estimated four million Americans of Philippine ancestry in the United States, and more than 250,000 American citizens in the Philippines.

7.6 Economy

Skyline of Ortigas Center in the foreground with Makati in the background on the left

The Philippine economy is the 39th largest in the world, with an estimated 2014 gross domestic product (nominal) of $289.686 billion. Primary exports include semiconductors and electronic products, transport equipment, garments, copper products, petroleum products, coconut oil, and fruits. Major trading partners include the United States, Japan, China, Singapore, Republic of Korea, the Netherlands, China's Hong Kong, Germany, China's Taiwan, and Thailand. Its unit of currency is the Philippine peso (₱ or PHP).

The economy is heavily reliant upon remittances from overseas filipinos, which surpass foreign direct investment as a source of foreign currency. Remittances peaked in 2010 at 10.4% of the national GDP, and were 8.6% in 2012. Regional development is uneven, with Luzon—Metro Manila in particular—gaining most of the new economic growth at the expense of the other regions, although the government has taken steps to distribute economic growth by promoting investment in other areas of the country. Despite constraints, services industries such as tourism and business process outsourcing have been identified as areas with some of the best opportunities for growth for the country.

Goldman Sachs includes the country in its list of the "Next Eleven" economies but China and India have emerged as major economic competitors. Goldman Sachs estimates that by the year 2050, it will be the 20th largest economy in the world. HSBC also projects the Philippine economy to become the 16th largest economy in the world, the 5th largest economy in Asia and the largest economy in the South East Asian region by 2050. The Philippines is a member of the World Bank, the International Monetary Fund, the World Trade Organization (WTO), the Asian Development Bank which is headquartered in Mandaluyong, the Colombo Plan, the G-77 and the G-24 among other groups and institutions.

The unemployment rate as of December 14, 2014 stands at 6.0%. Meanwhile, due to lower charges in basic necessities, the inflation rate eases to 3.7% in November. Gross international reserves as of October 2013 are $83.201 billion. The debt-to-GDP ratio continues to decline to 38.1% as of March 2014 from a record high of 78% in 2004. The country is a net importer but it is also a creditor nation.

Agriculture

A newly industrialized country, the Philippine economy has been transitioning from one based upon agriculture to an economy with more emphasis upon services and manufacturing. Of the country's total labor force of around 40.813 million, the agricultural sector employs close to 32% of the labor force, and accounts for 14% of GDP. The industrial sector employs around 14% of the workforce and accounts for 30% of GDP. Meanwhile, 47% of the workers involved in the services sector are responsible for 56% of GDP.

Arable farmland comprises more than 40 percent of the total land area. Although the Philippines is rich in agricultural potential, inadequate infrastructure, lack of financing, and government policies have limited productivity gains. Philippine farms produce food crops for domestic consumption and cash crops for export.

Decades of uncontrolled logging and slash-and-burn agriculture in marginal upland areas have stripped forests, with critical implications for the ecological balance. Although the government has instituted conservation programs, deforestation remains a severe problem.

With its 7,107 islands, the Philippines has a very diverse range of fishing areas. Not withstanding good prospects for marine fisheries, the industry continues to face a difficult future due to destructive fishing methods, a lack of funds, and inadequate government support.

Agriculture generally suffers from low productivity, low economies of scale and inadequate infrastructure support. Agricultural output increased by 5.1% in real terms during 2004 but stagnated to 2.24% in 2005 due to drought and intermittent weather disturbances. Despite the adverse effects of successive and very strong typhoons in the last four months of 2006, the overall annual farm output expanded by 3.8%. In 2007, the sector grew by 4.68%, led by gains in the fisheries sub-sector.

Industry

Industrial production is centered on the processing and assembly operations of the following: food, beverages, tobacco, rubber products, textiles, clothing and footwear, pharmaceuticals, paints, plywood and veneer, paper and paper products, small appliances, and electronics. Heavier industries are dominated by the production of cement, glass, industrial chemicals, fertilizers, iron and steel, and refined petroleum products. Newer industries, particularly production of semiconductors and other intermediate goods for incorporation into consumer electronics are important components of Philippine exports and are located in special export processing zones.

The industrial sector is concentrated in urban areas, especially in the metropolitan Manila region, and has only weak linkages to the rural economy. Inadequate infrastructure, transportation, and communication have so far inhibited faster industrial growth, although significant strides have been made in addressing the last of these elements.

The Philippines is a newly industrialized country with an economy anchored on agriculture but with substantial contributions from manufacturing, mining, remittances from overseas Filipinos, and services industries such as tourism, and increasingly, business process outsourcing.

The Philippines is one of the world's most highly mineralized countries, with untapped mineral wealth estimated at more than $840 billion. Philippine copper, gold, and chromate deposits are among the largest in the world. However, despite its rich mineral deposits, the Philippine mining industry is just a fraction of what it was in the 1970s and 1980s when the country ranked among the ten leading gold and copper producers worldwide. Low metal prices, high production costs, and lack of investment in infrastructure have contributed to the industry's overall decline. A December 2004 Supreme Court decision upheld the constitutionality of the 1995 Mining Act, thereby allowing up to 100 percent foreign-owned companies to invest in large-scale exploration, development, and utilization of minerals, oil, and gas.

Services

The services industry plays a very important role in the Philippines, which provides employment for over 14 million people (taking up more than 40% of the employment in the whole country). In 2010, the economic growth had increased by 12% contributing to the development of services industry. Nowadays, services industry is still one of the most important ones in the Philippines.

Tourism

Tourism is one of the major contributors to the economy of the Philippines, contributing 7.1% share in the Philippine GDP, employing 1,226,500 jobs, and accounting for 3.2 percent of total employment in the country in 2013. The industry had grown by US$4.8 billion in 2013. 2,433,428 international visitors have arrived in the country from January to June 2014, up by 2.22% in the same period in 2013. Republic of Koreans, Chinese, and Japanese accounted for 58.78% while Americans accounted for 19.28% and Europeans 10.64%. The Department of Tourism has the responsibility for the management and promotion of the tourism sector. On January 6, 2012, it launched a new slogan named "It's More Fun in the Philippines" and ranked third in world's best marketing campaigns according to Warc 100.

As an archipelago consisting of 7,107 islands, the Philippines has numerous beaches, caves and other rock formations. Tourist attractions in the country include the white sand beaches of Boracay, named as the best island in the world by Travel + Leisure in 2012, commercial shopping malls located in Manila including the SM Mall of Asia, Festival Supermall, etc., Banaue Rice Terraces in Ifugao, historic town of Vigan, Chocolate Hills in Bohol, Magellan's Cross in Cebu, Tubbataha Reef in Visayas and others in the rest of the country.

7.7 Culture

Languages

According to the 1987 Philippine Constitution, Filipino and English are the official languages. About 180 languages and dialects are also spoken in the islands, almost all of them belonging to the Borneo-Philippines group of the Malayo-Polynesian language branch of the Austronesian language family.

Filipino is the standard version of Tagalog, spoken mainly in Metro Manila, and other urban regions. Both Tagalog and English are used in government, education, print and broadcast media, and business.

Other major regional languages include Cebuano, Ilocano, Hiligaynon, Waray-Waray, Kapampangan, Bikol, Pangasinan, Kinaray-a, Maranao, Maguindanao, Tausug, and Chavacano. Other languages include Spanish, and Arabic which are recognized as auxiliary languages in the Philippine Constitution. The use of Spanish is prevalent among Hispanic mestizos; and Arabic is used by Filipino Muslims, and taught in madrasah (Muslim) schools.

Ethnics

The majority of Philippine nationals are descended from the Austronesian (Malayo-

Polynesian) people who settled in over a thousand years ago from southern China's Taiwan, genetically most closely related to the Ami tribe. The Malayo-Polynesian-speaking people, a branch of the Austronesian-speaking peoples, migrated to the Philippines, and brought their knowledge of agriculture, and ocean-sailing technology. Filipinos to this day are composed of various Malayo-Polynesian ethnic groups, including the Visayans, the Tagalog, the Ilocano, the Moro, the Kapampangan, the Bicolano, the Pangasinense, the Igorot, the Lumad, the Mangyan, the Ibanag, the Badjao, the Ivatan, and the Palawan tribes. [4] The Negritos, including the Aetas and the Ati, are considered as the aboriginal inhabitants of the Philippines though they are estimated to be fewer than 30,000 people (0.03%).

Filipinos of Chinese descent currently form the largest non-Austronesian ethnic group, forming 1.5% of the population, followed by Filipinos of Spanish descent. Other significant minorities include American, British, European, Japanese, Asian Indian, Korean, Arab, Indonesian, and other ethnic groups.

Throughout the country's history, various ethnic groups as well as immigrants and colonizers have intermarried with the native population, producing Filipino mestizos. These mestizos, apart from being of mixed Malayo-Polynesian and European ancestry, can be descended from any ethnic foreign forebears. The official percentage of Filipinos with foreign ancestry is unknown since there are no credible sources for the percentage of Philippine mestizos residing in the Philippines. The number of Filipino mestizos that reside outside the Philippines is also unknown. However, due to major historical factors, such as the Spanish colonization, the American occupation, and Chinese immigration after World War Ⅱ, most Filipino mestizos that reside in the Philippines are now of Spanish, American, European, Chinese, and other foreign descent.

Religion

The Islamic religion was brought to the Philippines by traders and proselytizers from Malaysia, Indonesia, and Arabia. By the 13th century, Islam was established in the Sulu Archipelago(苏禄群岛), and spread from there to Mindanao; it had reached parts of the Visayas, and Luzon region by 1565. Muslim converts established Islamic communities and states ruled by Datus, Rajahs, or Sultans.

Basilica Minore de San Sebastián, Manila

When the Spaniards arrived in the 16th century, the majority of the estimated 500,000 people in the islands lived in independent settlements.

The Philippines is one of two countries in Asia and the Asia-Pacific region with Roman Catholic majorities; the other is East Timor. The Philippines is separated into dioceses of which the Archdiocese of Manila is the main primacy. About 90% of Filipinos identify themselves as Christians, with 81% belonging to the Roman Catholic Church. 2% are composed of Protestant denominations, and 11% either belong to the Philippine Independent Church, Iglesia ni Cristo, or others.

The Philippines is also well-known for its Baroque-style churches.[5] Approximately 5% of Filipinos are Muslims, and are locally known as Moros, having been dubbed this by the Spaniards due to their sharing Islam with the Moors of North Africa. They primarily settle in parts of Mindanao, Palawan, and the Sulu archipelago, but are now found in most urban areas of the country. Most lowland Muslim Filipinos practice Islam, although the practices of some Mindanao's highland Muslim populations reflect a mixture with Animism. There are also small populations of Buddhists, Baha'i, Hindus, Sikhs, and animists, which, along with other non-Christians, non-Muslims and those with no religion, collectively comprise 2.5% of the population.

Customs

Philippine culture is a fusion of pre-Hispanic Austronesian (Malayo-Polynesian) civilizations mixed with Hispanic, and American. It has also been influenced by Chinese, Arab, and Indian cultures.

The Hispanic influences on Philippine culture are derived from the culture of Spain. These Hispanic influences are most evident in literature, folk music, folk dance, language, food, art, and religion.

Ethnic and folk dancing is an indispensable part in Philippine culture. Dancing varies from region to region. "Carinosa" (also called Love Dance) is considered the national dancing, which reflects the characteristics of the people of friendliness, loveliness and kindheartedness.

Spanish colonialists introduced Iberian, and Mexican dishes, such as arroz valenciana, to those of the Mexican cuisine. Philippine cuisine is a mixture of Asian, Oceanian, European, and American dishes. The main food for most of the people (70%) is rice, and a few take corns as the main food in their daily life because of the geographical features. In many areas, people eat with their hands. The people prefer the light flavor and fresh food, choosing Western style food for breakfasts, and Chinese food for lunch and dinner. There is also a wide influence of American pop cultural trends, such as the love of fast-food; many street corners exhibit fast-food outlets. Another feature in food culture is that people specially like beer.

Various sports are also enjoyed, including boxing, basketball, badminton, billiards, football (soccer) etc., and

Polynesian) people who settled in over a thousand years ago from southern China's Taiwan, genetically most closely related to the Ami tribe. The Malayo-Polynesian-speaking people, a branch of the Austronesian-speaking peoples, migrated to the Philippines, and brought their knowledge of agriculture, and ocean-sailing technology. Filipinos to this day are composed of various Malayo-Polynesian ethnic groups, including the Visayans, the Tagalog, the Ilocano, the Moro, the Kapampangan, the Bicolano, the Pangasinense, the Igorot, the Lumad, the Mangyan, the Ibanag, the Badjao, the Ivatan, and the Palawan tribes.[4] The Negritos, including the Aetas and the Ati, are considered as the aboriginal inhabitants of the Philippines though they are estimated to be fewer than 30,000 people (0.03%).

Filipinos of Chinese descent currently form the largest non-Austronesian ethnic group, forming 1.5% of the population, followed by Filipinos of Spanish descent. Other significant minorities include American, British, European, Japanese, Asian Indian, Korean, Arab, Indonesian, and other ethnic groups.

Throughout the country's history, various ethnic groups as well as immigrants and colonizers have intermarried with the native population, producing Filipino mestizos. These mestizos, apart from being of mixed Malayo-Polynesian and European ancestry, can be descended from any ethnic foreign forebears. The official percentage of Filipinos with foreign ancestry is unknown since there are no credible sources for the percentage of Philippine mestizos residing in the Philippines. The number of Filipino mestizos that reside outside the Philippines is also unknown. However, due to major historical factors, such as the Spanish colonization, the American occupation, and Chinese immigration after World War II, most Filipino mestizos that reside in the Philippines are now of Spanish, American, European, Chinese, and other foreign descent.

Religion

Basilica Minore de San Sebastián, Manila

The Islamic religion was brought to the Philippines by traders and proselytizers from Malaysia, Indonesia, and Arabia. By the 13th century, Islam was established in the Sulu Archipelago(苏禄群岛), and spread from there to Mindanao; it had reached parts of the Visayas, and Luzon region by 1565. Muslim converts established Islamic communities and states ruled by Datus, Rajahs, or Sultans. When the Spaniards arrived in the 16th century, the majority of the estimated 500,000 people in the islands lived in independent settlements.

The Philippines is one of two countries in Asia and the Asia-Pacific region with Roman Catholic majorities; the other is East Timor. The Philippines is separated into dioceses of which the Archdiocese of Manila is the main primacy. About 90% of Filipinos identify themselves as Christians, with 81% belonging to the Roman Catholic Church. 2% are composed of Protestant denominations, and 11% either belong to the Philippine Independent Church, Iglesia ni Cristo, or others.

The Philippines is also well-known for its Baroque-style churches.[5] Approximately 5% of Filipinos are Muslims, and are locally known as Moros, having been dubbed this by the Spaniards due to their sharing Islam with the Moors of North Africa. They primarily settle in parts of Mindanao, Palawan, and the Sulu archipelago, but are now found in most urban areas of the country. Most lowland Muslim Filipinos practice Islam, although the practices of some Mindanao's highland Muslim populations reflect a mixture with Animism. There are also small populations of Buddhists, Baha'i, Hindus, Sikhs, and animists, which, along with other non-Christians, non-Muslims and those with no religion, collectively comprise 2.5% of the population.

Customs

Philippine culture is a fusion of pre-Hispanic Austronesian (Malayo-Polynesian) civilizations mixed with Hispanic, and American. It has also been influenced by Chinese, Arab, and Indian cultures.

The Hispanic influences on Philippine culture are derived from the culture of Spain. These Hispanic influences are most evident in literature, folk music, folk dance, language, food, art, and religion.

Ethnic and folk dancing is an indispensable part in Philippine culture. Dancing varies from region to region. "Carinosa" (also called Love Dance) is considered the national dancing, which reflects the characteristics of the people of friendliness, loveliness and kindheartedness.

Spanish colonialists introduced Iberian, and Mexican dishes, such as arroz valenciana, to those of the Mexican cuisine. Philippine cuisine is a mixture of Asian, Oceanian, European, and American dishes. The main food for most of the people (70%) is rice, and a few take corns as the main food in their daily life because of the geographical features. In many areas, people eat with their hands. The people prefer the light flavor and fresh food, choosing Western style food for breakfasts, and Chinese food for lunch and dinner. There is also a wide influence of American pop cultural trends, such as the love of fast-food; many street corners exhibit fast-food outlets. Another feature in food culture is that people specially like beer.

Various sports are also enjoyed, including boxing, basketball, badminton, billiards, football (soccer) etc., and ten-pin bowling is a popular game in the country.

Upper-class society prefers the American life style. The family is the centre of the social structure. Philippine people like talking and praising families. People shake hands when meeting friends and guests. In the Philippines, different minorities have different costumes. Nowadays, people of upper-class society like Western suits while ordinary men like white shirts and Western style pants. Women prefer colorful dressing without colons or have Sarong wrapped around the waist. Old people still wear slippers made from wood, hemp or straw.

Firecracker for celebrating the New Year

Important holidays include New Year's Day (January 1), Labor Day (May 1), Good Friday (last Sunday of May), Independence Day (June 12, 1898 was the date of declaration of independence from Spain; July 4, 1946 was the date of independence from the US), National Heroes Day (August 27), Christmas Day (December 25), Rizal Day (December 30).

The number tattoo is "13" for Philippine people, which to them means bad luck and disaster. Their left hands are thought to be dirty, and people do not use left hands to pass on things or food. For the religious reasons, Islamic communities do not have pork or pork products as well as milk and strong alcohol. Philippine people are not interested in having ginger, viscera of animals and whole fish.

Notes

[1] According to official sources, the white triangle stands for equality and fraternity; the blue field for peace, truth and justice; and the red field for patriotism and valor. The eight primary rays of the sun represent the first eight provinces (Batangas, Bulacan, Cavite, Laguna, Manila, Nueva Ecija, Pampanga, and Tarlac) that sought independence from Spain and were placed under martial law by the Spaniards at the start of the Philippine Revolution in 1896. The three stars represent the three major geographical divisions of the country: Luzon, Visayas, and Mindanao.

[2] The Spanish military fought off various indigenous revolts, and several external threats, especially from the British, Dutch, and Portuguese. Roman Catholic missionaries

converted most of the inhabitants to Christianity, and founded numerous schools, universities and hospitals. In 1863 a Spanish decree introduced public education, creating free public schooling in Spanish.

[3] In November 1975, the government deicded to include the city of Manila into Metro Manila, by joining several other cities and municipalities such as Navotas and Caloocan City, Quezon City, San Juan and Mandaluyong City, Makati City, and Pasay City, etc. With a total area of about 656.58 square kilometers and a population of about 10 million, Metro Manila became one of the biggest cities in Asia.

[4] Tagalog 28.1%, Cebuano 13.1%, Ilocanon 9%, Bisaya/Ilokano/Visayan 7.6%, Hiligaynon Ilonggo 7.5%, Bikol 6%, Waray 3.4%, others 25.3% (2000 census)

[5] They are a part of the long list of UNESCO World Heritage Sites. These churches are: San Agustin Church in Intramuros, Manila; Paoay Church in Paoay, Ilocos Norte; Nuestra Señora de la Asuncion (Santa Maria) Church in Santa Maria, Ilocos Sur; and the Santo Tomas de Villanueva Church in Iloilo.

Exercises

1. **Explain the following in English.**
   (1) archipelago
   (2) "Tag-ulan"
   (3) the Philippine Constitution
   (4) UN Peacekeeping Operations
   (5) Hispanic

2. **Fill in the blanks.**
   (1) The national flag is displayed with the blue field on top _____, and with the red field on top _____.
   (2) The Philippines, which is located in _____, constitutes a(n) _____ of _____ islands.
   (3) The islands are commonly divided into three island groups: _____, _____,

Chapter 7 The Philippines

_____.

(4) It is also the biggest _____ in Southeast Asia and among the top ten producers of _____ in the world.

(5) _____ is the most active volcano in the Philippines.

(6) _____ are part of the Rice Terraces of the Philippine Cordilleras, ancient sprawling man-made structures from _____ years old, which is a(n) _____ .

(7) _____ is the _____ and current president of the Philippines.

(8) Philippine culture is a fusion of pre-Hispanic Austronesian (Malayo-Polynesian) civilizations mixed with _____ . It has also been influenced by _____ cultures.

(9) People _____ when meeting friends and guests.

(10) Their left hands are thought to be _____ , and they do not use left hands to pass on things or food.

3. Answer the following questions.

(1) What is the implication of the blue and red fields on the national flag?

(2) How many island groups are there in the Philippines? What are they?

(3) How was the history of colonization in the Philippine history?

(4) Where is the Rice Terraces located in the Philippine? Why is Mindanao the most exciting tourist destinations in Southeast Asia?

(5) What are the main languages and dialects spoken in the islands? How do they influence society in your opinion?

4. Discussion.

(1) How does the location and climate affect the plantation in the Philippines?

(2) How many recognized seasons are there in a year in the Philippines? How is it different from your own country?

(3) What is your favorite tourist destination in the Philippines? Why?

(4) What are the features of the culture in the Philippines as a whole? How is it influenced by other nations?

CHAPTER 8

Singapore

8.1 Country Name

conventional long form: Republic of Singapore
conventional short form: Singapore
local long form: Republic of Singapore
local short form: Singapore

8.2 National Symbols

National Flag

The flag is horizontally divided into two equal horizontal bands of red (top) and white; near the hoist side of the red band, there is a vertical, white crescent (closed portion is toward the hoist side) partially enclosing five white five-pointed stars arranged in a circle.

National Emblem

Singapore's emblem came in existence on December 3, 1959 and with that was introduced the national flag of the country and its national anthem. It basically consists of a shield with a white crescent moon and five stars on a red background. Red is the symbol of universal brotherhood and equality of man, while the white part shows prevailing and everlasting purity and virtue.

The moon shows the emerging of a new nation and the five stars show the five ideals of democracy, peace, progress, justice and equality. On the left and right are a lion and a tiger, supporting the shield. There is a blue ribbon underneath it inscribed with the Republic's motto "Majulah Singapura" in gold, meaning "Onward, Singapore".

8.3 Geography

Location

Singapore, officially the Republic of Singapore, is an island city-state located at the southern tip of the Malay Peninsula. The microstate lies 137 kilometers (about 85 mi) north of the equator, south of the Malaysian State of Johor and north of Indonesia's Riau Islands. At 714 km^2, Singapore, the smallest nation in Southeast Asia, is by orders of magnitude the largest of the three remaining sovereign city-states in the world [the others being Monaco(摩纳哥) and Vatican(梵蒂冈) City].

Area

Singapore consists of 63 islands, including mainland Singapore. There are two man-made connections to Johor(柔佛), Malaysia: the Johor-Singapore Causeway in the north, and the Tuas Second Link in the west. Jurong Island(裕廊岛), Pulau Tekong(德光岛), Pulau Ubin(乌敏岛) and Sentosa(圣陶沙) are the largest of Singapore's many smaller islands. The highest natural point of Singapore is Bukit Timah Hill(武吉知马山) at 166 m (about 537 ft).

The south of Singapore, an area around the mouth of the Singapore River and what is now the Downtown Core, used to be the only concentrated urban area, while the rest of the land was either undeveloped tropical rainforest or used for agriculture. Since the 1960s, the government has constructed new residential towns in outlying areas, resulting in an entirely built-up urban landscape. The Urban Redevelopment Authority was established on April 1, 1974, responsible for urban planning.

Singapore Botanic Gardens, a 67.3-hectare (about 166 acre) garden, includes the National Orchid Garden, has a collection of more than 3,000 species of orchids.

Singapore has on-going land reclamation projects with earth obtained from its own hills, the seabed, and neighboring countries. As a result, Singapore's land area grew from 581.5 km² (about 224.5 sq mi) in the 1960s to 714 km² (about 275 sq mi) today, and may grow by another 100 km² (about 38.6 sq mi) by 2030. The projects sometimes involve some of the smaller islands being merged together through land reclamation in order to form larger, more functional islands, such as in the case of Jurong Island.

Climate

Under the Köppen (热带气候区) climate classification system, Singapore has a tropical rainforest climate with no distinctive seasons. Its climate is characterized by uniform temperature and pressure, high humidity, and abundant rainfall. Temperatures range from 22℃ to 34℃ (71.6℉ to 93.2℉). On average, the relative humidity is around 90% in the morning and 60% in the afternoon. During prolonged heavy rain, relative humidity often reaches 100%. The lowest and highest temperatures recorded in its maritime history are 19.4℃ (66.92℉) and 35.8℃ (96.44℉) respectively. June and July are the hottest months, while November and December make up the wetter monsoon season. From August to October, there is often haze, sometimes severe enough to prompt public health warnings, due to bushfires in neighboring Indonesia. Singapore does not observe daylight saving time or a summer time zone change. The length of the day is nearly constant year round due to the country's location near the equator.

About 23% of Singapore's land area consists of forest and nature reserves. Urbanization has eliminated many areas of former primary rainforest, with the only remaining area of primary rainforest being Bukit Timah Nature Reserve. A variety of parks are maintained with human intervention, such as the Singapore Botanic Gardens.

Natural Resources

Only fishing and deepwater ports are the local natural resources.

Water Resource

Without natural freshwater rivers and lakes, rainfall is the primary domestic source of water supply in Singapore. About half of Singapore's water comes from rain collected in reservoirs and catchment areas while the rest comes from Malaysia. The two countries have long argued of the legality of agreements to supply water that were signed in colonial times.

Singapore has a network of reservoirs and water catchment areas. In 2001, there were 19 raw water reservoirs, 9 treatment works and 14 storage or service reservoirs locally to serve domestic needs. Marina Barrage is a dam being constructed around the estuary of three Singapore rivers, creating a huge freshwater reservoir by 2009, the Marina Bay reservoir. This will increase the rainfall catchment to two-thirds of the country's surface area.

Historically, Singapore relied on imports from Malaysia to supply half of its water consumption. However, two water agreements that supply water to Singapore are due to expire by 2011 and 2061 respectively. The two countries are engaged in a dispute on the price of water. Without a resolution in sight, the government of Singapore decided to increase self-sufficiency in its water supply. Presently, more catchment areas, facilities to recycle water (producing NEWater) and desalination plants are being built. This "four tap" strategy aims to reduce reliance on foreign supply and to diversify its water sources. In 2008, a water barrage name—The Marina Barrage was built across the Marina Channel between Marina East and Marina South. The barrage aims to provide additional water supply catchment area, improve flood control and serve as an outdoor attraction for tourists and Singaporeans.

Oil and Gas

Singapore has no oil and gas production or reserves, but its strategic location and attractive foreign investment regime have established it as Southeast Asia's largest oil refining and petrochemical centre. In 2007, the country consumed around 917,000 barrels of oil per day (bpd). Singapore's four main refineries—Esso Singapore Pte Ltd, Mobil Oil Singapore Pte Ltd, Shell Eastern Petroleum (Pte) Ltd and Singapore Refining Co Ltd [managed by BP (British Petroleum Company, Ltd) but jointly owned by BP, Caltex and the Singapore Petroleum Co]—have a combined refining capacity of more than 1.3 million bpd. This is expected to rise to around 1.4 million bpd by the end of 2008 when new capacity comes on line. Competition from new Asian refineries, notably in India [at Jāmnagar(贾姆纳格尔)] and Malaysia (at Melaka), has put the sector under increasing pressure and is likely to lead to consolidation and some loss of capacity. By early 2007, Singapore's various refiners and storage operators could hold more than 100 million barrels of crude oil and refined products, with more capacity added in 2008. At least 35 percent of the oil is used for bunker ships. The main upstream producer is the Petrochemical Corporation of Singapore (PCS), owned by Shell Eastern Petroleum and a Sumitomo-led Japanese consortium. Largest among the seven downstream companies are Phillips Petroleum and the Polyolefin Company (30% by Shell and 70% Japanese). Singapore's primary refining and petrochemical plants are located on a group of islands off the southwest coast in Jurong at the extreme.

All Singapore's natural gas is imported through three pipelines linking its electricity power generation plants to Malaysian and Indonesian gas fields. The northern pipeline delivers approximately 4 million m³ of natural gas per day from gas fields in Malaysia to Senoko Power Ltd. Another pipeline supplies approximately 9.2 million m³ of natural gas per day to SembCorp Gas Pte. Ltd from Indonesia's West Natural gas fields. The third pipeline transports approximately 9.9 million m³ of natural gas per day from South Sumatra to Singapore. The agreements are believed to expire around 2023. All Singapore's natural gas is imported. In 2002, Singapore Power imported 4.39 million m³ of natural gas through a pipeline from Malaysia, the first transnational natural gas pipeline built in East Asia. The rapid increase in the use of natural gas reflects the government's policy of reducing carbon dioxide and sulphur emissions while promoting Singapore as the centre of an integrated gas pipeline network. A desire to reduce over-dependence upon one source has seen Singapore develop links with Indonesia's Pertamina for the purchase of 9.2 million m³ per day of natural gas from the state company's West Natural gas field through a 640-km-pipeline (which came on stream in 2001) and 4.25 million m³ per day of gas from West Sumatra via a 477 km, US$420 million pipeline completed in August, 2003. Singapore is expected to increase its purchase of the Sumatran gas to 9.91 million m³ per day by 2009.

Tourist Sites

(1) History and origins

The Merlion was designed as an emblem for the Singapore Tourism Board (STB) in 1964. The designer was Mr. Fraser Brunner, a member of the souvenir committee and a curator of the Van Kleef Aquarium. The Merlion has a lion head and a fish body resting on a crest of waves. The lion head symbolizes the legend of the rediscovery of Singapore, as recorded in the "Malay Annals". In ancient times, Singapore was known as Temasek, a Javanese word for sea.

The Merlion

(2) Underwater World

The main attraction is dugong, sea cow that entertains visitors with its acrobatic movements. You may observe them through a series of interactive, feeding and training sessions specially designed to demonstrate their natural abilities of tail-walking synchronization.

Underwater World

(3) Night Safari

This is the world's premier night zoo. The twilight holds many surprises at Night Safari, where you can look a rhinoceros in the eye or hear the howls of a pack of striped hyenas. There are over 1,200 animals of over 110 exotic species to watch out for.

(4) Statues of Sir Stamford Raffles

The statue of Singapore's founder, Sir Stamford Raffles, cast in dark bronze by Thomas Woolmer, stands in front of Victoria Theatre. Its replica, made of pure polymarble white(多种花纹的白色天然大理石), stands at North Boat Quay.

Statues of Sir Stamford Raffles

Changi Chapel and Museum

(5) Changi Chapel and Museum

Honoring the spirit and commitment of those who rose from the depths of adversity, the Museum inspires future generations to come and deepen their appreciation of the heroic.

(6) Sentosa

Beach lovers can enjoy exciting games and sea sports along the 3.2-km long sandy beaches in Sentosa stretching across Siloso, Palawan and Tanjong.

Sentosa Island

(7) East Coast Park

East Coast Park, located off the East Coast Parkway, is a favorite play area for Singaporeans, either at the beach or on its landscaped vistas and terrains where cycling is much enjoyed.

East Coast Park

8.4 Brief History

The first records of settlement in Singapore are from the 2nd century AD. Between the 16th and early 19th centuries, Singapore Island was part of the Sultanate of Johor. During the Malay-Portugal wars in 1613, the settlement was set ablaze by Portuguese troops. The Portuguese subsequently held control in that century and the Dutch in the 17th, but throughout most of this time the island's population consisted mainly of fishermen.

The founding of Singapore by Sir Stamford Raffles in 1819 catapulted the island out from its fishing village status. The British had first established its presence in the Straights of Melaka (Malacca) in the 18th century and part of its policy in the region included the East India Company setting out to secure and protect its line of trade from China to India. Fearing encroaching Dutch presence, Raffles argued for an increased British presence in the region through Singapore.

In 1826, Singapore, Malacca and Penang (collectively known as the Straits Settlements) came under the control of British India. By 1832, Singapore had become the centre of government for the Straits Settlements; and in 1867, the Straits Settlements became a Crown Colony under the jurisdiction of the Colonial Office in London.

The outbreak of the Second World War and the invasion of Singapore by Japan in 1941 quickly changed things. The peace and prosperity thus came to an abrupt end when Singapore was surrendered to the Japanese on February 15, 1942, and was renamed Syonan-to (Light of the South). When the British returned three years later, they were welcomed back but their right to rule was no longer assured. Singapore was moving slowly towards self-government by the 1950s.

In 1959, the People's Action Party was elected with Lee Kuan Yew as Prime Minister (a position he would continue to hold for the next 31 years). A union was formed with Malaya (now Malaysia) in 1963, which proved short-lived. Almost unwillingly, Singapore became a sovereign, democratic and independent nation on the 9th of August 1965—a date that has since been celebrated as National Day.

Singapore gained independence as the Republic of Singapore (remaining within the Commonwealth of Nations) on August 9, 1965. Race riots broke out once more in 1969. In 1967, the country co-founded ASEAN, the Association of Southeast Asian Nations, and in 1970 it joined the Non-Aligned Movement. Lee Kuan Yew became Prime Minister. His emphasis on rapid economic growth, support for business entrepreneurship, limitations on internal democracy, and close relationships with China set the new nation's policies for the next half century.

In 1990, Goh Chok Tong succeeded Lee Kuan Yew as Prime Minister, while Lee continued serving in the Cabinet as Senior Minister until 2004, and then Minister Mentor until May 2011. During his tenure, the country faced the 1997 Asian Financial Crisis, the 2003 SARS outbreak and terrorist threats posed by Jemaah Islamiyah. On March 23, 2015, Lee Kuan Yew passed away and is recognized as the founding father of independent Singapore. In 2004, Lee Hsien Loong, the eldest son of Lee Kuan Yew, became the country's third Prime Minister.

In 2011, the ruling PAP suffered its worst election results since independence, winning about 60% of votes.

In 2015, Singapore celebrated its Golden jubilee—its 50th year of independence, with a year-long series of events branded SG50. PAP returned to power in the September general elections. Lee Hsien Loong became the Prime Minister for a second time.

8.5 Politics

In 2011, the World Justice Project's Rule of Law Index ranked Singapore among the top countries surveyed with regard to "Order and Security", "Absence of Corruption", and "Effective Criminal Justice".

Parliament House

Singapore is a parliamentary democracy with a Westminster system of unicameral parliamentary government representing different constituencies. The bulk of the executive powers rest with the Cabinet, headed by the Prime Minister, currently Mr. Lee Hsien Loong. The office of President of Singapore, historically a ceremonial one, was granted some veto powers as of 1991 for a few key decisions such as the appointment of positions. The position is to be elected by popular vote. The election was held in 2011 and Tony Tan Keng Yam became the president of Singapore.

Parliament House

The legislative branch of government is the Parliament. Parliamentary elections in Singapore are plurality-based for group representation constituencies since the Parliamentary Elections Act was modified in 1991.

The Members of the Parliament (MPs) consist of either elected, non-constituency or nominated Members(NCMP). The majority of the Members of Parliament is elected into Parliament at a general election on a first-past-the-post basis and represents either Single Member or Group Representation Constituencies (GRCs).

The elected Members of the Parliament act as a bridge between the community and the government by ensuring that the concerns of their constituents are heard in Parliament. The present Parliament was formed in September, 2015 with 92 members, 83 Members of the People's Action Party, 6 Members of the Workers' Party of Singapore, and 3 NCMP.

The People's Action Party (PAP) has been the ruling party in Singapore since self-government was attained. There are several opposition parties in Singapore, the most notable being the Workers' Party of Singapore, the Singapore Democratic Party (SDP) and the Singapore Democratic Alliance (SDA). The Economist Intelligence Unit describes Singapore as a "hybrid regime" of democratic and authoritarian elements. Freedom House ranks the country as "partly free". Although general elections are free from irregularities and vote rigging, the PAP has been criticized by some for manipulating the political system through its use of censorship, gerrymandering, and civil libel suits against opposition politicians.

Singapore has a successful and transparent market economy. Government-linked companies are dominant in various sectors of the local economy, such as media, utilities, and public transport. Singapore has consistently been rated as the least corrupt country in Asia and among the world's ten most free from corruption by Transparency International.

Although Singapore's laws are inherited from British and British Indian laws, including many elements of English common law, the government has also chosen not to follow some elements of liberal democratic values. There are no jury trials and there are laws restricting the freedom of speech that may breed ill will or cause disharmony within Singapore's multiracial, multi-religious society. Criminal activity is often punished with heavy penalties including heavy fines or caning and there are laws which allow capital punishment in Singapore for first-degree murder and drug trafficking. The Singapore government argues that Singapore has the sovereign right to determine its own judicial system and impose what it sees as an appropriate punishment, including capital punishment for the most serious crimes.

Executive Branch

Head of state: President Tong Tan Keng Yam (since September 1, 2011).

Head of government: Prime Minister Lee Hsien Loong (since September 11, 2015).

Cabinet: appointed by president, responsible to Parliament.

Elections: president elected by popular vote for a six-year term; appointed in August, 2011 (next election to be held in August 2017); following legislative elections, leader of majority party or leader of majority coalition is usually appointed prime minister by president; deputy prime ministers appointed by president.

8.6 Economy

Today, Singapore has a highly developed market economy, based historically on extended entrepôt trade. The Singaporean economy is known as one of the freest, most innovative, most competitive, and most business-friendly. The 2015 Index of Economic Freedom ranks Singapore as the second freest economy in the world. According to the Corruption Perceptions Index, Singapore is consistently ranked as one of the least corrupt countries in the world, along with New Zealand and the Scandinavian countries.

In recent years, the country has been identified as an increasingly popular tax haven for the wealthy due to the low tax rate on personal income and tax exemptions on foreign-based income and capital gains. Australian millionaire retailer Brett Blundy, with an estimated personal wealth worth AU$835 million, and multi-billionaire Facebook co-founder Eduardo Saverin are two examples of wealthy individuals who have settled in Singapore (Blundy in 2013 and Saverin in 2012). Singapore ranked fifth on the Tax Justice Network's 2013 Financial Secrecy Index of the world's top tax havens, scoring narrowly ahead of the United States.

Singapore has a highly developed market-based economy, which has historically revolved around extended entrepot trade. Along with China's Hong Kong, the Republic of Korea and China's Taiwan, Singapore is one of the Four Asian Tigers. The economy depends heavily on exports and refining imported goods, especially in manufacturing. Manufacturing constituted 25% of Singapore's GDP in 2014. The manufacturing industry is well-diversified with significant electronics, petroleum refining, chemicals, mechanical engineering and biomedical sciences manufacturing sectors. In 2006, Singapore produced about 10% of the world's foundry wafer output. Singapore has one of the busiest ports in the world and is the world's fourth largest foreign exchange trading centre after London, New York City and Tokyo.

Singapore has been rated as the most business-friendly economy in the world, with thousands of foreign expatriates working in multi-national corporations. Singapore is also considered to be one of the top centers of finance in the region and the world. In addition to this, the city-state also employs tens of thousands of foreign blue-collared workers from around the world.

Singapore is a world leader in several economic areas. The country is the world's fourth leading financial centre, one of the world's top three oil-refining centres, the world's largest oil-rig producer,

Singapore's Central Business District (CBD)

and a major hub for ship repair services. The economy depends heavily on financial services, manufacturing, oil-refining. Its top exports are refined petroleum, integrated circuits and computers which constituted 27% of the country's GDP in 2010. Tourism also forms a large part of the economy, with over 15 million tourists visiting the city-state in 2014. Singapore is an education hub. In 2009, 20% of all students in Singaporean universities were international students, who were mainly from ASEAN, China and India.

The per capita GDP in 2014 was US$56,284. As of September 2014, the unemployment rate is 2%, which is the lowest in a decade, having improved to around pre-Asian crisis level. Employment continued to grow strongly as the economy maintained its rapid expansion.

8.7 Culture

Languages

The official languages are English, Malay, Chinese (Mandarin) and Tamil (泰米尔语). The national language of Singapore is Malay for historical reasons, and it is used in the national anthem, "Majulah Singapura".

English is the main language of Singapore and has been heavily promoted as such since the country's independence. The English used is primarily based on British English, with some American English influences. The use of English became widespread in Singapore after it was implemented as a first language medium in the education system, and English is the most common language in Singaporean literature. In school, children are required to learn English and one of the three other official languages. By law, all signs and official publications are required to be primarily in English, although there are occasionally translated versions into the other official languages. However, most Singaporeans speak a localized hybrid form of English known as "Singlish" (Singapore English), which has many creole (克里奥耳化语言, 混合语)-like characteristics, incorporating vocabulary and grammar from Standard English, various Chinese dialects, Malay, and Indian languages.

The second most common language in Singapore is Mandarin, with over fifty percent of the population having it as a second language. Most Singapore Chinese are, however, descended from immigrants who came from the southern regions of China where other dialects were spoken, such as Hokkien, Teochew and Cantonese. Mandarin use has spread largely as a result of government efforts to support its adoption and use over the dialects.

Ethnics

Chinese occupies 74.2% of the total population, Malay 13.3%, Indian 9.1%, and others 3.4%.

Religion

Singapore is a multi-religious country. According to Statistics Singapore, around 44% of resident Singaporeans (excluding significant numbers of visitors and migrant workers) practice Buddhism and Taoism. About 18%, mostly Chinese, Eurasians, and Indians, practice Christianity—a broad classification including Catholicism, Protestantism and other denominations. Muslims constitute 15%, of whom Malays account for the majority with a substantial number of Indian Muslims and Chinese Muslims. Smaller minorities practice Sikhism, Hinduism and others, according to the 2010 census.

About 15% of the population declared no religious affiliation.

Customs

Singapore is popular because of the way it has economically evolved and progressed and at the same time preserved its age-old traditions and customs. Though it appears extremely modern and polished from the outside, the local customs and traditions in Singapore are still dominant there, kept alive by the older generations. Owing to the presence of diverse religions and ethnicities such as the Indians, the Malays and the Muslims, there is a kaleidoscope of diverse local customs and traditions in Singapore.

Some of the local customs and traditions in Singapore insist that people always present the business card with both hands and not have the card in black, which is an inauspicious color for the Chinese people. The custom in Singapore is generally not to adapt handshakes as greetings, but other forms such as bowing, salaaming, saluting, etc. Another popular custom in Singapore is that the people here enter barefoot inside their homes and shoes are removed outside as a sign of respect. There are many other local customs and traditions in Singapore that vary from religion to religion.

The different religions in Singapore respect the traditions and customs of each other and thus contribute to the stability of the multicultural society of Singapore.

Exercises

1. **Explain the following in English.**

    (1) Island city-state

    (2) Jurong Island

    (3) monsoon

    (4) the Merlion

    (5) Sir Stamford Raffles

2. **Fill in the blanks.**

    (1) The three remaining sovereign city-states in the world are _____, _____ and _____; and the largest of them is _____.

    (2) _____ is recognized as the founding father of independent Singapore.

    (3) During World War II, the _____ invaded Malaya, culminating in the Battle of Singapore.

    (4) Singapore is a _____ democracy with a _____ of unicameral parliamentary government representing different constituencies.

    (5) Singapore has a successful and transparent market economy. Government-linked companies are dominant in various sectors of the local economy, such as _____, _____, and _____.

    (6) Along with _____, _____ and _____, Singapore is one of the Four Asian Tigers.

    (7) Singapore has a highly developed _____ economy, based historically on extended entrepôt trade.

    (8) The official languages of Singapore are _____, _____, _____ and _____. The national language of Singapore is Malay for historical reasons.

    (9) Most Singapore Chinese are, however, descended from immigrants who came from the southern regions of China where other dialects were spoken, such as _____, _____ and _____.

    (10) The custom in Singapore is generally not to adapt _____ as greetings, but other forms such as _____, _____, _____, etc.

3. **Answer the following questions.**

    (1) Why are there no distinctive seasons in Singapore? What is the climate like in this country?

    (2) How did the Singapore solve the water oil and gas shortage problems?

    (3) Give five of main tourist sites in Singapore.

    (4) Why has Singapore consistently been rated as the least corrupt country in Asia?

(5) Give a brief introduction to the customs and traditions in Singapore.

4. **Discussion.**

   (1) "When in Rome, do as the Romans do." As a Chinese, what habits should you pay special attention to in order to avoid local punishment if you have a chance to visit Singapore?

   (2) In terms of economy, what can China learn from Singapore to transform our country into a developed one?

   (3) What do you think are the differences between the mainland Chinese and the Singapore Chinese? What makes the differences?

CHAPTER 9

Thailand

9.1 Country Name

Full Name: the Kingdom of Thailand
Short Name: Thailand
Used Name: Siam

9.2 National Symbols

National Flag

The flag of the Kingdom of Thailand shows five horizontal stripes in the colours of red, white, blue, white and red, with the middle blue stripe being twice as wide as each of the other four. The three colours red-white-blue stand for nation-religion-king, an unofficial motto of Thailand. The flag was adopted on September 28, 1917, according to the royal decree about the flag in that year. The Thai name for the flag is *Thong Trairong*, which simply means tricolour flag.

National Emblem

The national emblem of Thailand features the Garuda[1], a figure from both Buddhist and Hindu[2] mythology. In Thailand, this figure is used as a symbol of the royal family and authority. This version of the figure is referred to as Krut Pha, meaning "garuda acting as the vehicle (of Vishnu)(毗湿奴,印度教主神

之一）". The national emblem is also the emblem of the King of Thailand[3].

The Garuda also features in the coat of arms of Indonesia and the city of Ulan Bator (the capital of Mongolia). The coat of arms of Indonesia is different from that of Thailand in one respect the former does not feature a heraldic shield.

9.3 Geography

Location

At 513,115 km², Thailand is the world's 50th largest country in land mass, whilst it is the world's 20th largest country in terms of population. It is comparable in population to countries such as France and the United Kingdom, and is similar in land size to France and California in the US.

Thailand is a country at the centre of the Indo-China Peninsula. It is bordered to the north by Myanmar and Laos, to the east by Laos and Cambodia, to the south by the Gulf of the Thailand and Malaysia, and to the west by the Andaman Sea and the southern extremity of Myanmar.

Thailand is home to several distinct geographic regions, partly corresponding to the provincial groups. The north of the country is mountainous, with the highest point being Doi Inthanon(因他暖山) at 2,565 meters (about 8,415 ft) above sea level. The northeast, Isan, consists of the Khorat Plateau(呵叻高原), bordered to the east by the Mekong River. The centre of the country is dominated by the predominantly flat Chao Phraya/Mae Nam(昭披耶河/湄南河) river valley, which runs into the Gulf of Thailand. The south consists of the narrow Kra Isthmus(克拉地峡) that widens into the Malay Peninsula.

 Climate

The local climate is tropical and characterized by monsoons. There is a rainy, warm, and cloudy southwest monsoon from mid-May to September, as well as a dry, cool northeast monsoon from November to mid-March. The southern Isthmus is always hot and humid. Countrywide, temperatures normally range from an average annual high of 38℃ (100.4℉) to a low of 19℃ (66.2℉). During the dry season, the temperature rises dramatically in the second half of March, spiking to well over 40℃ (104℉) in some areas by mid-April when the sun passes its zenith.

Tourist Sites

Thailand offers a great variety of attractions. These include diving sites, sandy beaches, hundreds of tropical islands, varied night-life, archaeological sites, museums, hill tribes, exceptional flora and bird life, palaces and World Heritage sites.

(1) **Bangkok**

Bangkok is the capital of Thailand and one of the most cosmopolitan cities of the whole Asian continent. Bangkok is not only the capital of Thailand but also the national treasure house, spiritual, political, cultural, educational, commercial and diplomatic centre.

Bangkok

The Baiyoke Tower II, the tallest building in Thailand

(2) **Grand Palace**

The Grand Palace is a complex of buildings in Bangkok, Thailand. It has served as the official residence of the Kings of Thailand from the 18th century onwards. Construction of the Palace began in 1782, during the reign of King Rama I, when he moved the capital across the river from Thonburi(吞武里) to Bangkok. The Palace has been constantly expanded and many additional structures were added over time. The present King of Thailand, King Rama IX, however, does not currently reside there but at the Chitralada Palace(奇托拉达宫).

(3) **Wat Phra Kaew**

The Wat Phra Kaew, generally called the Temple of the Emerald Buddha, is regarded as the most sacred Buddhist temple (wat) in Thailand. It is located in the historic center of Bangkok (district Phra Nakhon), within the grounds of the Grand Palace.

The construction of the temple started when King Buddha Yodfa Chulaloke (Rama I) moved the capital from Thonburi to Bangkok in 1785. Unlike other temples it does not contain living quarters for monks; rather, it has only the highly decorated holy buildings, statues, and pagodas.

(4) Pattaya

Located in a crescent on Thailand's Eastern Seaboard, only 147 km from Bangkok, Pattaya is the closest of Thailand's major beach resorts to the capital city. The combination of its big, wide beaches, water sports, interesting attractions, sightseeing, shopping, great hotels and resorts, international dining experiences, together of course with a raucous and naughty nightlife scene that's talked about the world over, makes Pattaya's formula for fun a big winner.

(5) Phuket Island

Phuket is Thailand's largest island, approximately the size of Singapore. The island is connected to mainland Thailand by a bridge. It is situated off the west coast of Thailand in the Andaman Sea. The region has an area of approximately 570 km^2 and is made up of 1 large and 39 small islands. Phuket formerly derived its wealth from tin and rubber. The island was on one of the major trading routes between India and China, and was frequently mentioned in foreign trader's ship logs. The region now derives much of its income from tourism.

9.4 Brief History

The region known as Thailand has been inhabited by humans since the Paleolithic period, about 10,000 years ago. Prior to the fall of the Khmer Empire in the 13th century, various states thrived there, such as the various Tai, Mon, Khmer and Malay kingdoms, as seen through the numerous archaeological sites and artifacts that are scattered throughout the Siamese landscape. Prior to the 12th century however, the first Thai or Siamese State is traditionally considered to be the Buddhist Kingdom of Sukhothai, which was founded in 1238.

Following the decline and fall of the Khmer empire in the 13th – 14th centuries, the Buddhist Tai Kingdoms of Sukhothai, Lanna and Lan Xhang were on the ascension. However, a century later, Sukhothai's power was overshadowed by the new Kingdom of Ayutthaya, established in the mid-14th century.

After the fall of the Ayutthaya in 1767 to the Burmese, King Taksin the Great moved the capital of Thailand to Thonburi for approximately 15 years. The current Rattanakosin era of Thai history began in 1782, following the establishment of Bangkok as capital of the Chakri Dynasty under King Rama Ⅰ the Great.

Thailand retains a tradition of trade with its neighboring states, and the cultures of the Indian ocean and the South China Sea. European trade and influence arrived in Thailand in the 16th century, beginning with the Portuguese. Despite European pressure, Thailand is the only Southeast Asian nation that has never been colonized. Two main reasons for this were that Thailand had a long succession of very able rulers in the 1800s and that it was able to exploit the rivalry and tension between the French and the British. As a result, the country remained as a buffer state between parts of Southeast Asia that were colonized by the two colonial powers. Despite this, Western influence led to many reforms in the 19th century and major concessions, most notably being the loss of large territory on the east side of the Mekong to the French and the step-by-step absorption by Britain of the Shan (Thai Yai) States(掸邦)(now in Myanmar) and the Malay Peninsula. The loss initially included Penang and Tumasik(单马锡,即新加坡) and eventually culminated in the loss of four predominantly ethnic-Malay southern provinces, which later became Malaysia's four northern states, under the Anglo-Siamese Treaty of 1909[4].

In 1932, a bloodless revolution resulted in a new constitutional monarchy. During World War Ⅱ, the Empire of Japan demanded the right to move troops across Thailand to the Malayan frontier. Japan invaded the country and engaged the Thai army for six to eight hours before Phibunsongkhram ordered an armistice. Shortly thereafter Japan was granted free passage, and on December 21, 1941, Thailand and Japan signed a military alliance with a secret protocol wherein Tokyo agreed to help Thailand regain territories lost to the British and French. Subsequently, Thailand undertook to "assist" Japan in its war against the Allies(同盟国), while at the same time maintaining an active anti-Japanese resistance movement known as the Seri Thai. After the war, Thailand emerged as an ally of the United States. As with many of the developing nations during the Cold War, Thailand then went through decades of political transgression characterized by coups d'état as one military regime replaced another, but eventually progressed towards a stable prosperity and democracy in the 1980s.

The official calendar in Thailand is based on Eastern version of the Buddhist Era[5], which is 543 years ahead of the Gregorian (Western) calendar. For example, the year 2008 AD is called 2551 BE(Buddhist Era) in Thailand.

9.5 Politics

(1) **Constitution and election**

The politics of Thailand currently takes place within a framework of constitutional monarchy, whereby the prime minister is head of government and a hereditary monarch is head of state. The judiciary is independent of the executive and the legislative branches.

Thailand has been ruled by kings since the thirteenth century. In 1932, the country officially became a constitutional monarchy. The country's current constitution was promulgated in 2007.

On December 23, 2007, a general election was held. The People's Power Party, led by Somchai Wongsawat, won the majority of seats in the Parliament. A civilian coalition government was formed on January 28, 2008 with five other minor parties leaving the Democrats, led by Mr. Abhisit Vejjajiva, as the only opposition party.

(2) **2008 – 2010 political crisis**

The People's Power Party (Thailand), led by Samak Sundaravej, formed the government with five smaller parties. In September 2008, Sundaravej was found guilty of conflict of interest by the Constitutional Court of Thailand (due to hosting a TV cooking program), and thus ended his term in office. He was replaced by PPP member Somchai Wongsawat. As of October 2008, Wongsawat was unable to gain access to his offices, which were occupied by protesters from the People's Alliance for Democracy. On December 2, 2008, Thailand's Constitutional Court in a highly controversial ruling found the People's Power Party guilty of electoral fraud, which led to the dissolution of the party according to the law. However, in June, 2010, supporters of the eventually disbanded PPP were charged with tapping a judge's phone. The leader of the Democrat Party, and former leader of the opposition, Abhisit Vejjajiva was appointed and sworn in as the 27th Prime Minister, together with the new cabinet on December 17, 2008.

On July 3, 2011, the oppositional Pheu Thai Party, led by Yingluck Shinawatra (the youngest sister of Thaksin Shinawatra), won the general election by a landslide (265 out of 500 seats in the House of Representatives). She had never previously been involved in politics, Pheu Thai campaigning for her with the slogan "Thaksin thinks, Pheu Thai acts". Yingluck is the nation's first female prime minister and her role was officially endorsed in a ceremony presided over by King Bhumibol Adulyadej. The Pheu Thai Party is a continuation of Thaksin's Thai Rak Thai Party.

(3) **2013 – 2014 political crisis**

Protests recommenced in late 2013, as a broad alliance of protestors, led by former opposition deputy leader Suthep Thaugsuban, demanded an end to the so-called Thaksin regime. A newly named group, the People's Democratic Reform Committee (PDRC) along with allied groups, escalated the pressure, with the opposition Democrat Party resigning en masse to create a parliamentary vacuum.

In response to the intensive protests, Yingluck dissolved the Parliament on December 9, 2013 and proposed a new election for February 2, 2014, a date that was later approved by the election commission (EC). Yingluck insisted that she should continue her duties until the scheduled election in February, 2014, urging the protesters to accept her proposal.

In response to the electoral commission's registration process for party-list candidates—for the scheduled election in February, 2014—anti-government protesters marched to the Thai-Japanese sports stadium, the venue of the registration process, on December 22, 2013. Suthep and the PDRC led the protest, of which security forces claimed that approximately 270,000 protesters joined. Yingluck and the Pheu Thai Party reiterated their election plan and anticipated presenting a list of 125 party-list candidates to the EC.

On May 7, 2014, the Constitutional Court ruled that Yingluck would have to step down as the Prime Minister as she was deemed to have abused her power in transferring a high-level government official. On August 21, 2014, she was replaced by army chief General Prayut Chan-o-cha.

(4) **2014 coup d'état**

On May 20, 2014, the Thai army declared martial law and began to deploy troops in the capital. They denied that it was a coup attempt. On May 22, the army announced that it was a coup and that it was taking control of the country and suspending the country's constitution. On the same day, the military imposed a curfew between the hours of 22:00 – 05:00, ordering citizens and visitors to remain indoors during this period. On August 21, 2014, the National Assembly of Thailand elected the army chief, General Prayut Chan-o-cha, as Prime Minister. Martial law was declared formally ended on April 1, 2015.

Government

According to the constitution, the three major independent authorities holding the balance of power are executive, legislative, and judicial.

The King has little direct power under the constitution but is a symbol of national identity and unity. The present monarch has a great deal of popular respect and moral authority, which has been used to attempt to resolve political crises.

The head of government is the Prime Minister. Under the present constitution, the Prime Minister must be a Member of the Parliament. Cabinet members do not have to be Members of the Parliament. The legislature can hold a vote of non-confidence against the Premier and members of his Cabinet if it has sufficient votes.

## Diplomacy

Thailand's foreign policy includes support for ASEAN—in the interest of regional stability and emphasizes a close and longstanding security relationship with the United States.

Thailand participates fully in international and regional organizations. It has developed increasingly close ties with other ASEAN members—Indonesia, Malaysia, the Philippines, Singapore, Brunei, Laos, Cambodia, Myanmar, and Vietnam—whose foreign and economic ministers hold annual meetings. Regional cooperation is progressing in economic, trade, banking, political, and cultural matters. In 2003, Thailand served as APEC host. Supachai Panitchpakdi, the former Deputy Prime Minister of Thailand, currently serves as Director-General of the World Trade Organization (WTO). In 2005 Thailand attended the inaugural East Asia Summit.

In recent years, Thailand has taken an active role on the international stage. Thailand has contributed troops to the international peace-keeping effort.

9.6 Economy

Thailand is an emerging economy and considered as a newly industrialized country. After enjoying the world's highest growth rate from 1985 to 1996—averaging 12.4% annually—increased pressure on Thailand's currency, the baht, in 1997, the year in which the economy contracted by 1.9% led to a crisis that uncovered financial sector weaknesses. This collapse prompted the Asian Financial Crisis.

Thailand's economy started to recover in 1999, expanding by 4.2%–4.4% in 2000, largely due to strong exports. Growth (2.2%) was dampened by the softening of the global economy in 2001, but picked up in the subsequent years due to strong growth in Asia, a relatively weak baht encouraging exports and increasing domestic spending as a result of several mega projects and incentives of Prime Minister Thaksin Shinawatra, known as Thaksinomics. Growth in 2002, 2003 and 2004 was 5%–7% annually. Growth in 2005, 2006 and 2007 hovered around 4%–5%.

Thailand exports an increasing value of over US $105 billion worth of goods and services annually. Major exports include Thai rice, textiles and footwear, fishery products, rubber, jewelry, automobiles, computers and electrical appliances. Thailand is the world's No.1 exporter of rice, exporting more than 6.5 million tons of milled rice annually. Rice is the most important crop in the country. Thailand has the highest percent of arable land (27.25%) of any nations in the Greater Mekong Subregion. About 55% of the available land area is used for rice production. Substantial industries include electric appliances, components, computer parts and automobiles, while tourism makes up about 6% of the Thai economy.

Thailand uses the metric system but traditional units of measurement and imperial measure (feet, inches) are still much in use, particularly for agriculture and building materials. Years are numbered as BE (Buddhist Era) in education, the civil service, government, and on contracts and newspaper datelines; in banking, however, and increasingly in industry and commerce, standard Western year (Christian or Common Era) counting prevails.

Thailand had a 2013 GDP of US$673 billion (on a purchasing power parity [PPP] basis). Thailand is the 2nd largest economy in Southeast Asia after Indonesia. Thailand ranks midway in the wealth spread in Southeast Asia as it is the 4th richest nation according to GDP per capita, after Singapore, Brunei, and Malaysia.

Thailand functions as an anchor economy for the neighbouring developing economies of Laos, Myanmar, and Cambodia. In the third quarter of 2014, the unemployment rate in Thailand stood at 0.84% according to Thailand's National Economic and Social Development Board (NESDB).

9.7 Culture

The culture of Thailand is heavily influenced by Buddhism. Other influences have included Hinduism, business and trade with Southeast Asian neighbors such as Laos, Cambodia and Myanmar, and repeated influxes of Chinese immigrants.

Languages

The official language of Thailand is the Thai language, a Tai-Kadai language closely related to Lao, Shan in Myanmar, and numerous smaller languages spoken in an arc from Hainan and Yunan south of China to the Malaysian border. It is the principal language of education and government and spoken throughout the country. The standard is based on the dialect of the Central Thai people, and it is written in the Thai alphabet, an abugida script that evolved from the Khmer script. Several other dialects exist, and coincide with the regional designations. Southern Thai is spoken in the southern provinces, and Northern Thai is spoken in the provinces that were formally part of the independent Kingdom of Lannathai.

Thailand is also host to several other minority languages, the largest of which is the Lao dialect of Isan spoken in the northeastern provinces. Although sometimes considered a Thai dialect, it is a Lao dialect, and the region where it is traditionally spoken was historically part of the Lao Kingdom of Lan Xhang. In the far south, Yawi, a dialect of Malay, is the primary language of the Malay Muslims. Chinese dialects are also spoken by the large Chinese population, Teochew being the dialect best represented.

Numerous tribal languages are also spoken, including those belonging to the Mon-Khmer family, such as Mon, Khmer, Viet, Mlabri, the Austronesian family, such as Cham, Moken, and Orang Asli, the Sino-Tibetan family such as Hmong, Lawa, Akhan, and Karen, and other Tai languages such as Nyaw, Phu Thai, and Saek.

English is a mandatory school subject, but the number of fluent speakers remains very low, especially outside the cities.

Ethnics

Thailand is a country with many distinct ethnic groups, just like other countries, including the majority Thai and numerous hill tribes living primarily in the mountains of the north. The Thai (or ethnic Thai) make up approximately 75% of the nation's population in 2014. The remaining of the population include Thai Chinese (14%), and others (Malay, Mon, Khmer, etc., 12%).

Thailand's population is relatively homogeneous, with more than 85% speaking a Thai language and sharing a common culture. This core population includes the Central Thai, Northeastern Thai, Northern Thai, and Southern Thai.

Religion

According to the last census (2000), 94.6% of the total population is Buddhists of the Theravada tradition. Muslims are the second largest religious group in Thailand at 4.6%. Thailand's southernmost provinces—Pattani(北大年), Yala(也拉/惹拉), Narathiwat(那拉提瓦) and part of Songkhla(宋卡), Chumphon(春蓬) have dominant Muslim populations, consisting of both ethnic Thai and Malay. Most often Muslims live in separate communities from non-Muslims. The southern tip of Thailand is mostly ethnically Malay, and most Malays are Sunni Muslims. Christians, mainly Catholics, represent 0.75% of the population. A tiny but influential community of Sikhs in Thailand and some Hindus also live in the country's cities. There is also a small Jewish community in Thailand, dating back to the 17th century.

Customs

The culture of Thailand incorporates a great deal of influence from India, China, Cambodia, and the rest of Southeast Asia. Thailand's national theology, Theravada Buddhism(小乘佛教的信徒), is central to modern Thai identity and belief. In practice, Thai Buddhism has evolved over time to include many regional beliefs originating from Hinduism, animism as well as ancestor worship. In areas in the southernmost parts of

Thailand, Islam is prevalent. Several different ethnic groups, many of which are marginalized, populate Thailand. Some of these groups overlap into Myanmar, Laos, Cambodia, and Malaysia and have mediated between their traditional local culture, national Thai, and global cultural influence. Overseas Chinese also form a significant part of Thai society, particularly in and around Bangkok. Their successful integration into Thai society has allowed for this group to hold positions of economic and political power.

The most important thing that you must know while visiting Thailand is *wai* or the Thai mode of greeting. The Thais join the palms of their hands and bow their heads in order to show a respectful greeting. However, such greetings are not to be used for a child! There are yet many other things about Thailand's customs and traditions.

Apart from greeting each other with the *wai* gesture, the people of Thailand address to the elders by adding a before their names. On the other hand, *nong* is added before the name of a child to show endearment.

Head is considered to be the highest and purest part of human body by the Thai people. Therefore, pointing at someone or touching someone with feet is considered to be highly disrespectful. It is for the same reason that stepping on the Thai coin that contains the king's head or sitting in a temple with feet pointed to the religious icon is considered sacrilegious.

It is mandatory to open one's footwear before entering a temple or a house. Finding heaps of shoes in front of a shop or a restaurant in Thailand is a usual phenomenon.

The custom of eating food is also singular. Tradition demands that there should be several dishes on the table and the guest is expected to taste a little bit of everything.

Public display of affection by couples is forbidden by the Thai custom.

Women are supposed to make way for Buddhist monks so as to prevent an accidental physical contact.

It has been the tradition of Buddhist families in Thailand to send the boy to endure a 3-month's monk hood when they were 20 years of age.

Traditional Buddhist marriages demand that the couple must at first bow before the idol of Buddha. Also, the presence of a monk during a marriage ceremony was considered to be ominous.

Thai funerals usually last for a week and the grieved are requested not to cry so that the soul of the departed is not troubled. The monks chant hymns and then after the cremation of the body, the ashes were put in an urn and kept in a *Ched*(泰语) in the local temple.

The Thai folks celebrate various festivals throughout the year such as the New Year, maka(泰语) and songkran(泰语). These festivals are part of the Thai tradition.

Notes

[1] Garuda: The Garuda is a large mythical bird or bird-like creature that appears in both Hindu and Buddhist mythology.

[2] Hindu: Hinduism is the predominant religion of the Indian subcontinent. Hinduism is often referred to as Sanātana Dharma, a Sanskrit phrase meaning "the eternal law", by its adherents.

[3] The King of Thailand: It refers to the constitutional monarchy and monarch of the Kingdom of Thailand (formerly Siam). The King of Thailand is the head of state and head of the ruling Royal House of Chakri. As a constitutional monarch the powers of the King is limited to a symbolic figurehead, however the institution elicits huge amount of respect and reverence from the Thai people.

[4] The Anglo-Siamese Treaty of 1909: or called Bangkok Treaty of 1909, was a treaty between the United Kingdom and Thailand signed in Bangkok on March 10, 1909.

[5] The Buddhist Era: It is used on mainland Southeast Asia in the countries of Cambodia, Laos, Thailand, Myanmar and Sri Lanka in several related forms. It is a lunisolar calendar having months that are alternately 29 and 30 days, with an intercalated day and a 30-day month added at regular intervals.

Exercises

1. Explain the following in English.

(1) monsoon
(2) the Buddhist calendar
(3) ESA
(4) The Grand Palace
(5) *wai*

2. Fill in the blanks.

(1) The flag of the Kingdom of Thailand shows five horizontal stripes in the colours red, white, blue, white and red. The three colours red-white-blue stand for _____, an unofficial motto of Thailand.

(2) The national emblem of Thailand features _____, a figure from both Buddhist and Hindu mythology. In Thailand, this figure is used as a symbol of _____.

(3) The local climate of Thailand is tropical and characterized by _____.

(4) _____ is not only the capital of Thailand but also the national treasure house, spiritual, political, cultural, educational, commercial and diplomatic centre.

(5) _____ is a complex of buildings in Bangkok, Thailand. It has served as the official residence of the Kings of Thailand from the 18th century onwards.

(6) _____, is regarded as the most sacred Buddhist temple (wat) in Thailand. It is located in the historic center of _____, within the grounds of _____.

(7) _____ is the Thai representation of the Hindu god Brahma.

(8) According to the constitution, the three major independent authorities holding the balance of power are _____, _____, and _____.

(9) In Thailand, 94.6% of the total population is _____. _____ are the second largest religious group.

3. Answer the following questions.

(1) What is the national emblem of Thailand?

(2) What are the main tourist sites of Thailand?

(3) What is Thailand's largest island? Please give a brief introduction to it.

(4) What do you think of Thailand's economy?

(5) Please state the political system of Thailand.

4. Discussion.

(1) Which is your most favorite scenic spot in Thailand? Why?

(2) What is the most important characteristic of Thailand?

(3) Thailand is one of the most devoutly Buddhist countries in the world. The national religion is Theravada Buddhism which is practiced by 95% of all Thais. What do you think of the influence of Buddhism on Thai people's life?

CHAPTER 10

Vietnam

10.1 Country Name

Full Name: the Socialist Republic of Vietnam
Short Name: Vietnam
Local Full Name: the Socialist Republic of Vietnam
Local Short Name: Vietnam

10.2 National Symbols

National Flag

The national flag of the Socialist Republic of Vietnam is rectangular in shape. Its width equals to two-thirds of its length. In the middle of a red background is a golden star. The red stands for the revolution and victory, the golden star represents the Communist Party of Vietnam. The five points of the golden star are the symbols of the workers, farmers, soldiers, intellectuals and the youth.

National Emblem

The Vietnam national emblem is a circular pattern, with red background, which has a golden five-pointed star near the top. A gear, which stands for industry, is at the bottom, surrounded by symbols of golden rice ears, representing agriculture. A red sash on the lower end of the emblem is inscribed with the words " the

Socialist Republic of Vietnam".

10.3 Geography

Location

Vietnam is located in the eastern part of the Indo-China peninsula, between 8°30′N – 23°22′N, 102°E – 109°29′E bordering Guangxi, Yunnan of China to the north, Laos and Cambodia to the west with a long land border of 4,550 km. Facing the South China Sea to the southeast and the Gulf of Thailand to the southwest, it has more than 3,260 km of coastline. On the map, Vietnam is seen as an s-shaped long strip of land. The country's total length is 1,650 km from the northernmost point to the southernmost point. Its width, stretching from the eastern coast to the western border, is about 500 km at the widest part and about 50 km at the narrowest part.

Area

Vietnam is approximately 329,556 km² in area, larger than the UK or Italy, but smaller than Germany.

The country's territory is made up of hills, mountains, deltas, coastlines and continental shelf. Three quarters of Vietnam's territory is made up of low mountains and hilly regions. Regions with elevations less than 1,000 metres above sea level make up 85% of the territory. Mountainous regions over 2,000 metres above sea level account for only 1%. Only one fourth of the Vietnamese territory is covered by deltas separated in many regions by mountains and hills. There are two major deltas with fertile arable land in Vietnam. One is the Red River delta, locally known as the Northern delta, spreading 16,700 sq km, and the other is the Mekong River delta or the Southern delta, covering 40,000 sq km. Between these two major deltas is a chain of small deltas located along the central coast with a total area of 15,000 sq km.

Climate

Vietnam is located in the tropical and temperate zone. Its climate is characterized by generally high temperature and humidity all year round, a tropical monsoon climate. Vietnam's weather varies by seasons and by regions. There are different regions with different climates. There are two major climate regions in Vietnam. Northern Vietnam has a highly humid tropical monsoon climate with four distinguishable seasons (spring, summer, autumn and winter) and is influenced by the northeast and southeast monsoon. Southern Vietnam has a rather moderate tropical climate and is characterized by dry and rainy seasons and warm weather all year round. Vietnam's climate is also characterized by a considerable amount of sunshine with the number of sunny hours varying between 1,400 and 3,000 per year. The average rainfall each year stands between 1,500 mm and 2,000 mm. Air humidity is 80%. Given the influence of the monsoon and a complex topography, Vietnam is often prone to natural disasters such as storms, floods and droughts. Each year, the country suffers from 6 to 10 tropical storms.

Natural Resources

Vietnam is rich in natural resources. "One shoulder-pole carries two baskets of rice" and "gold mountains and silver seas" are the general praises which give us a vivid description. "One shoulder-pole" refers to the long-narrow center of Vietnam, while "two baskets of rice" stands for the Mekong Plain and the Red River Plain, which are the two well-known grain-producing areas. The northern and western mountain area of Vietnam is covered with forest, rich in valuable timber and other forest products, where a variety of rare birds and animals live. At the same time, there are different kinds of mineral resources in Vietnam, such as coal, iron, copper, tin, zinc, lead, chromium and antimony, especially coal. All these resources account for the "Gold Mountains". The rivers and lakes of Vietnam give it the reputation of "Silver Seas" because of their wide range of aquatic resources. Since the Mekong Plain and the Red River Plain are located in the sub-tropical area, which provide a hot climate, adequate rainfall, fertile soil and irrigation facilities, it is easy to make progress in agriculture. Vietnam is suitable for the cultivation of rice. Most of the places have 2 harvests during a year, while some can get 3. Vietnam exports rice to many countries, ranking third of all the rice-exporting countries in the world.

Tourist Sites

In the recent years, Vietnam's tourism has enjoyed great progress. The northern tourism zone consists of provinces from Ha Giang(河江) to Ha Tinh(河静). Ha Noi (Hanoi) is the center. The key axis is Ha Noi-Hai Phong(海防)-Ha Long (下龙).

The southern central and southern tourism area consists of provinces from Kon Tum (昆嵩) to Ca Mau(金瓯). Ho Chi Minh City is the center, and the key axes are Ho Chi Minh City-Can Tho(芹苴)-Ha Tien(河仙)-Phu Quoc(富国岛) and Ho Chi Minh City-Vung Tau(头顿)-Phan Thiet(潘切).

(1) **Bating Square**

Bating Square is located in the center of Ha Noi City, the capital of Vietnam, to the northwest of Hoan Kiem Lake(还剑湖). It is 320 meters long and nearly 100 meters wide and can hold 200,000 people. It's the place for festival activities and gatherings of Ha Noi people. On September 2, 1945, President Ho Chi Minh read there the  Declaration of Independence, declaring the founding of the Democratic Republic of Vietnam (in 1976, it was renamed the Socialist Republic of Vietnam).

(2) **Ha Long Bay**

Ha Long Bay(下龙湾), the most unusual tourist site, is one of the wonders of the world.

It is located on the western coast of the Beibu Gulf, which is over 100 km east of Ha Noi, and more than 100 km from the border between China and Vietnam. It is famous for its beautiful scenery, and it is called "the sea of Guilin" because its beauty is just like that in Guilin, China. At the 18th Session of the UNESCO's  Council of World Heritage held on December 17, 1994 in Thailand, Ha Long Bay was officially recognized as one of the World Natural Heritages.

(3) **Hoi An Ancient Town**

The ancient town of Hoi An(会安), 30 km south of Da Nang(岘港), lies on the banks of the Thu Bon River(秋盆河). It is famous for its ancient architecture. Hoi An has a distinct Chinese atmosphere with low, tile-roofed houses and narrow streets; the original structure of some of these streets still remains almost intact. All the houses were  made of rare wood, decorated with lacquered boards and panels engraved with Chinese characters. Pillars were also carved with ornamental designs. Hoi An Ancient Town was recognized as a World Cultural Heritage in December, 1999.

Tourists can visit the relics of the Sa Huynh(沙登) and Cham cultures. They can also enjoy the beautiful scenery of the romantic Hoi An River, Cua Dai Beach, and Cham

Island(占族岛).

Over the last few years, Hoi An has become a very popular tourist destination in Vietnam.

(4) **Ancient Capital of Hue**

The ancient capital of Hue(顺化) was the capital of the Nguyen Dynasty (1802 – 1945), the final feudal regime of Vietnam. On December 11, 1993, the UNESCO recognized the architectural ensemble of Hue as a World Cultural Heritage. That is the first time a Vietnamese city ever received such a title. Situated 638 km to the south of Ha Noi, with an area of 15 square kilometers and a population of nearly 20,000, this historical ancient capital has become a cultural and tourism center of Vietnam and the world.

10.4　Brief History

Vietnam is a country with a long history. It began around 2,700 years ago. In 968 AD Vietnam became an independent feudal country. France assumed control over the whole of Vietnam in 1884. On September 2, 1945, Ho Chi Minh declared Vietnam independent under the new name of the Democratic Republic of Vietnam (DRV). In 1976, Vietnam was officially unified and renamed Socialist Republic of Vietnam, with its capital in Ha Noi.

10.5　Politics

Capital

Ha Noi, the capital of Vietnam, is an elegant city located on the banks of the Red River with a population of 6.92 million (according to the 2012 Population Census). As the capital of Vietnam for almost a thousand years, it is considered to be the political, economic and cultural centre of Vietnam, where every dynasty has left behind its imprint. Ha Noi experiences the typical climate of highly humid tropical monsoon region, where

Ho Chi Minh Mausoleum

summers are hot and humid, and winters are relatively cool and dry. The average temperature is 28.9 ℃ in summer, and 18.9 ℃ in winter.

Parties

The leading force of the state and society, the Communist Party of Vietnam (CPV), which was established on February 3, 1930, is the only political party in Vietnam. Over the years of its existence, the Party has been renamed several times: the Communist Party of Indo-China (October 1930), the Vietnam Workers' Party (February 1951), and the Communist Party of Vietnam(CPV)(December 1976).

The aim of the CPV is to make Vietnam a strong, independent, prosperous and democratic country with an equitable and civilized society, to realize socialism and ultimately, communism. The Party's activities are governed by the Constitution and laws.

The present General Secretary of the Communist Party of Vietnam is Nguyen Phu Trong.

Leaders

The president is the head of state, elected by the National Assembly from among its deputies to represent the Socialist Republic of Vietnam in domestic and foreign affairs, to head all people's armed forces and take charge of the position of Chairman of the Security and National Defense Council. The term of office of the President of the state is 5 years. The first President was Ho Chi Minh, and the present President is Truong Tan Sang.

Government

The government is based on the executive body of the National Assembly and the highest body of state Administration of the Socialist Republic of Vietnam. In August 2011, Vietnam held the first meeting of the Thirteenth National Assembly and elected a new government. They are Prime Minister Nguyen Tan Dung, Standing Deputy Prime Minister Nguyen Xuan Phuc, Deputy Prime Minister and Minister of Foreign Affairs Pham Binh Minh.

Administrative Divisions

Vietnam is divided into 5 centrally-controlled municipalities(Ha Noi, Ho Chi Minh City, Hai Phong, Da Nang and Can Tho) and 58 provinces.

Constitution

The current constitution is the Fourth Constitution, which was adopted by the 8th

National Assembly in 1992 and was supplemented and amended in 2013 at the 6th session of the 13th National Assembly. The Constitution inherits from and builds on previous Constitutions(1946, 1959, and 1980). It institutionalizes basic viewpoints of the Communist Party of Vietnam on economic and political reforms, socialist democracy and civil freedoms reaffirming the goal of building socialism. The constitution clearly indicates that the state power is in the hands of the people.

Legislature

The National Assembly is the highest organ of state power of the Socialist Republic of Vietnam, the sole organ that has the constitutional and legislative rights. The term of each session of the National Assembly is five years, and meetings are convened twice a year. It has the power to draw up, adopt, and amend the constitution and to make and amend laws. It also has the responsibility to legislate and implement state plans and budgets. It appoints the president (chief of state), the prime minister (head of government), chief procurators of the Supreme People's Court and the Supreme People's Office of Supervision and Control. It has the power to initiate or conclude wars. The 13th National Assembly was held in May,2011, with 500 deputies directly elected by the people. The present Assembly Chairman is Nguyen Sinh Hung.

Justice

The Supreme People's Court, local People's Courts, Military Tribunals and the other tribunals established by law are the judicial organs of the Socialist Republic of Vietnam. Under special circumstances, the National Assembly may decide to set up a Special Tribunal. The Supreme People's Court is the highest judicial organ of the Socialist Republic of Vietnam. It supervises and directs the judicial work of local People's Courts, Military Tribunals and Special Tribunals.

The Supreme People's Procuracy oversees the enforcement of the law by Ministries, Ministerial-level organs, other Government agencies, local administration, economic entities, mass organizations, people's military organs and citizens. It exercises the right to prosecution and ensures serious and uniform implementation of the law. Local People's Procuracy and Military Procuracy oversee the execution of the law and exercise the right to prosecution as stipulated by the law.

Diplomacy

Vietnam has endorsed the foreign policy of openness, diversification and multi-lateralization of international relations. By August 2014, Vietnam had established diplomatic relations with 180 countries, including the United States, which normalized relations in 1995. Vietnam holds membership of 63 international organizations, including the United Nations, ASEAN, NAM, Francophonie and the WTO. It is furthermore a member of around 650 non-government organizations.

Vietnam-China Relations

Traditional friendship between China and Vietnam as well as the people of the two countries has enjoyed a long history. On January 18, 1950, the two countries established diplomatic relations. The Chinese Government and people rendered full support to the long-term revolutionary struggle of Vietnam against France and the US, and provided Vietnam with huge economic aid. Vietnam regards China as its strong supporters, and the two countries have developed extensive cooperation in the political, military and economic fields. In the late 1970s, however, Sino-Vietnamese relations deteriorated. In November 1991, at the invitation of General Secretary Jiang Zemin and Premier Li Peng, General Secretary of the Central Committee of the Vietnamese Communist Party Do Muoi and Chairman of the Council of Minister Vo Van Kiet visited China, and both sides declared an end to the past strains and the start of a positive future. The party and state relations between the two countries were normalized.

Since then, the party and state relations between China and Vietnam have seen an overall restoration and in-depth development. There were frequent contacts and exchanges of visits between the leaders of the two countries, and friendly exchanges and mutually beneficial cooperation in various fields. At the start of 1999, the general secretaries of the two parties set "long-standing stability, future orientation, neighborliness and friendship, all-round cooperation" as the framework guiding Sino-Vietnamese relations in the new century. In 2000, the two countries issued the Joint Statement on all-round cooperation in the new century, drawing up a concrete programme for the development of friendly relations and cooperation between them. Since 2000, the leaders of the two countries have paid state visits to each country. The governments of the People's Republic of China and the Socialist Republic of Vietnam issued a joint communiqué. The two sides agreed to ceaselessly foster the friendly and cooperative relations between the two countries, and continue to increase exchange, friendship and cooperation in different fields and enhance mutual understanding and trust, making Vietnam and China forever good neighbors, good friends, good comrades and good partners. Both sides are glad to see that guided by the principle of "long-term stability, orientation to the future, good-neighborliness and friendship and all-round cooperation" defined by the leaders of the two countries, Sino-Vietnamese relations are developing rapidly, comprehensively and deeply.

Vietnam in ASEAN

Vietnam became a full member of ASEAN on July 28, 1995. Vietnam has actively contributed to the unity and cooperation in ASEAN, striving for an ASEAN of peace, stability and development since joining the Association. In December 1998, Vietnam successfully hosted the 6th ASEAN Summit in Ha Noi. From Janurary 1, 2013, former Deputy Minister of Foreign Affairs Le Luong Minh acted as the 13th Secretary General of ASEAN.

Vietnam in ASEM

Vietnam was one of the 26 founding members of ASEM in March 1996. Since then, together with other partners in ASEM, Vietnam has made efforts to help ASEM evolve towards its set targets and bring Asia-Europe ties to a new height with more effective and practical significance for the development of both continents. Vietnam was the successful host of the Fifth Asia-Europe Meeting (ASEM 5) in Ha Noi from 6 – 9 October 2004. This event has helped further to substantiate and revitalize Asia-Europe cooperation and bring it to a new height.

Vietnam in APEC

Vietnam joined APEC in November 1998. Since then Vietnam has actively participated in cooperation programs on free trade and trade-investment facilitation as well as technical cooperation within APEC. Vietnam successfully hosted Vietnam APEC 2006 and the 14th APEC Economic Leaders' Meeting (AELM) in Ha Noi in November, 2006.

10.6 Economy

In 2012, Vietnam's nominal GDP reached US$138 billion, with a nominal GDP per capita of US$1,527, according to the International Monetary Fund (IMF). According to a December 2005 forecast by Goldman Sachs, the Vietnamese economy will become the world's 21st largest by 2025, with an estimated nominal GDP of US$436 billion and a nominal GDP per capita of US$4,357. According to a 2008 forecast by PricewaterhouseCoopers, Vietnam may be the fastest-growing of the world's emerging economies by 2025, with a potential growth rate of almost 10% annually in real dollar terms. In 2012, HSBC predicted that Vietnam's total GDP would surpass those of Norway, Singapore and Portugal by 2050.

Agriculture, Forestry, and Fishing

In 2004 agriculture and forestry accounted for 21.8% of GDP, and during 1994 – 2004 the sector grew at an annual rate of 4.1%. However, agricultural employment was much higher than agriculture's share of GDP; in 2005 some 60% of the employed labor force was engaged in agriculture, forestry, and fishing. Agricultural products accounted for 30% of exports in 2005. The relaxation of the state monopoly on rice exports has transformed the country into the world's third largest rice exporter. Other cash crops(经济作物) are coffee, cotton, peanuts, rubber, sugarcane, and tea.

In 2003 Vietnam produced an estimated 30.7 million cubic meters of roundwood. Production of sawnwood was more modest 2,950 cubic meters. In 1992, in response to dwindling forests, Vietnam imposed a ban on the export of logs and raw timber. In 1997 the ban was extended to all timber products except wooden artifacts. During the 1990s, Vietnam began to reclaim land for forests with a tree-planting program.

Vietnam's fishing industry, which has abundant resources given the country's long coastline and extensive network of rivers and lakes, has experienced moderate growth overall. In 2003 the total catch was about 2.6 million tons. However, seafood exports expanded fourfold from 1990 to 2002 to more than US$2 billion, driven in part by shrimp farms in the south and "catfish", a different species from their American counterpart but marketed in the United States under the same name. By concentrating on the US market for the sale of vast quantities of shrimp and catfish, Vietnam triggered antidumping complaints by the United States, which imposed tariffs in the case of catfish and is considering doing the same for shrimp. In 2005 the seafood industry began to focus on domestic demand to compensate for declining exports.

Industry and Manufacturing

Although industry contributed 40.1% of GDP in 2004, it employed only 12.9% of the workforce. In 2000, 22.4% of industrial production was attributable to non-state activities. During 1994 – 2004, industrial GDP grew at an average annual rate of 10.3%. Manufacturing contributed 20.3% of GDP in 2004, while employing 10.2% of the workforce. During 1994 – 2004, manufacturing GDP grew at an average annual rate of 11.2%. The top manufacturing sectors—food processing, cigarettes and tobacco, textiles, chemicals, and electrical goods—experienced rapid growth. Almost a third of manufacturing and retail activity is concentrated in Ho Chi Minh City.

Services

Services keeps growing fast during past years, at an average rate of 6%. In the first half of 2014, GDP of services sector increases by 10.7%.

Other Industries

Mining and Minerals: In 2003 mining and quarrying accounted for a 9.4% share of GDP; the sector employed 0.7% of the workforce. Petroleum and coal are the main mineral exports. Also mined are antimony, bauxite, chromium, gold, iron, natural phosphates, tin, and zinc.

Energy: Crude oil is Vietnam's leading export, totaling 17 million tons in 2002; in 2004 crude oil represented 22% of all export earnings. Petroleum exports are in the form of crude petroleum because Vietnam has a very limited refining capacity. Vietnam's only operational refinery, a facility at Cat Hai(吉海县) near Ho Chi Minh City, has a capacity of only 800 barrels per day.

Trade and Investment

Vietnam's customs office reported in July 2013 that the total value of international merchandise trade for the first half of 2013 was US$124 billion, which was 15.7% higher than the same period in 2012. Mobile phones and their parts were both imported and exported in large numbers, while in the natural resources market, crude oil was a top-ranking export and high levels of iron and steel were imported during this period. The US was the country that purchased the highest amount of Vietnam's exports, while Chinese goods were the most popular Vietnamese import.

As a result of several land reform measures, Vietnam has become a major exporter of agricultural products. It is now the world's largest producer of cashew nuts, with a one-third global share; the largest producer of black pepper, accounting for one-third of the world's market; and the third largest rice exporter in the world, after Thailand, India. Vietnam is the world's second largest exporter of coffee. Vietnam has the highest proportion of land use for permanent crops—6.93%—of any nation in the Greater Mekong Subregion. Other primary exports include tea, rubber, and fishery products.

10.7 Culture

Languages

In addition to their unique cultures, 54 ethnic groups in Vietnam have different languages. 24 ethnic groups have their own scripts such as Thai, Hmong, Tay, Nung and Khmer. And some of these scripts are used at schools. The Vietnamese language has been selected as the common language for the education system from pre-school to tertiary education. Vietnamese is the universal language, an instrument for transferring knowledge and a means of communication and state management for all ethnic groups in Vietnam.

The written Vietnamese language today has its origin in the 17th century when a group of European missionaries headed by priest Alexandre de Rhodes introduced in Vietnam a system of Latin-based scripts. Since then, the written Vietnamese language has evolved into a complete writing system and become the official script of Vietnam since the early 20th century. After gaining national independence, Vietnam has used the Vietnamese language and its scripts in all aspects of social life.

Ethnics

Vietnam is a multi-ethnic country with 54 ethnic groups coexisting peacefully, among which the Viet or Kinh people[越(京)族] account for 86% of the population. Among ethnic minorities, the most populous are Tay(岱依族), Thai, Muong(芒族), Hoa[华(汉)族], Khmer, and Nung(侬族) with a population of around 1 million each, while the least populous are Brau and Odu with several hundred people each. Chinese account for 3% of the population. The Kinh people mainly inhabit in the lowland and deltas. The majority of the other 53 ethnic groups are scattered over mountainous areas and the midlands spreading from the north to the south. Most ethnic groups coexist in the same regions, particularly the ethnic minorities in northern and northern central region.

Religion

Vietnam has a diverse mix of major religions with a large number of followers, religious figures, and monks such as Buddhism, Christianity and Islam (Muslims) and some indigenous religions such as Caodaism and Hoa Hao(和好教), etc.

Chapter 10 Vietnam

 **Customs**

With the perception that every object has a soul, since ancient times, the Vietnamese have worshiped a large number of gods, especially those related to agriculture such as the sun, the moon, land, mountain, river and forest, etc., for good luck. Each ethnic minority in Vietnam has its own way of practicing their beliefs, which is still maintained by some ethnic groups such as Tay, Thai, Hmong, and Khmer.

In addition, the most popular and time-honoured custom of the Vietnamese and some ethnic minorities is ancestor worship and commemoration of death anniversaries. Every Vietnamese family has an altar to worship their ancestors and attaches importance to the commemoration of death anniversaries and acknowledgement of the service rendered by their predecessors. Besides ancestor worship in each family and each clan, many villages have a communal house and a temple to worship the village Deity. The custom of worshiping the village Deity and the communal house are the unique features of Vietnamese villages. The village Deity worshiped in the village's temple or communal house can be a mythical Deity or an outstanding figure who rendered great service such as the forefather of a traditional handicraft or a national hero who recorded glorious feats in national buildings and in the wars against foreign aggression. The Vietnamese people also worship other gods such as the kitchen god or god of the soil, etc.

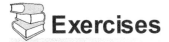 **Exercises**

1. **Explain the following in English.**
   (1) "One shoulder-pole carries two baskets of rice"
   (2) "Gold mountains and silver seas"
   (3) "the sea of Guilin"
   (4) the Communist Party of Vietnam
   (5) the national flag of the Socialist Republic of Vietnam

2. **Fill in the blanks.**
   (1) Vietnam is divided into _____ centrally-controlled municipalities and _____.
   (2) The term of each session of the National Assembly of Vietnam is _____ years, and meetings are convened _____ a year.
   (3) The Supreme People's Court is the _____ judicial _____ of the Socialist Republic of Vietnam.
   (4) The Vietnamese have worshiped a large number of _____, especially those related to _____, such as the sun, the _____, land, mountain, river and forest, etc.,

for good _____.

3. **Answer the following questions.**

    (1) Where is Vietnam located and which city is its capital?

    (2) What is the highest organ of state power of the Socialist Republic of Vietnam?

    (3) What is the climate like in Vietnam?

    (4) Which is the biggest commercial city in Vietnam? What is its former name?

    (5) How many ethnic groups are there in Vietnam and which has the biggest population?

4. **Discussion.**

    (1) What are the main natural resources in Vietnam?

    (2) Do you think Vietnamese tourism contributes greatly to its economy? Why or why not?

    (3) What is the Vietnamese foreign policy and how does it work?

CHAPTER 11

Malaysia

11.1 Brief Introduction

Malaysia is a federation that consists of thirteen states and three federal territories in Southeast Asia with a total area of 330,257 square kilometers (about 127,350 sq mi). The country is separated into two regions—Peninsular Malaysia and Malaysian Borneo—by the South China Sea. Malaysia borders Thailand, Indonesia, Singapore, Brunei and the Philippines. The name "Malaysia" was adopted in 1963 when the Federation of Malaya, Singapore, North Borneo and Sarawak formed a 14-state federation. However, the name itself had been vaguely used to refer to the areas in Southeast Asia prior to that. Other names were contemplated for the 1963 federation. Among them was Langkasuka (Langkasuka was an old kingdom located at the upper section of the Malay Peninsula in the first millennium of the Common Era).

11.2 National Symbols

National Flag

The flag of Malaysia, also known as the Jalur Gemilang ("Stripes of Glory"), comprises a field of 14 alternating red and white stripes along the flag and a blue canton bearing a crescent and a 14-point star known as the Bintang Persekutuan or Federal Star. The 14 stripes, of equal width, represent the equal status in the federation of the 13 member states and the federal government, while the 14 points of the star  represent the unity between these entities. The crescent represents Islam, the country's official religion; the blue canton symbolizes the unity of the Malaysian people; the yellow of the star and crescent is the royal color of the Malay rulers. In blazon, the Malaysian flag is described as "A banner Gules, seven bars Argent; the canton Azure charged with decrescent(下弦月亮) and mullet(星形图案) of fourteen points". This means "a red flag with seven horizontal white stripes; the upper-left (hoist) quarter is blue with a yellow waning crescent (i.e. horns pointing to sinister) and a yellow 14-pointed star".

National Emblem

The national emblem of Malaysia (*Jata Negara* in Malay), or the coat of arms (盾徽,盾形纹章) of Malaysia, comprises five major elements: a shield (as the escutcheon), two tigers (as supporters), a yellow crescent and a yellow 14-pointed star (as the crest), and a banner (as the motto). As the Malaysian emblem descended from the coat of arms of the Federated Malay States (FMS) during British colonial rule, the current  design of the Malaysian arms bears numerous elements of Western heraldry. The yellow color of the crest, a crescent and a 14-pointed federal star, symbolizes the country's monarchy. The crescent also represents Islam as the official religion while the federal star represents the thirteen states and the Federal Territories of Malaysia. The escutcheon, represented by a shield, is primarily intended to serve as a representation of states unified under the Malaysian federation and is subdivided into ten divisions. The two rampant tigers symbolize strength and courage. The motto of the arms, located below the shield, consists of a banner with the phrase "Unity is Strength" (*Bersekutu Bertambah Mutu*) written in both romanized Malay and Jawi. The original English words were replaced by romanized Malay some time after independence.

11.3 Geography

Location and Climate

Located between 2° and 7° north of the equator, 330,257 square km, Peninsular Malaysia is separated from the States of Sabah and Sarawak by the South China Sea. To the north of Peninsula Malaysia is Thailand while its southern neighbor is Singapore. Sabah and Sarawak are north of Indonesia in Borneo while Sarawak also shares a border with Brunei.

Its weather is tropical with warm weather all year round. Temperatures in the lowlands range from 21℃ (70℉) to 32℃ (89.6℉). The highlands are cooler, where temperatures range between 15℃ (59℉) to 25℃ (77℉). Annual rainfall varies from 2,000 mm to 2,500 mm.

Natural Resources

Malaysia is well-endowed with natural resources in areas such as agriculture, forestry and minerals. In terms of agriculture, Malaysia is one of the top exporters of natural rubber and palm oil, which together with sawn logs and sawn timber, cocoa, pepper, pineapple and tobacco dominate the growth of the sector. Palm oil is also a major generator of foreign exchange.

Regarding forestry resources, it is noted that logging only began to make a substantial contribution to the economy during the 19th century. Today, an estimated 59% of Malaysia remains forested. The rapid expansion of the timber industry, particularly after the 1960s, has brought about a serious erosion problem in the country's forest resources. However, in line with the government's commitment to protect the environment and the ecological system, forestry resources are being managed on a sustainable basis, and accordingly, the rate of tree felling has been on the decline.

In addition, substantial areas are being culturally treated and reforestation of degraded forest land is also being carried out. The Malaysian government provides plans for the enrichment of some 312.30 square kilometers (about 120.58 sq mi) of land with rattan under natural forest conditions and in rubber plantations. To further enrich forest resources, fast-growing timber species such as *meranti* (*Shorea*) *tembaga* (铜色娑罗双树), *merawan* (*Hopea*) (坡垒树) and *sesenduk* are also being planted. At the same time, the cultivation of high-value trees like teak and other trees for pulp and paper are also encouraged. Rubber, once the mainstay of the Malaysian economy, has been largely replaced by oil palm as Malaysia's leading agricultural export.

Tin and petroleum are the two main mineral resources that are of major significance in the Malaysian economy. Malaysia was once the world's largest producer of tin until the collapse of the tin market in the early 1980s. In the 19th and 20th centuries, tin played a predominant role in the Malaysian economy. It was only in 1972 that petroleum and natural gas took over from tin as the mainstay of the mineral extraction sector. Meanwhile, the contribution by tin has declined. Petroleum and natural gas discoveries in oil fields off Sabah, Sarawak and Terengganu have contributed much to the Malaysian economy. Other minerals of some importance or significance include copper, bauxite, iron-ore and coal together with industrial minerals like clay, kaolin, silica, limestone, barite, phosphates and dimension stones such as granite as well as marble blocks and slabs. Small quantities of gold are produced. In 2004, a minister in the Prime Minister's Department, Mustapa Mohamed, revealed that Malaysia's oil reserves stood at 4.84 billion barrels (about 769,000,000 m^3) while natural gas reserves increased to 89 trillion cubic feet (about 2,500 km^3), with an increase of 7.2%. As of January 1, 2007, Petronas reported that oil and gas reserves in Malaysia amounted to 20.18 billion barrels (about 3.208 ×109 m^3) equivalent. The government estimates that at current production rates Malaysia will be able to produce oil up to 18 years and gas for 35 years. In 2004, Malaysia is ranked 24th in terms of world oil reserves and 13th for gas. 56% of the oil reserves exist in the Peninsula while 19% exist in East Malaysia. The government collects oil royalties of which 5% are passed to the states and the rest retained by the federal government.

11.4 Brief History

As a unified state, Malaysia did not exist until 1963. Previously, a set of colonies were established by the United Kingdom from the late-18th century, and the western half of modern Malaysia was composed of several separate kingdoms. This group of colonies was known as British Malaya until its dissolution in 1946, when it was reorganized as the Malayan Union. Due to widespread opposition, it was reorganized again as the Federation of Malaya in 1948 and later gained independence on August 31, 1957. Singapore, Sarawak, British North Borneo and the Federation of Malaya joined to form Malaysia on September 16, 1963. However, less than two years later Singapore seceded from the federation and became an independent republic on August 9, 1965.

Archaeological remains have been found throughout Peninsular Malaysia, Sabah and Sarawak. The Semang have a deep ancestry within the Malay Peninsula, dating to the initial settlement from Africa over 50,000 years ago. The Senoi appear to be a composite group, with approximately half of the maternal lineages tracing back to the ancestors of the Semang and about half to Indo-China.

There were numerous Malay kingdoms in the 2nd and 3rd centuries CE—as many as 30 according to Chinese sources.

The Buddhist kingdom of Ligor took control, and its King Chandrabhanu used it as a base to attack Sri Lanka in the 11th century. During the first millennium, the people of the Malay Peninsula adopted Hinduism and Buddhism and the use of the Sanskrit language until they eventually converted to Islam.

In the early 15th century, the Malacca Sultanate was established under a dynasty founded by Parameswara or Sultan Iskandar Shah, a prince from Palembang with bloodline related to the royal house of Srivijaya, who fled from Temasek (now

Singapore).

Britain established its first colony in the Malay Peninsula in 1786. In 1826, Britain established the crown colony of the Straits Settlements, uniting its four possessions in Malaya: Penang, Malacca, Singapore and the island of Labuan(纳闽岛/拉布安岛). During the late 19th century, many Malay states decided to obtain British help in settling their internal conflicts.

Following the Japanese Invasion of Malaya and its occupation during World War II, popular support for independence grew. The Malayan Union, established in 1946 and consisting of all the British possessions in Malaya with the exception of Singapore, was dissolved in 1948 and replaced by the Federation of Malaya, which restored the autonomy of the rulers of the Malay states under British protection.

In 1963, Malaya along with the then-British crown colonies of Sabah (British North Borneo), Sarawak and Singapore, formed Malaysia. After the 13 May race riots of 1969, the controversial New Economic Policy was launched by Prime Minister Abdul Razak. Malaysia has since maintained a delicate ethno-political balance, with a system of government that has attempted to combine overall economic development with political and economic policies that promote equitable participation of all races.

Between the 1980s and the mid-1990s, Malaysia experienced significant economic growth under the premiership of Mahathir bin Mohamad. The period saw a shift from an agriculture-based economy to one based on manufacturing and industry in areas such as computers and consumer electronics. In the late 1990s, Malaysia was shaken by the Asian Financial Crisis.

11.5 Politics

Capital

The capital city is Kuala Lumpur, while Putrajaya is the seat of the federal government. The population stands at over 30 million (2015).

Leaders

Malaysia is a federal constitutional elective monarchy. The federal head of state of Malaysia is the Yang di-Pertuan Agong, commonly referred to as the King of Malaysia. The current head of state is Abdul Halim Mu'adzam Shah, who took office in December, 2011. The Yang di-Pertuan Agong is elected to a five-year term among the nine hereditary Sultans of the Malay states; the other four states, which have titular governors, do not participate in the election. The system of government in Malaysia is closely modeled on that of Westminster parliamentary system, a legacy of British colonial rule. In practice however, more power is vested in the executive branch of government than in the legislative, and the judiciary has been weakened by sustained attacks by the government during the Mahathir era. Since independence in 1957, Malaysia has been governed by a multi-party coalition known as the Barisan Nasional (formerly known as the Alliance).

Legislation

Legislative power is divided between federal and state legislatures. The bicameral parliament consists of the lower house, the House of Representatives or Dewan Rakyat (literally the "Chamber of the People") and the upper house, the Senate or Dewan Negara (literally the "Chamber of the Nation"). The 222-member of House of Representatives is elected for a maximum term of five years from single-member constituencies that are drawn based on population. All 70 senators sit for three-year terms; 26 are elected by the 13 state assemblies, two represent the federal territory of Kuala Lumpur, one is from federal territories of Labuan and one from Putrajaya, and 40 are appointed by the king upon the prime minister's recommendation. Besides the Parliament at the federal level, each state has a unicameral state legislative assembly (Malay: *Dewan Undangan Negeri*) whose members are elected from single-member constituencies. Parliamentary elections are held at least once every five years, with the last general election being in May, 2013. Registered voters of age 21 and above may vote for the members of the House of Representatives and in most of the states, the state legislative chamber as well. Voting is not compulsory.

Cabinet

Executive power is vested in the Cabinet led by the Prime Minister; the Malaysian Constitution stipulates that the Prime Minister must be a member of the House of Representatives who, in the opinion of the Yang di-Pertuan Agong, commands a majority in Parliament. The Cabinet is chosen from among members of both houses of Parliament and is responsible to that body. The Prime Minister is both the head of Cabinet and the head of government. The incumbent, Najib Razak, appointed in 2009, is the sixth Prime Minister.

 Government

The federal government has authority over external affairs, defense, internal security, justice (except civil law cases among Malays or other Muslims and other indigenous peoples, adjudicated under Islamic and traditional law), federal citizenship, finance, commerce, industry, communications, transportation, and other matters.

State governments are led by Chief Ministers (*Menteri Besar* in Malay States or *Ketua Menteri* in States without hereditary rulers), who are state assembly members from the majority party in the Dewan Undangan Negeri. In each of the states with a hereditary ruler, the Chief Minister is required to be a Malay Muslim, although this rule is subject to the rulers' discretions.

Political Parties

There are more than 40 registered political parties, including the foregoing, not all of which are represented in the federal parliament. For example, Barisan Nasional (National Front)—a coalition comprising the United Malays National Organization (UMNO) and 12 other parties, most of which are ethnically based; Democratic Action Party (DAP); Parti Islam se Malaysia (PAS); and Parti Keadilan Rakyat (PKR).

Malaysia's predominant political party, the United Malays National Organization (UMNO), has held power in coalition with other parties continuously since independence in 1957. The UMNO coalition's share of the vote declined in national elections held in May 1969. In the years that followed, Malaysia undertook several initiatives that became integral parts of its socioeconomic model. The New Economic Policy (NEP), launched in 1971, contained a series of affirmative action policies designed to benefit Malays and certain indigenous groups (together known as *bumiputera* or "sons of the soil"). The constitution was amended to limit dissent against the specially-protected and sensitive portions of the Constitution pertaining to the social contract. The government identified intercommunal harmony as one of its official goals. The previous alliance of communally based parties was replaced with a broader coalition—the Barisan Nasional or National Front. The BN won large majorities in the 1974 federal and state elections.

Malaysia held general elections on May 5, 2013 following the dissolution of the Parliament announced on April 3, 2013. Both the House of Representatives and 12 out of 13 state legislative assemblies (with the exception of Sarawak) were renewed.

The federal ruling Barisan Nasional (BN) coalition, dominated by the United Malays National Organization (UMNO) party, whose leader is Prime Minister Najib Razak, formed the federal government with 60% of parliamentary seats. BN coalition won a mere 47.38% of the popular vote while the Pakatan Rakyat (PR) coalition led by Anwar Ibrahim formed the bulk of the opposition in Parliament after winning 50.87% of the popular vote. The election was Barisan Nasional's worst ever showing, outmatching even the 1969 election which triggered the May 13 riots. Despite winning the popular vote and making gains in the number of parliamentary seats, the Pakatan Rakyat coalition failed to win a majority of seats to form the federal government. For state legislative assemblies elections, Barisan Nasional won 9 out of 12 states, including Kedah and Perak which were won by Pakatan Rakyat in the last elections.

Diplomacy

Regional cooperation is a cornerstone of Malaysia's foreign policy. It was a founding member of the Association of Southeast Asian Nations and served as the group's chair from 2005 – 2006. It hosted the ASEAN Summit and East Asia Summit in December 2005, as well as the ASEAN Ministerial and the ASEAN Regional Forum in July 2006.

Malaysia is an active member of the Asia Pacific Economic Cooperation (APEC) forum, the Organization of the Islamic Conference (OIC), the Non-Aligned Movement (NAM), and the United Nations. It had been chair of the OIC until March 2008 and has also chaired the NAM.

Malaysia is a frequent contributor to the UN and other peacekeeping and stabilization missions, including recent deployments to Lebanon(黎巴嫩), Timor-Leste, the Philippines, Indonesia, Pakistan, Sierra Leone, and Kosovo.

11.6 Economy

The Malay Peninsula and Southeast Asia have been a centre of trade for centuries. Various items such as porcelain and spices were actively traded even before Malacca and Singapore rose to prominence. In the 17th century, they were found in several Malay states. Later, as the British started to take over as administrators of Malaya, rubber and palm oil trees were introduced for commercial purposes. Over time, Malaya became the world's largest major producer of tin, rubber, and palm oil. These three commodities, along with other raw materials, firmly set Malaysia's economic tempo well into the mid-20th century.

Instead of relying on the local Malays as a source of labor, the British brought in Chinese and Indians to work in the mines, plantations and fill up the void in professional expertise. Although many of them returned to their respective home countries after their agreed tenure ended, some remained in Malaysia and settled permanently.

As Malaya moved towards independence, the government began implementing economic five-year plans, beginning with the First Malayan Five-Year Plan in 1955. Upon the establishment of Malaysia, the plans were re-titled and renumbered, beginning with the First Malaysia Plan in 1965.

In the 1970s, Malaysia began to imitate the Four Asian Tiger economies (China's Taiwan, the Republic of Korea, China's Hong Kong and Singapore) and committed itself to a transition from being reliant on mining and agriculture to an economy that depended more on manufacturing. With Japanese investment, heavy industries flourished and in a matter of years, Malaysian exports became the country's primary growth engine. Malaysia consistently achieved more than 7% GDP growth along with low inflation in the 1980s and the 1990s. During the same period, the government tried to eradicate poverty with the controversial New Economic Policy. Its main objective was the elimination of the association of race with economic function, and the first Five-Year Plan to begin implementing the NEP was the Second Malaysia Plan. The success or failure of the NEP is the subject of much debate, although it was officially retired in 1990 and replaced by the National Development Policy (NDP).

Malaysia experienced an economic boom and underwent a rapid development during the late 20th century and has GDP per capita (nominal) of US$11,062.043 in 2014, and is considered a newly industrialized country. In 2009, the Purchasing power parity (PPP) GDP was US$383.6 billion, about half the 2014 amount, and the PPP per capita GDP was US$8,100, about one third the 2014 amount.

 Agriculture

Agriculture remains an important sector of Malaysia's economy, contributing 12% to the national GDP and providing employment for 16% of the population. The British established large-scale plantations and introduced new commercial crops (rubber in 1876, palm oil in 1917, and cocoa in the 1950s). The 3 main crops—rubber, palm oil, and cocoa—have dominated agricultural exports ever since, although the Malaysian share of the world's production of these crops declined steadily during the last 2 decades. In addition to these products, Malaysian farmers produce a number of fruits and vegetables for the domestic market, including bananas, coconuts, durian, pineapples, rice, rambutan (a red, oval fruit grown on a tree of the same name in Southeast Asia), and others. The Malaysian tropical climate is very favorable for the production of various exotic fruits and vegetables, especially since Malaysia seldom experiences hurricanes or droughts.

As rice is a staple foodstuff in the everyday diet of Malaysians and is a symbol of traditional Malay culture, the production of rice, which stood at 1.94 million metric tons in 1998, plays an important part in the country's agriculture. However, the overall production of rice does not satisfy the country's needs, and Malaysia imports rice from neighboring Thailand and Vietnam.

In 1999, Malaysia produced 10.55 million metric tons of palm oil, remaining one of the world's largest producers. Almost 85% or 8.8 million metric tons of palm oil was exported to international market. Malaysia is one of the world's leading suppliers of rubber, producing 767,000 metric tons of rubber in 1999. However, in the 1990s, large plantation companies began to turn to the more profitable palm oil production. Malaysia is also the world's fourth-largest producer of cocoa.

Logging in the tropical rainforest is an important export revenue earner in East Malaysia and in the northern states of Peninsular Malaysia. In 2000, Malaysia produced 21.94 million cubic meters of sawn logs, earning RM 1.7 billion (about US$450 million) from exports. Malaysia sells more tropical logs and sawn tropical timber abroad than any other country and is one of the biggest exporters of hardwood. Despite attempts at administrative control and strict requirements regarding reforestation in the early 1990s, logging companies often damage the fragile tropical environment. Sharp criticism from local and international environmentalist groups gradually led to bans on the direct export of timber from almost all states, except Sarawak and Sabah. In December 2000, the government and representatives of indigenous and environmentalist groups agreed that there was a need to adopt standards set by the international Forest Stewardship Council (FSC), which certifies that timber comes from well-managed forests and logging companies have to be responsible for reforestation.

Industry

The early years of the new union were marred by an armed conflict with Indonesia and the expulsion of Singapore. The Southeast Asian nation experienced an economic boom and underwent rapid development during the late 20th century. With rapid growth averaging 8% from 1991 to 1997, it has, from time to time, been considered a newly industrialised country. Because Malaysia is one of the three countries that control the Strait of Malacca, international trade plays a large role in its economy. At one time, it was the largest producer of tin, rubber and palm oil in the world. Manufacturing has a large influence on the country's economy. Malaysia has a biodiverse range of flora and fauna and is also considered one of the 17 most Megadiverse countries in the world.

11.7 Culture

Ethnics

Malaysia is a multi-ethnic, multi-cultural and multilingual society. The population was estimated 30 million in 2015 consisting of 50.1% Malays, 22.6% Chinese, 6.7%

Indians, with other minorities and indigenous peoples (Department of Statistics, Malaysia). The Malays, who form the largest community, are defined as Muslims in the Constitution of Malaysia. The Malays play a dominant role politically and are included in a grouping identified as the Bumiputra. Their native language is Malay (*Bahasa Melayu*) which is the national language of the country.

Malaysia is a multi-religious society and Islam is the official religion. According to the Population and Housing Census 2010 figures, approximately 61.3% of the population practiced Islam; 19.8% Buddhism; 9.2% Christianity; 6.3% Hinduism; and 1.3% traditional Chinese religions. And other faiths while 1.1% either 0.7% declared no religion and the remaining 1.4% practiced other religions or did not provide any information.

Holiday

Malaysians observe a number of holidays and festivities throughout the year. Some holidays are federal gazetted public holidays and some are public holidays observed by individual states. Other festivals are observed by particular ethnic or religion groups, but are not public holidays.

The most celebrated holiday is the "Hari Kebangsaan" (Independence Day) on August 31 commemorating the independence of the Federation of Malaya in 1957, while Malaysia Day is only celebrated in the state of Sabah on September 16 to commemorate the formation of Malaysia in 1963. Hari Merdeka, as well as Labour Day (May 1), the King's birthday (first Saturday of June) and some other festivals is federal gazetted public holidays.

Muslims in Malaysia celebrate Muslim holidays. The most celebrated festival, Hari Raya Puasa(斋戒节,封斋节), is the Malay translation of Eid al-Fitr. It is generally a festival honoured by the Muslims worldwide marking the end of Ramadan, the fasting month. In addition to Hari Raya Puasa, they also celebrate Hari Raya Haji (also called Hari Raya Aidiladha, the translation of Eid ul-Adha,古尔邦节), Awal Muharram (Islamic New Year) and Maulidur Rasul (birthday of the Prophet).

Chinese in Malaysia typically celebrate festivals that are observed by Chinese around the world. Chinese New Year is the most celebrated among the festivals. It lasts for fifteen days and ends with Chap Goh Mei. Other festivals celebrated by Chinese are the Qingming Festival, the Dragon Boat Festival and the Mid-Autumn Festival. In addition to traditional Chinese festivals, Buddhists Chinese also celebrate Vesak.

The majority of Indians in Malaysia are Hindus and they celebrate Deepavali, the festival of light, while Thaipusam is a celebration during which pilgrims from all over the country flock to Batu Caves. Apart from the Hindus, Sikhs celebrate the Vaisakhi, the

Sikh New Year. Other festivals such as Good Friday (East Malaysia only), Christmas, Hari Gawai of the Ibans (Dayaks), Pesta Menuai (Pesta Kaamatan) of the Kadazan-Dusuns are also celebrated in Malaysia.

Despite most of the festivals being identified with a particular ethnic or religious group, all Malaysians celebrate the festivities together, regardless of their background. For years when the Hari Raya Puasa and Chinese New Year coincided, a portmanteau Kongsi Raya was coined, which is a combination of Gong Xi Fa Cai (a greeting used on the Chinese New Year) and Hari Raya (which could also mean "celebrating together" in Malay). Similarly, the portmanteau Deepa Raya was coined when Hari Raya Puasa and Deepavali coincided.

Exercises

1. **Explain the following in English.**

    (1) legislative power

    (2) Hari Kebangsaan

    (3) the Malay Peninsula

    (4) Malaysia Day

    (5) Kuala Lumpur

    (6) Yang di-Pertuan Agong

2. **Fill in the blanks.**

    (1) Malaysia is a _____, _____, _____ society. The population was estimated _____, consisting of 50.1% Malays, 22.6% _____, 6.7% _____, with other minorities and indigenous peoples.

    (2) Malaysia Day is only celebrated in the state of _____ on September 16 to commemorate the _____ in 1963.

    (3) Over time, Malaya became the world's largest major producer of _____, _____, and _____. These three commodities, along with other raw materials, firmly set Malaysia's _____ well into the mid-20th century.

    (4) Malaysia is a _____ that consists of _____ and _____ in Southeast Asia with a total landmass of _____. The country is separated into two regions—Peninsular Malaysia and Malaysian Borneo—by _____.

    (5) The Malays, who form the largest community, are defined as _____ in the Constitution of Malaysia.

    (6) The government is headed by _____. The government is closely modeled after the _____.

    (7) In terms of agriculture, Malaysia is one of the top exporters of _____ and

_____, which together with _____ and _____, _____, _____, _____, dominate the growth of the sector.

(8) The most celebrated holiday is the "Hari Kebangsaan" _____ on August 31 commemorating _____ in 1957.

(9) Malaysia is a _____ society and _____ is the official religion.

(10) Malaysia's predominant political party, _____, has held power in coalition with other parties continuously since independence in 1957.

3. **Answer the following questions.**

(1) What is the basic information concerning Malaysia?

(2) What is Malaysia famous for?

(3) How did Malaysia get her name?

(4) Why is Malaysia Day not a public holiday in Peninsular Malaysia?

(5) What are some major industries of Malaysia?

CHAPTER 12

ASEAN

ASEAN (the Association of Southeast Asian Nations) consists of 10 member nations, Brunei, Cambodia, Indonesia, Laos, Malaysia, Myanmar, the Philippines, Singapore, Thailand, and Vietnam. Its administrative body, the ASEAN Secretariat based in Jakarta, Indonesia, serves the 10 Southeast Asian nations in overseeing plans and programs initiated by the regional grouping.

12.1 Establishment and Development

ASEAN was preceded by an organization of the Association of Southeast Asia, commonly called ASA, an alliance consisting of the Philippines, Malaysia, and Thailand that was formed in 1961. The bloc itself, however, was established on August 8, 1967, when foreign ministers of five countries—Indonesia, Malaysia, the Philippines, Singapore, and Thailand—met at the Thai Department of Foreign Affairs  building in Bangkok and signed the ASEAN Declaration, more commonly known as the Bangkok Declaration. The five foreign ministers—Adam Malik of Indonesia, Narciso Ramos of the Philippines, Abdul Razak of Malaysia, S. Rajaratnam of Singapore, and Thanat Khoman of Thailand—are considered as the organization's founding fathers.

Brunei joined on January 8, 1984, Vietnam on July 28, 1995; Laos and Myanmar on July 23, 1997; and Cambodia on April 30, 1999. Two countries—East Timor and Papua New Guinea—are observers of ASEAN. the ASEAN region has a population of about 560 million, a total area of 4.5 million square kilometers, a combined gross domestic product of almost US $1,100 billion, and a total trade of about US$1,400 billion.

At the first ASEAN Summit, Bali, on February 24, 1976, Treaty of Amity and Cooperation in Southeast Asia and Declaration of ASEAN Concord—the well-known Bali Concord I—were signed, which reaffirm the ASEAN objectives and principles. On

October 7, 2003, a series of documents known as Bali Concord Ⅱ were signed at the nineth ASEAN Summit, Bali, including ASEAN Security Community (ASC), ASEAN Economic Community (AEC), ASEAN Socio-Cultural Community (ASCC) and so on, putting forward the establishment of the ASEAN Community in 2020 similar to European Communities.

The ASEAN + 3 cooperation began in December 1997 with the convening of an informal summit among the leaders of ASEAN and their counterparts from East Asia, namely China, Japan and the Republic of Korea (ROK) at the sidelines of the Second ASEAN Informal Summit in Malaysia. On November 6, 2001, the ASEAN leaders held three separate meetings in Brunei with the leaders of China, Japan and the Republic of Korea and began the ASEAN + 1 cooperation, which was enhanced at the summits in Bali, Indonesia, on October 8, 2003 respectively with China, Japan, the ROK and India.

ASEAN continues to develop cooperative relations with its dialogue partners, namely, Australia, Canada, China, the European Union, India, Japan, the ROK, New Zealand, the Russian Federation, the United States of America, and the United Nations Development Program. ASEAN also promotes cooperation with Pakistan in some areas of mutual interest.

The ASEAN Charter was signed on November 20, 2007, by the leaders of the 10 ASEAN member states at the 13th ASEAN Summit in Singapore. It comes as ASEAN celebrates its 40th anniversary of its founding in 1967. The charter transforms ASEAN into a rules-based legal entity like the European Union, nailing down for the first time the ASEAN community strategic aims, developing objectives, principles and framework.

12.2 Aims and Purposes

The purpose of founding ASEAN is to promote the regional prosperity and stability. The ASEAN Declaration (1967) states that the aims and purposes of the association are:

- To accelerate the economic growth, social progress and cultural development in the region through joint endeavours in the spirit of equality and partnership in order to strengthen the foundation for a prosperous and peaceful community of Southeast Asian Nations;

- To promote regional peace and stability through abiding respect for justice and the rule of law in the relationship among countries of the region and adherence to the principles of the United Nations Charter;

- To promote active collaboration and mutual assistance on matters of common interest in the economic, social, cultural, technical, scientific and administrative fields;

● To provide assistance to each other in the form of training and research facilities in the educational, professional, technical and administrative spheres;

● To collaborate more effectively for the greater utilization of their agriculture and industries, the expansion of their trade, including the study of the problems of international commodity trade, the improvement of their transportation and communications facilities and the raising of the living standards of their peoples;

● To promote Southeast Asian studies;

● To maintain close and beneficial cooperation with existing international and regional organizations with similar aims and purposes, and explore all avenues for even closer cooperation among themselves.

In the middle of 1990s, ASEAN advanced the integrative aims of cooperation in politics, economy and culture among the member states. The ASEAN Vision 2020, adopted by the ASEAN leaders at the 30th Anniversary of ASEAN in 1997, agreed on a shared vision of ASEAN as a concert of Southeast Asian nations, outward looking, living in peace, stability and prosperity, bonded together in partnership in dynamic development and in a community of caring societies. In 2003, the ASEAN leaders resolved that an ASEAN community should be established comprising three pillars, namely, ASEAN Security Community, ASEAN Economic Community and ASEAN Socio-Cultural Community.

12.3 Organization

ASEAN Organizational Structure

```
                        ASEAN Summit
                             |
        ┌──────────┬─────────┼─────────┬──────────┐
       AEM        AMM              AFMM         Others
        |      ┌───┼───┐             |            |
      SEOM   ASC     SOM          ASFOM      Committees
        |     |       |             |            |
   Sub-comm/ Working Working    Sub-comm/    Sub-comm/
   Working   Groups  Groups     Working      Working
   Groups                        Groups       Groups
              |
       ASEAN Secretariat
```

AEM: ASEAN Economic Ministers
AMM: ASEAN Ministerial Meeting

AFMM: ASEAN Finance Ministers Meeting
SEOM: Senior Economic Officials Meeting
ASC: ASEAN Standing Committee
SOM: Senior Officials Meeting
ASFOM: ASEAN Senior Finance Officials Meeting

ASEAN Summit: The highest decision-making body in ASEAN is the nonscheduled meeting of the ASEAN heads of state and government. Whenever decided, the ASEAN Summit is preceded by a Joint Ministerial Meeting (JMM) composed of foreign and economic ministers. Since the first ASEAN Summit in Bali on February 23-24, 1976, ASEAN has held 26 formal summits and four informal summits.

ASEAN Economic Ministers (AEM): AEM is composed of all ASEAN member countries and primarily discusses issues of economic situation and ASEAN economic cooperation. The first ASEAN Economic Ministers Meeting was held in Jakarta in November, 1975. Up to 2015, the annual meeting of AEM has been held 47 times.

ASEAN Ministerial Meeting (AMM): The AMM is an annual meeting of the ASEAN foreign ministers held in July of each year and hosted on a rotational basis by ASEAN member nations in alphabetical order, following the rotation of chairmanship of the ASEAN Summit. The ASEAN senior officials and directors-general hold a series of preparatory meetings before the AMM. Up to 2014, ASEAN has held forty-six meetings and 1991 was the first year for China to attend the AMM.

ASEAN Standing Committee (ASC): The ASC, under the chairmanship of the foreign minister of the country-in-chair, is mandated to prepare and host the ASEAN Ministerial Meeting. After the meeting it is in charge of supervising and implementing the resolutions made by AMM and entitled to release statements on behalf of ASEAN.

The ASEAN Secretariat: The ASEAN Secretariat is the administrative body for ASEAN, based in Jakarta, Indonesia. The Secretary-General is selected by ASEAN member countries on a rotational basis in two-year tenure of office. The basic mandate of the ASEAN Secretariat is to provide greater efficiency in the coordination of ASEAN organs and more effective implementation of ASEAN projects and activities.

The ASEAN Dialogue Partners Meeting: Known as the post ministerial conference, the ASEAN Dialogue Partners Meeting, founded in 1999, is a forum on discussion about politics and securities and cooperation between ASEAN and dialogue-partner countries. It consists of ten member states from ASEAN and 10 dialogue partners, namely Australia, Canada, China, EU, India, Japan, the Republic of Korea, New Zealand, Russia, and US. In 1996, China became the dialogue-partner country.

The ASEAN Regional Forum (ARF): The 26th ASEAN Ministerial Meeting and Post Ministerial Conference, held in Singapore on July 23-25, 1993, agreed to establish the ASEAN Regional Forum (ARF). ARF was established in Bangkok on July 25, 1994 with the intent to "foster constructive dialogue and consultation on political and security issues of common interest and concern" and to "make significant contributions to efforts towards confidence-building and preventive diplomacy in the Asia-Pacific region". The Chairman's Statements at the 3rd ARF, Jakarta, on July 23, 1996 declared that ARF would "cover all of East Asia, both Northeast and Southeast Asia, as well as Oceania". Up to now, the participants in the ARF are 10 member states and other 17 countries or organs—Australia, Bangladesh, Canada, China, European Union, India, Japan, Democratic People's Republic of Korea, the Republic of Korea, Mongolia, New Zealand, Pakistan, Papua New Guinea, Russian Federation, Sri Lanka, Timor-Leste, and the United States. In 1994, China attended the first ARF as a consultation-partner country.

ASEAN Plus Three Cooperation (10 +3): The ASEAN Plus Three Cooperation began in December 1997 with the convening of an informal summit among the leaders of ASEAN and their counterparts from East Asia, namely China, Japan and the Republic of Korea at the sidelines of the Second ASEAN Informal Summit in Malaysia. The ASEAN Plus Three Summits are primarily held after each ASEAN Summit.

ASEAN Plus One Cooperation (10 +1): The ASEAN Plus One Cooperation is held alongside the ASEAN Plus Three Cooperation. The ASEAN Plus One Summits are the three ASEAN +3 summits that ASEAN respectively meets with China, Japan, and the Republic of Korea. In October, 2003, the ASEAN-India Summit was added to the fourth ASEAN +1 summits.

ASEAN-EU Ministerial Meeting (AEMM): The participants for AEMM are all ASEAN member states and 15 country ministers or deputies from the EU.

ASEAN-US Dialogue Meeting: It mainly discusses the ASEAN and US bilateral relations, and issues affecting the two sides in the region and international affairs.

The ASEAN Business Advisory Council (ASEAN-BAC): It was inaugurated in April 2003 at the ASEAN Secretariat in Jakarta, Indonesia. ASEAN-BAC is mandated by the ASEAN leaders to provide private sector feedback and guidance to boost ASEAN's efforts towards economic integration and to identify priority areas for consideration by the ASEAN leaders. In May, 2013, the 52nd ASEAN-BAC Council Meeting was held in Kuala Lumpur, Malaysia.

ASEAN Investment Area (AIA) Council: It is a ministerial body composed of ASEAN secretary-general and economic ministers from ASEAN member states, to oversee the implementation of the framework agreements to promote the flow of investment, agreed in a joint statement issued at the end of the meeting to create an even more liberal, facilitative, transparent and competitive investment environment.

ASEAN Free Trade Area (AFTA) Council: AFTA Council, composed of ASEAN secretary-general and economic ministers from ASEAN member countries, is in charge of issues in ASEAN Free Trade Area.

Furthermore, ASEAN holds ministerial meetings in other areas to discuss the relevant cooperation. These include ASEAN Health Ministers Meeting, ASEAN Environment Ministers Meeting, ASEAN Transport Ministers Meeting, ASEAN Tourism Ministers Meeting and so on.

12.4 Major Events and Achievements

In more than 40 years since its founding, ASEAN has kept enhancing the cooperation among the member states and that between ASEAN and relevant countries in politics, economy, regional security, culture, technology, society and so on, resulting in significant achievements such as accelerating ASEAN integration and enlarging regional and external cooperation.

Progress in ASEAN Integration

(1) **Regional cooperation in security**

The initial intention to found ASEAN is based on the regional security. In course of dealing with its internal affairs and relationship, ASEAN insists on the principles of consensus, equal reciprocity, seeking common points while reserving difference, "non-interference in the internal affairs of one another", and "renunciation of the threat or use of force" (Treaty of Amity and Cooperation in Southeast Asia, 1976). ASEAN has played a positive role in interceding its internal affairs such as the intercession of the Sabah sovereignty issue between Malaysia and the Philippines, objection to regional hegemonism by demanding the withdraw of Vietnamese troops from Cambodia, The Agreement on the Safety of Navigation in the Straits of Malacca signed by Indonesia, Malaysia and Singapore to ensure navigation safety in the Straits of Malacca and the Straits of Singapore during the ministerial meeting in Manila on February 24, 1977, which urged to settle Cambodian issues in political way, and implementing nonintervention of Indonesian interior.

On November 27, 1971, the foreign ministers of the then five ASEAN members met in Kuala Lumpur and signed the zone of peace, freedom and neutrality (ZOPFAN) declaration. It commits all ASEAN members to "exert efforts to secure the recognition of and respect for Southeast Asia as a zone of peace, freedom and neutrality, free from any manner of interference by outside powers", and to "make concerted efforts to broaden the areas of cooperation, which would contribute to their strength, solidarity and closer relationship".

Another five years passed before the next major development in political cooperation came about—the First ASEAN Summit in Bali, when the ASEAN leaders signed three major documents: the Declaration of ASEAN Concord, the Treaty of Amity and Cooperation in Southeast Asia, and the Agreement Establishing the ASEAN Secretariat.

(2) **Regional cooperation in non-traditional security**

In recent years, such transnational crimes as illegal drug selling, money laundering, terrorism, sea piracy, weapon smuggling and human trafficking have become international issues of non-traditional security, and ASEAN has reinforced the cooperation in the field.

Since the September 11 attack in 2001, terrorism has become a global security problem. Southeast Asia is not only a victim region but also a region of bases for terrorists' training. The ASEAN members are on the side of the UN against terrorism. As for strikes against terrorism, ASEAN has organized and precipitated consultations and cooperation in many ways.

The heads of state/government of the ASEAN at the 7th ASEAN Summit in Bandar Seri Begawan, Brunei, in November 2001 issued 2001 ASEAN Declaration on Joint Action to Counter Terrorism, to strengthen national mechanisms to combat terrorism.

On November 15, 2001 the heads of the armies of the ASEAN member states convened a meeting in Manila, the Philippines, working out the plan of strike against terrorism in the ASEAN region.

From July 29 to August 1, 2002, in Bandar Seri Begawan, the capital of Brunei, the 35th ASEAN Ministerial Meeting, the ASEAN Regional Forum and a series of annual meetings between ASEAN and the dialogue partners laid stress on countering international terrorism. The Ministerial Meeting declared to be fully committed to strengthening bilateral, regional and international cooperation to counter terrorism in a comprehensive manner and to make Southeast Asia a more stable and safer place. At the ARF 23 participating states issued a statement to cooperate together in the fight against terrorism.

The 3rd annual ASEAN Senior Official Meeting on Transnational Crimes and the ASEAN Dialogue Partner Meeting held from June 6 – 8, 2003 in Hanoi, Vietnam, stand for the first time for ASEAN, China, Japan and the Republic of Korea to convene senior official dialogue meetings on combating transnational crimes. The five meetings of senior officials on transnational crimes, namely the 3rd annual SOMTC; the 1st ASEAN + 3 (with Japan, China, and the Republic of Korea); ASEAN + China, ASEAN + European Union (EU), and ASEAN + US Senior Official Meetings on Transnational Crimes reviewed and worked out concrete measures to strengthen the cooperation among ASEAN member states and between ASEAN and its dialogue partners. The cooperation covers combating transnational crimes, such as terrorism, people smuggling, narcotics-related, money laundering, sea piracy, and high-tech crimes.

The 36th ASEAN Ministerial Meeting and a series of ministerial meetings on June 17, 2003 in Phnom Penh discussed counter-terrorism as one of the issues. The Ministers renewed their resolve to counter all kinds of terrorism and all the combination of terrorism with religious, racial and national issues, and their resolve to continue reinforcing the cooperation with the world to combat international terrorism, and their resolve to fight against the transnational crimes such as sea piracy, human trafficking, drugs trafficking, money laundering and their resolve to support the commitment to a drugs-free ASEAN by 2015.

The Southeast Asia Regional Centre for Counter Terrorism (SEARCCT), set up in July 2003 in Malaysia, serves as a major centre in the region to train and build the capacity of enforcement and security officials from governments in the region and beyond, with collaboration with other governments and international organizations and to research on the radical actions in the region in order to promote the regional security.

(3) **Constant progress in ASEAN economic integration**

In the 1970s and 1980s the ASEAN economic cooperation lay mainly in trade and industry. On February 24, 1977 in Manila, foreign ministers of ASEAN signed Agreement on ASEAN Preferential Trading Arrangements. The agreement provides a series of preferential trading arrangements. Besides, ASEAN also achieves remarkable results by reinforcing the cooperation in traffic, communication, finance, insurance, oil, rubber industry, wood industry and grain production.

Since the 1990s ASEAN economic cooperation is mainly the progress in its economic integration and it goes on smoothly. ASEAN Free Trade Area has kept adjusting its course and schedule according to the changes of internal and external situations. The 4th ASEAN Summit in January, 1992 decided that "all member states agree to establish and participate in the ASEAN Free Trade Area (AFTA) within 15 years", implementing the Common Effective Preferential Tariff (CEPT) Scheme stage by stage. At the 26th ASEAN Economic Ministers Meeting in September, 1994, the ministers endorsed the Fifth AFTA Council decision to accelerate the realization of AFTA from 15 to 10 years by January 1, 2003 instead of 2008, and would recommend the decision to ASEAN heads of government. The 6th ASEAN Summit in December 1998 decided to advance the implementation of AFTA by one year from 2003 to 2002. The CEPT rates are reduced to 0%-5% by the year 2000 (2003 for Vietnam, 2005 for Laos and Myanmar and 2010 for Cambodia). The 3rd ASEAN Informal Summit in Manila, the Philippines, November 28, 1999 agreed that all import duties were to be eliminated by 2010, ahead of the original 2015 schedule, for the six original members of ASEAN, and that the schedule was to be in principle advanced from 2018 to 2015 for the new members of ASEAN, but allowing some sensitive products to follow the original date of 2018. In January 2002, the six original members of ASEAN formally began AFTA reducing the CEPT rates to below 5%.

The participants at the ASEAN Economic Ministers Meeting in Phnom Penh, Cambodia, in September 2003 agreed to accelerate the proceeding of AFTA by adjusting the prices of some preferential industrial products.

ASEAN has now largely completed the "easy phase" of intra-regional trade liberalization. As of 2009, zero tariffs applied to 64% of the products in the Inclusion List of the ASEAN-6. The average tariff for ASEAN-6 under the CEPT scheme is down to 1.5%, from 12.8% when the tariff cutting exercise commenced in 1993.

The 47th Meeting of the ASEAN Economic Ministers in Malaysia on August 22, 2015 underscored the significance of the year 2015 as a key milestone in ASEAN's community building process. Noting the challenges faced collectively by the region as well as by individual ASEAN Member States, the meeting expressed ASEAN's continued resolve to establish the ASEAN Economic Community (AEC) at the end of this year and its commitment towards deeper integration under the AEC post-2015 agenda.

The ASEAN Economic Community (AEC) is envisioned to be the realization of ASEAN economic integration by 2015. Several initiatives have been undertaken to bring the region closer to the goals of the AEC 2015. The ASEAN Trade in Goods Agreement (ATIGA), in force since May 2010, has led to significant tariff elimination among ASEAN countries, and has contributed to the on-going efforts to address non-tariff measures in the region. The ASEAN Framework Agreement on Services (AFAS), signed in 1995, has eased restrictions to cross-border services trade in various sectors such as business services, construction, health care, maritime transport, telecommunications, tourism, and financial services. The ASEAN Comprehensive Investment Agreement (ACIA), which came into effect in March 2012, articulates member states' commitments in terms of liberalizing and protecting cross-border investment activities while embracing international best practices in the treatment of foreign investors and investment.

ASEAN has made great progress in the tourism cooperation. The implementation of the ASEAN Tourism Strategic Plan (ATSP) 2011-2015 has been well progressing, where 75% measures for 2013 have been duly completed. In further promoting sustainable tourism to support timely realization of the ASEAN Economic Community, measures under ASTP were updated to ensure its relevance to its on-going efforts. Important progress was also made in developing comprehensive tourism standards for green hotel, homestay, spa services, public toilet, clean tourist city and community based tourism, and their certification process, which would help enhancing quality of tourism human resources, services and facilities in the region. In facilitating full implementation of those standards by 2015, capacity building for auditors and pilot testing would be carried out in 2014. The ASEAN Tourism Forum (ATF) 2014 held on January 16-23, 2014 in Kuching, Malaysia, with the theme of "ASEAN: Advancing Tourism Together", was attended by 462 international buyers and 879 sellers with 353 booths as well as 75 media.

ASEAN has implemented numerous cooperation projects in food, agriculture and forestry sectors, which cover a wide spectrum of activities ranging from exchange of information, crop production, postharvest and handling, training and extension, research and development as well as trade promotion in the areas of crops, livestock, fisheries, and forestry. In order to respond to trade globalisation, ASEAN cooperation in food, agriculture and forestry is now more focused on the enhancement of food, agricultural and forestry products competitiveness in international markets, while sustaining agricultural production. Harmonisation of quality and standards, assurance of food safety, and standardisation of trade certification are amongst the priorities being addressed, building upon the experience of some Member States and existing international standards. Most of the ASEAN programmes and projects are implemented under a networking arrangement, where cooperation is implemented through the focal point in each ASEAN Member State and utilises national funds.

ASEAN also intensifies the sub-regional economic cooperation to promote the development of the members and narrow the economic gap among them. Since 1990 the sub-regional cooperation as a new form has appeared in ASEAN, such as the South ASEAN Triangle of Growth composed of Singapore, Indonesia and Malaysia, the North ASEAN Triangle of Growth composed of Indonesia, Malaysia and Thailand, the Brunei-Indonesia-Malaysia-The Philippines East ASEAN Growth Area (BIMP-EAGA), and the ASEAN-Mekong Basin Development Cooperation involving China, Myanmar, Laos, Cambodia and Vietnam.

(4) **The intensification of social cooperation**

ASEAN has a positive progress in socio-cultural cooperation, especially in prevention and control of HIV/AIDS and drug abuse, environment protection, health, social welfare, youth and children and so on.

Drug abuse is an issue that has existed in Southeast Asia for far too long, particularly in the Indo-China Peninsula. Owing to the unstable political situation, long-standing local armed forces in some countries and severe lagged effect of social economic development in border minority areas, "Golden Triangle" was formed as a base for drugs planting, processing and selling in the border land of Laos, Myanmar and Thailand. Hence, prevention and control of drug abuse is one of the important cooperation in ASEAN member states and other countries. At the International Congress in Thailand in October, 2000, entitled "In Pursuit of a Drug-Free ASEAN 2015 Sharing the Vision, Leading the Change", the congress issued documents such as the ASEAN and China on a Joint Regional Plan to Achieve a Drug-Free ASEAN by 2015, and Bangkok Political Declaration in Pursuit of a Drug-Free ASEAN 2015. In August, 2001, China, Laos, Myanmar and Thailand held a ministerial meeting in Beijing and issued Beijing

Declaration, which emphasized closer coordination and consultation at both high level and working level and announced a partnership among them.

Due to social unrests and economic crisis, drugs have been spreading as well as HIV/AIDS. In recent years, the number of HIV/AIDS sufferers in ASEAN member states is increasing rapidly. The cooperation of prevention and control of HIV/AIDS has been strengthened by adopting the 7th ASEAN Summit Declaration on HIV/AIDS and a four-year ASEAN Work Programme on HIV/AIDS (2002 - 2005) to combat the spread of AIDS in ASEAN countries. In 2008, ASEAN and the United Nations Regional Task Force on Mobility and HIV Vulnerability Reduction in Southeast Asia and Southern Provinces of China (UNRTF) presented key findings and recommendations of a rapid assessment conducted on HIV and mobility issued in the ten ASEAN countries in 2007 - 2008. Joint ASEAN-UN Press Release Rising Southeast Asia Mobility Highlights Need for Better Coordinated HIV Efforts is the first such publication to include information on current migration patterns along with the HIV situation across the region.

The 12th ASEAN Health Ministers Meeting on September 18, 2014 commits to mobilise and diversify all resources at national, regional and international levels to sustain and improve the achievement in curbing HIV and AIDS new infections, prevalence, and deaths, and to accelerate progress in achieving the ASEAN Declaration of Commitment: Getting to Zero New HIV Infections, Zero Discrimination, Zero AIDS-Related Deaths and the Millennium Development Goal 6 relevant to HIV and AIDS. Further, to achieve the commitment to the Declaration, there is a need to review, where appropriate, the HIV and AIDS programmes, policies and progress towards ending HIV and AIDS as a public health threat.

The cooperation in family and community organizations has increased. ASEAN Ministers Responsible for Social Welfare Meeting was held in Jakarta 1977, Kuala Lumpur 1990, Manila 1993. At the 4th meeting held in August 2001 in Singapore, the ministers noted that the family and the community were instrumental to building society's capacity to withstand societal changes and challenges. They agreed to change the name as "ASEAN Ministerial Meeting for Social Welfare and Development" (AMMSWD) to better reflect the increasing importance of integrating social development with national policies and plans. The 5th AMMSWD was held in December 2004, under the theme "Enhancing a Community of Caring Societies". The Ministers reviewed the progress made on implementing the ASEAN Work Programme for Social Welfare, Family and Population, and set priorities for future cooperation in several areas, including capacity building in the social sector and strengthening the family. The contribution of volunteers as well as the role of NGOs and community organizations towards ASEAN's goals on social welfare and development role was recognized. The 6th AMMSWD was held on December 6, 2007, with the theme of "mainstreaming persons with disabilities in development: Lessons and actions for the future". The ministers welcomed Brunei to host the Seventh ASEAN Ministerial Meeting for Social Welfare and Development in 2010.

With the rapid development of economy, many countries have got rid of poverty, but have to face many environmental problems. In recent years, transboundary haze pollution became the most obvious issue in ASEAN region. With the support of the United Nations Environment Programme (UNEP), ASEAN's earliest initiative on environmental cooperation was the ASEAN Sub-regional Environment Programme (ASEP I) of 1977. This set the framework for regional cooperation in terms of priorities, specific projects and day-to-day activities. During the First ASEAN Ministerial Meeting on Environment in Manila on April 30, 1981, they adopted the ASEAN Declaration on the Environment to ensure the protection of the ASEAN environment and the sustainability of its natural resources so that it can sustain continual development with the aim of eradicating poverty and attaining the highest possible quality life for the people of the ASEAN countries. After that, many declarations were unveiled to prescribe the collaborations and actions in ASEAN member states, for instance, Yangon Resolution on Sustainable Development and ASEAN Declaration on Heritage Parks in 2003, Agreement on the Establishment of ASEAN Centre for Biodiversity in 2005, Cebu Resolution on Sustainable Development in 2006, ASEAN Declaration on Environmental Sustainability and ASEAN Declaration on the 13th Session of the Conference of the Parties to the UNFCCC and the 3rd Session of the CMP to the Kyoto Protocol in 2007, Clear Air for Smaller Cities in the ASEAN Regions in 2009, the Roadmap for Haze-Free ASEAN in 2015. Currently, ASEAN environmental cooperation focuses on ten priority areas of regional importance as reflected in the Blueprint for the ASEAN Socio-Cultural Community (ASCC Blueprint) 2009 – 2015. Besides, environment protection activities were carried out in ASEAN Environment Year (AEY). The ASEAN Environment Year (AEY) is a celebration held once every three years to showcase ASEAN's achievements as well achievements made by individual ASEAN member countries, in the field of environmental protection and management. AEY was first initiated in 1995 and following the success of the 1995 AEY, ASEAN Member States (AMS) agreed to celebrate in 2000 the second AEY as an ASEAN Flagship Project and every three years thereafter. In 2015, the event was held in Nay Pyi Taw, Myanmar on July 29 – 30.

In the field of health, the collaborations between ASEAN member states and other countries or regions have been strengthening. In 2003, facing up to the formidable challenge posed by the spread of SARS, they combated and prevented it together with obvious effects. ASEAN Health Ministers Special Meeting was held in Kuala Lumpur, Malaysia, on April 26, 2003, which issued Joint Statement ASEAN +3 Ministers of Health Special Meeting on SARS. At the Special ASEAN-China Leaders Meeting on SARS in Bangkok, they negotiated further cooperation in SARS prevention and issued Joint

Statement of the Special ASEAN-China Leaders Meeting on SARS, emphasizing the importance of strong leadership, political commitment, multi-sectoral collaboration and partnership at the national and regional levels to fight epidemic.

The 14th ASEAN summit was held from February 26 to March 1, 2009 in Hua Hin, Thailand. It was originally scheduled for December 2008, but was postponed due to the political crisis in Thailand. At the summit, the ASEAN leaders signed the Cha-am Hua Hin Declaration on the Roadmap for an ASEAN Community and adopted various other documents, including the ASEAN Political-Security Community Blueprint and the ASEAN Socio-Cultural Community Blueprint. The ASEAN-Australia-New Zealand Free Trade Area was established. It is one of Asia's largest trade arrangements and covers trade in goods, investment and services, financial services, telecommunications, electronic commerce and intellectual property.

(5) **The intensification of cooperation in technological information**

A series of plans of action in science and technology (S&T) have been developed since the ASEAN Committee on Science and Technology (COST) was established in 1978. The current S&T cooperation in ASEAN focuses on nine programme areas, namely ① food science and technology, ② biotechnology, ③ meteorology and geophysics, ④ marine science and technology, ⑤ non-conventional energy research, ⑥ microelectronics and information technology, ⑦ material science and technology, ⑧ space technology and applications, and ⑨ S & T infrastructure and resources development.

ASEAN International Cooperation

In the field of external relations, ASEAN pursues solidarity and speaking in "One Voice". It puts forward an object of building "zone of peace, freedom and neutrality", carries out a balanced diplomatism with great powers and emphasizes the diplomatism among Asian countries.

(1) **Cooperation between ASEAN and Asian countries**

The diplomatic cooperation between ASEAN and Asian countries has increasingly enhanced. The importance of carrying out the strategy of great powers is to develop the bilateral relations between ASEAN and China, Japan, Russia, the United States and European Union respectively. Since the Financial Crisis of 1997, ASEAN pays special attention to cooperating with Asian countries, especially the friendship development between East Asian countries. ASEAN Plus Three Summits (10 +3) and ASEAN Plus One Summits (10 +1) are annually held with the purpose of strengthening cooperation in economic, political and social fields between ASEAN and East Asian countries. In recent years, the relation between ASEAN and China is intensive. Their cooperation has been strengthened in various fields, including politic and security cooperation, economic cooperation and functional cooperation and regional and international cooperation.

① Cooperation between ASEAN and Japan

ASEAN and Japan first established informal dialogue relations in 1973, which was later formalised in March 1977 with the convening of the ASEAN-Japan Forum. Since then, significant progress has been made in ASEAN-Japan relations and cooperation in the areas of political security, economic-finance and socio-culture.

The signing of the Tokyo Declaration for the Dynamic and Enduring ASEAN-Japan Partnership in the New Millennium together with the ASEAN-Japan Plan of Action (ASEAN-Japan POA) at the ASEAN-Japan Commemorative Summit, held in December, 2003 in Tokyo, have contributed to the strengthening of relations between the two sides. The 2003 Tokyo Declaration and the ASEAN-Japan POA served as the roadmap in moving ASEAN-Japan relations forward until 2010.

At the ASEAN-Japan Commemorative Summit held on December 14, 2013, the leaders adopted a Joint Statement with the theme hand in hand, facing regional and global challenges and a Vision Statement on ASEAN-Japan Friendship and Cooperation and its Implementation Plan. This Implementation Plan serves to further strengthen cooperation to support the ASEAN Community building and contributes to ASEAN Community Post-2015 Vision. The Implementation Plan also built upon the Joint Declaration for Enhancing ASEAN-Japan Strategic Partnership for Prospering Together (Bali Declaration) and the ASEAN-Japan Plan of Action 2011 – 2015, which was adopted at the 14th ASEAN-Japan Summit in 2011.

ASEAN and Japan conduct their dialogue relations through various mechanisms, which include summits, ministerial meetings, senior officials and experts meetings, as well as broader ASEAN-initiated regional dialogue mechanisms such as the ASEAN Regional Forum (ARF), ASEAN Plus Three, the East Asia Summit and ASEAN Defense Ministers Meeting Plus (ADMM Plus).

② Cooperation between ASEAN and the Republic of Korea and India

In recent years, ASEAN enhances the cooperation with India and the Korean Peninsula. At ASEAN-India Senior Officials Meeting held in January 2001, New Delhi, ASEAN and India decided to strengthen the bilateral cooperation in human resource development, tourism, culture, transportation and telecom fields. At ASEAN-India Summit (10 + 1) in October, 2003, leaders from ASEAN member states and India signed the Framework Agreement on Comprehensive Economic Cooperation Between the Association of Southeast Asian Nations and the Republic of India. They had agreed on the importance of strengthening and enhancing economic, trade and investment cooperation between the two sides and to enter into negotiations in order to establish an ASEAN-India Regional Trade and Investment Area (RTIA). During the meeting, Prime Minister of India A. B. Vajpayee expressed that India would promote the elimination of tariff and non-tariff trade barriers between two parties and hoped that a Free Trade Area (FTA) in goods, services and investment would be established within 10 years. On October 9, 2003, India and Thailand inked the Framework Agreement for Establishing Free Trade Area Between the Republic of India and the Kingdom of Thailand, marking a new stage in bilateral relations. The FTA for zero duty imports was put into effect in 2010. At the third ASEAN + India Summit on November 30, 2004, they signed the ASEAN-India Partnership for Peace, Progress and Shared Prosperity, and adopted their Plan of Action to expand and deepen their partnership and cooperation in the new century. A Plan of Action (2004 - 2010) was also developed to implement the partnership. The 7th ASEAN-India Summit held in October 2009 also noted with satisfaction the steady progress of implementation of the ASEAN-India Partnership for Peace, Progress and Shared Prosperity. The Summit also agreed on a new and more enhanced phase of the Plan of Action to implement the said Partnership in order to seize the opportunities and overcome the challenges arising from the global financial crisis and evolving political and economic landscape. Subsequently, the new ASEAN-India Plan of Action for 2010 - 2015 was developed and adopted by the Leaders at the 8th ASEAN-India Summit in October 2010 in Ha Noi.

ASEAN and India signed the ASEAN-India Trade in Goods (TIG) Agreement in Bangkok on August 13, 2009 after six years of negotiations. The signing of the ASEAN-India Trade in Goods Agreement paves the way for the creation of one of the world's largest free trade areas (FTA)—market of almost 1.8 billion people with a combined GDP of US$4.6 trillion. The ASEAN-India FTA will see tariff liberalization of over 90% of products traded between the two dynamic regions. Tariffs on over 4,000 product lines will be eliminated by 2016 at the earliest. The ASEAN-India TIG Agreement entered into force on January 1, 2010.

During the 10th ASEAN-India Summit in November, 2012, the ASEAN-India leaders tasked their economic ministers to step up their efforts and flexibility to conclude the ASEAN-India Trade in Services and Investment Agreements at the earliest. Subsequently, an announcement on the conclusion of the negotiations on both Agreements was made at the ASEAN-India Commemorative Summit on December 20, 2012. By January, 2015, the Agreement has been signed by all ASEAN Member States and India. The Agreement entered into force on July 1, 2015.

Since 1997, ASEAN-Republic of Korea Summit (10 + 1) has been held after the meeting of ASEAN Plus Three (10 + 3) and their cooperation has strengthened and developed in the areas of trade, investment, tourism, science and technology, human resources and so on. Leaders from ROK presented many ministerial meetings as well. The ASEAN-ROK Joint Declaration on Comprehensive Cooperation Partnership was signed in November 2004 in Vientiane which had helped to consolidate the partnership and chart the future direction of the ASEAN-ROK relations. In July 2001, the Democratic People's

Republic of Korea (DPRK) first attended the ASEAN Regional Forum Foreign Minister Meeting. At the 11th ASEAN-Republic of Korea Summit in Singapore in November 2007, the leaders welcomed the progress made at the Six-Party Talks and expressed support for the Agreement in October 2007 as another important step toward the denuclearization of the Korean Peninsula.

In order to facilitate closer cooperation and mutual understanding between ASEAN and the ROK, the ROK established its Mission to ASEAN in Jakarta in September, 2012 and appointed its first resident Ambassador to ASEAN in October, 2012.

(2) **Cooperation between ASEAN and US and EU and other countries and regions**

The United States has traditional influence in Southeast Asia. In recent years, its relation with ASEAN has got enhanced. The first meeting of ASEAN-US dialogue was held in Manila in 1977. Both sides negotiated regional security, economic cooperation and many other fields. Since the event of September 11 in 2001, they have enhanced cooperation in combating international terrorism, unveiling Joint Press Statement of the 16th US-ASEAN Dialogue Washington D. C. and ASEAN-United States of America Joint Declaration for Cooperation to Combat International Terrorism.

At the ASEAN Post Ministerial Conference Session + 1 with the US, held on July 22, 2011 in Bali, Indonesia, the Meeting endorsed a Plan of Action to Implement the ASEAN-US Enhanced Partnership 2011 – 2015 for Enduring Peace and Prosperity, replacing the previous Plan of Action, the timeline of which had come to an end. Subsequently, at the Third ASEAN-US Leaders' Meeting in November 2011 in Bali, Indonesia, the leaders of ASEAN and the US adopted the Plan of Action to Implement the ASEAN-US Enhanced Partnership for 2011 – 2015. ASEAN-US development cooperation has currently implemented under the framework of the ASEAN-US Enhanced Partnership. During the course of 2008 – 2013, the US development assistance was channelled mainly through the ASEAN Development Vision to Advance National Cooperation and Economic Integration (ADVANCE).

The EU and ASEAN have been interacting with each other on the economic, trade and political levels for more than four decades. The partnership between the EU and ASEAN dates back to 1972 when the EU (then known as the European Economic Community) became ASEAN's first formal dialogue partner. Relations between the two regions are expanding, developing progressively on the economic, political and cultural fronts. Dialogue between the two regions has been enhanced with numerous technical level meetings and bi-annual ministerial meetings. Whereas in the past, much of the Europe-Southeast Asia relationship has focused on Southeast Asian development, the focus of cooperation has transformed to an emphasis on diplomacy, where the two sides discusses regional and international problems, and finally to a new emphasis on non-traditional risks and regional integration support.

The EU and ASEAN enjoy robust commercial relations. The EU is ASEAN's third largest trading partner, while ASEAN is the EU's 5th largest trading partner. Total trade in 2011 in goods and services amounted to $265 billion. ASEAN had a surplus of $25 billion in its trade with the EU. The EU is the biggest provider of foreign direct investment into ASEAN, 24% of the total.

Momentum has been building up over the last years in the EU-ASEAN relationship. Foreign Ministers of ASEAN and the EU adopted the Bandar Seri Begawan Plan of Action 2013 – 2017, defining ASEAN-EU cooperation for this period. Both 2012 and 2013 have seen an unprecedented number of visits by top-level EU officials to ASEAN and its Member States: by Presidents Van Rompuy and Barroso, High representative Ashton and several Commissioners as well as a marked rise in the visits by EU Member States. In July 2012, High representative Ashton signed the EU's accession to ASEAN's Treaty of Amity and Cooperation. The EU is an active member of the ASEAN Regional Forum (ARF).

In 2012 and 2013, High representative Ashton attended the ASEAN Regional Forum Meeting at Ministerial level. The EU and ASEAN have an intensifying dialogue on human rights. In May, 2013, EU Special Representative for Human Rights Stavros Lambrinidis met the ASEAN Intergovernmental Commission on Human Rights, while the same Commission is expected to visit the EU institutions soon on their second visit. Dialogue and cooperation is also starting in several security-related fields.

In addition, ASEAN has strengthened the cooperation with Australia, Russia and other countries. In 2002, Australia signed a Memorandum of Understanding with ASEAN—the ASEAN-Australia Development Cooperation Program (AADCP). On November 21, 2007, ASEAN and Australia issued an ASEAN-Australia Joint Press Statement on the Adoption of the Plan of Action to Implement the Joint Declaration on ASEAN-Australia Comprehensive Partnership in Singapore.

The first stand-alone ASEAN-Australia Summit was held in Hanoi in October 2010 in conjunction with the 17th ASEAN Summit and Related Summits, during which the leaders reaffirmed the significance of Australia's longstanding partnership with ASEAN. Trade, investment, and tourism between ASEAN and Australia continued to expand in the past year. Australia was the 6th largest trading partner of ASEAN, and ASEAN was Australia's second largest trading partner in 2014, with a total two-way trade reached US $ 70.4 billion, a 3.4% increase year-on-year.

In 2003, ASEAN and Russia signed the Joint Declaration of the Foreign Ministers of the Russian Federation and the Association of Southeast Asian Nations on Partnership for Peace and Security, and Prosperity and Development in the Asia-Pacific Region. Agreement Between the Governments of the Member Countries of the Association of Southeast Asian Nations and the Government of the Russian Federation on Economic and Development Cooperation was signed in Kuala Lumpur on December 10, 2005.

In 2012, the ASEAN-Russia Trade and Investment Cooperation Roadmap was endorsed by ASEAN and Russian Ministers on ad-referendum basis. The Roadmap comprises five key areas, namely high-level policy dialogue; consultations at the senior economic officials level; sectoral dialogues between ASEAN and Russian officials; Trade and investment facilitation; enhancing dialogue with business. Subsequently, the 2nd AEM-Russia Consultation held on August 21, 2013 in Bandar Seri Begawan, Brunei, endorsed the Work Programme for the ASEAN-Russia Trade and Investment Roadmap, which includes of the following areas: trade and investment facilitation and liberalisation, energy, logistics chain development, human resources development, tourism, SME development, innovation and modernisation and intellectual property creation, and business dialogue.

12.5 "10 +3" "10 +1"

ASEAN Plus Three (10 +3)

The ASEAN Plus Three Summits are annual meetings among the leaders of ASEAN and the their counterparts from East Asia, namely China, Japan and the Republic of Korea (ROK). The ASEAN Plus Three cooperation began in December, 1997. Since then, with the firm cooperation, ASEAN Plus Three has inaugurated the new patterns of neighbouring states collaboration and become a significant strength in promoting regional sustainable development of economy. The long-term objective is to establish East Asia Free Trade Area (EAFTA) containing ASEAN member countries and China, Japan and the ROK.

Since the process began in 1997, ASEAN Plus Three (APT) cooperation has broadened and deepened. It includes cooperation in the areas of political and security; transnational crime; economic; finance; tourism; agriculture and forestry; energy; minerals; small- and medium-sized enterprises; environment; rural development and poverty eradication; social welfare; youth; women; civil service; labour; culture and arts; information and media; education; science, technology, and innovation; and public health.

At the 11th APT Summit held in November 2007 in Singapore, the APT leaders adopted a Joint Statement on East Asia Cooperation and the APT Cooperation Work Plan (2007 – 2017). The documents provided strategic guidance for the future direction of APT cooperation.

In order to gain an overall picture of the progress as well as the gaps in the implementation of the APT Cooperation Work Plan, a Mid-Term Review of the APT Cooperation Work Plan (2007 - 2017) was conducted and its recommendations were adopted by the 14th APT Foreign Ministers Meeting on June 30, 2013. As a follow-up to the recommendations of the Mid-Term Review, the APT Cooperation Work Plan was revised with the new timeframe of 2013 - 2017. The revised Work Plan was adopted by the 16th APT Summit held on October 10, 2014 in Bandar Seri Begawan.

(1) **Political-security cooperation**

Against the backdrop of the 1997 Asian financial crisis, at the APT Summit in December, 1998, the formation of an "East Asia Vision Group" (EAVG) was proposed. The Vision Group was composed of eminent intellectuals charged with the task of drawing up a vision for mid-to-long term cooperation in East Asia for the 21st century. Its reports were submitted in a report to the APT Summit in 2001.

After one decade since the EAVG submitted its report to the APT leaders, the East Asia Vision Group II (EAVG II) was established in October, 2011 with the purpose of reviewing the APT cooperation over the past 15 years and provide future vision of the APT for the next decades. The EAVG II met four times in October, 2011, February 2012, May 2012 and September 2012. At its fourth meeting, the EAVG II finalised its Report. The Report was submitted to the 15th APT Commemorative Summit in Phnom Penh on November 19, 2012.

The APT leaders, at the 17th APT Summit held in November 2014 in Nay Pyi Taw, Myanmar, reiterated that APT cooperation would remain as a main vehicle in moving forward to realise its long-term goal of an East Asia community with ASEAN as the driving force in the evolving regional architecture.

Cooperation on non-traditional security matters is undertaken under the purview of the APT Ministerial Meeting on Transnational Crime (AMMTC + 3) and the APT Senior Officials Meeting on Transnational Crime (SOMTC + 3). Since then, six AMMTC + 3 and 12 SOMTC + 3 have been held. The Sixth AMMTC + 3 was held on September 18, 2013 in Vientiane and the 12th SOMTC + 3 was held on June 25, 2014 in Bandar Seri Begawan. Several activities have been carried out, such as seminars on law enforcement, law enforcement executive meetings, and a forum on non-traditional security issues.

(2) **Finance and economic cooperation**

ASEAN's trade with the Plus Three countries retained its momentum despites challenges derived from uncertainties in the global economy. In 2013, ASEAN total trade with the Plus Three countries recorded an increase of 1.8% year-on-year, amounting to US $726.4 billion and accounting for 28.9% of ASEAN's total trade. While ASEAN's imports from the Plus Three countries grew by 2.1% year on year in 2013, the rate has moderated from 11.2% the previous year. ASEAN's exports to the Plus Three countries grew by 1.5% year-on-year. Total foreign direct investment flows from the Plus Three countries into ASEAN reached US $35.1 billion or 28.7% of total, representing a 13.6% increase from the previous year.

In finance and monetary cooperation, progress has been steady and the focus continues to be on the implementation of the Chiang Mai Initiative Multilateralisation (CMIM) and the Asian Bond Market Initiative (ABMI).

On CMIM, further efforts to improve its readiness as a regional safety net are being undertaken. The amended CMIM Agreement came into effect on July 17, 2014 and the Agreement Establishing ASEAN +3 Macroeconomic Research Office (AMRO) was signed on October 10, 2014 in Washington D. C. to transform AMRO into an international organisation. The AMRO is the regional macroeconomic surveillance unit of the CMIM. AMRO's purposes are to monitor and analyse regional economies and to contribute to early detection of risks, swift implementation of remedial actions and effective decision-making of the CMIM.

On ABMI, progress has been made in developing local currency bond markets across the region so as to allow the region's large savings to be channelled to finance its own investment needs. Under the ABMI framework, the Credit Guarantee and Investment Facility (CGIF) and ASEAN +3 Bond Market Forum (ABMF) have contributed to the development of efficient and liquid bond markets in the region. On CGIF, the guarantee capacity has been scaled-up from US$700 million to US $1.75 billion to further promote issuance of local currency bonds.

On tourism, the APT Tourism Ministers at their 12th Meeting on January 21, 2013 in Vientiane adopted the APT Tourism Cooperation Work Plan 2013 – 2017 covering quality tourism, skills development, joint tourism marketing and promotion, cruise tourism, and tourism crisis communications. The adoption of the APT Tourism Cooperation Work Plan would further promote linkages and strengthen cooperation among National Tourism Organisations. The Ministers agreed to establish the APT e-Tourism Working Group to implement the Work Plan.

On agriculture and forestry, many projects have been implemented under the umbrella of the APT Cooperation Strategy (APTCS) Framework, including the implementation of APT Emergency Rice Reserve (APTERR) Agreement, ASEAN Food Security Information System (AFSIS), and ASEAN Plus Three Comprehensive Strategy on Food Security and Bio-energy Development (APTCS-FSBD). At the 14th Meeting of the ASEAN Ministers on Agriculture and Forestry (AMAF) Plus Three held on September 24, 2014 in Nay Pyi Taw, Myanmar, the Ministers noted the progress on the transformation of AFSIS into a permanent mechanism and the need for further work through stepwise approach, by firstly strengthening the mechanism at the national level.

The APT cooperation on energy has witnessed good progress. The cooperation covers a range of projects and activities, which include, among others, regular APT forum on oil market, APT forum on energy security, as well as APT forum on new and renewable energy and energy efficiency and conservation. At the 11th APT Ministers on Energy Meeting (AMEM + 3) on September 23, 2014 in Vientiane, the Ministers noted that capacity building, information sharing and exchange amongst the countries are key elements of deepening cooperation and promoting sustainable development and low-carbon growth economies.

(3) **Environment, climate change, and sustainable development cooperation**

Cooperation on environment continues to progress, particularly in addressing the issue of environment and sustainable development. The annual APT Leadership Programme on Sustainable Production and Consumption, a programme for the private sector to discuss green economy, has been held since 2008. The Seventh Programme was held on September 30-October 3, 2014 in Bali, Indonesia. A new project on ASEAN Integrated Water Resource Management (IWRM) Country Strategy Guidelines is currently on-going. This project is aimed at enabling ASEAN to measure regional performance and progress towards IWRM goals against a regionally consistent set of strategies.

(4) **Socio-cultural and development cooperation**

In the area of civil service, cooperation is undertaken under the purview of the APT Conference on Civil Service Matters (ACCSM +3). At the Inaugural ACCSM +3, held on October 29, 2010 in Luang Prabang, Lao PDR, the Heads of Civil Service of ASEAN Member States and the Plus Three countries adopted the Luang Prabang Joint Declaration on APT Civil Service Cooperation. Subsequently, two APT Heads of Civil Service Meeting have been held, in October, 2012 and in September 2014 in Yangon, Myanmar. At the Second Meeting, the Heads of Civil Service reviewed the nine pilot projects under the ACCSM +3. They agreed to work together on the development of APT projects on civil service matters for 2016 – 2020 in areas of mutual interest.

The APT cooperation on labour is progressing well. The Eighth APT Labour Ministers Meeting (ALMM + 3) was held on May 23, 2014 in Nay Pyi Taw, Myanmar. The Ministers agreed that closer cooperation among APT countries should be enhanced to promote quality vocational training and education, improve labour market information systems, and national competency standards.

The APT countries continue to strengthen their cooperation on culture. At the Sixth ASEAN Plus Three Ministers Responsible for Culture and Arts (AMCA + 3) on April 19 – 20, 2014 in Hue, Vietnam, the Ministers reiterated the importance of APT cooperation in the areas of culture and arts, especially on the sharing of the implementation of arts and culture policies, human resources development, cultural heritage and development of small-and medium-sized cultural enterprises, including creative industry projects. In addition, the Ministers noted that the Plus Three countries established the East Asian Cultural Cities in 2014 to further promote cultural cooperation and support friendship among the Plus Three countries.

In order to further promote APT cooperation on information, three Conferences of APT Ministers Responsible for Information (AMRI+3) have been held thus far. The Third Conference of AMRI+3 was held on June 12, 2014 in Nay Pyi Taw, Myanmar. The AMRI+3 reviewed the progress of the Work Plan on Enhancing APT Cooperation through Information and Media (2012-2017) and noted that several initiatives are being discussed to further enhance cooperation between ASEAN and the Plus Three countries.

At the Second APT Education Ministers Meeting held on September 12, 2014 in Vientiane, Lao PDR, the Ministers reaffirmed the general objective of the APT Plan of Action on Education (2010-2017) was to encourage APT countries to expand their efforts in implementing the Plan at the national and bilateral levels to the regional level. The Ministers welcomed the convening of the First Working Group on Mobility of Higher Education and Ensuring Quality Assurance of Higher Education among APT countries in September 2013 in Tokyo. The Second Working Group on Mobility of Higher Education and Ensuring Quality Assurance of Higher Education among APT countries was held on 16 October 2014 in Bali, Indonesia.

On science and technology, two major programmes are undertaken under the ASEAN Committee on Science and Technology Plus Three (COST+3), namely the ASEAN+3 Teachers' Training and Student Camp Gifted in Science and the APT Junior Science Odyssey (JSO). The Third APT JSO was held on June 23-26, 2014 in Thailand with a theme of "Innovative Agriculture for Global Sustainability" while the Sixth ASEAN+3 Teachers' Training and Student Camp Gifted in Science was held on January 11-18, 2015 in Changwon, the ROK.

The APT cooperation in health is also progressing well, particularly in the areas of traditional medicines, health-related issues of ageing, non-communicable diseases, disaster health management, maternal and child health, pandemic preparedness response, communicable diseases and emerging infectious diseases. The APT countries also continue to cooperate in the APT cooperation through the APT Field Epidemiology Training Network (FETN), APT Partnership Laboratories (APL), Animal and Human Health Cooperation, Risk Communication, and through the project activities addressing specific disease-interventions including malaria, rabies, and dengue. The Sixth APT Health Ministers Meeting was held on September 19, 2014 in Ha Noi under the theme of "Better Health for ASEAN Community Beyond 2015". At the Meeting, the Ministers reiterated the significance of Universal Health Coverage (UHC) and advocated UHC as one of the health priorities in ASEAN Post-2015 Health Development Agenda. The Ministers welcomed the establishment of the APT UHC Network and urged the Network to accelerate the implementation of its action plan.

On December 15, 2014, Thailand hosted an APT Health Ministers Special Meeting on Ebola Preparedness and Response in Bangkok. The Meeting resolved to strengthen national, regional (among the APT countries), and global collaboration and responses to Ebola outbreak through existing bilateral, regional, and multilateral channels. In this regard, the Ministers tasked the Senior Officials Meeting on Health Development (SOMHD) in coordination with ASEAN Working Group on Pandemic and Response and in close collaboration with APT Emerging Infectious Diseases (EID) Cooperation to keep updating and regularly review the progress on this matter and to work in close consultation with the APT Health Ministers with the support of the World Health Organisation (WHO) with a view to following-up on the implementation of the Joint Statement of the Meeting.

Apart from Track 1 cooperation in various areas outlined above, the APT countries also pursue networking of Track 2 and Track 1.5. Track 1.5 cooperation among the APT countries has been convened through the East Asia Forum (EAF) annually since 2003. For the period of 2008 – 2014, the 6th to 12th EAFs were held, covering various topics, including energy and food security issues, deepening of economic cooperation in East Asia, strengthening of social and cultural cooperation in East Asia, enhancing connectivity in East Asia, internal growth engine of East Asia, narrowing development gaps in rural and urban communities and revitalization of EAF, enhancing people-to-people connectivity: focusing on tourism cooperation, and the common purpose towards a peaceful, prosperous, and environmentally responsible East Asia. The 12th EAF was held on November 25 – 27, 2014 in Bandar Seri Begawan. Networking among the Track 2 of the APT countries is continued being pursued through the Network of East Asian Think Tanks (NEAT). Under NEAT, there are working groups' established and meet on regular or ad-hoc basis to discuss different issues relevant to the region. The outcomes of the working groups' discussion serve as inputs to the NEAT's annual recommendation to the APT Summit. The 21st NEAT Country Coordinator's Meeting (NEAT CCM) and the 12th NEAT Annual Conference were held in September 2014 in Phnom Penh.

ASEAN-China "10 +1"

During the "10 +3" summit meeting, the leaders from China, Japan and the ROK will meet leaders from member countries from ASEAN to strengthen dialogues and communications, discuss the mutual cooperation, and promote peace, stability and prosperity in the regions, thus forming three sets of "10 +1" frameworks. In the year 2003, ASEAN-India Summit became the fourth "10 +1" meeting. The following sections refer to the cooperation of ASEAN-China "10 +1", including the ASEAN-China Summit and other cooperation mechanisms under the framework of "10 +1".

(1) **ASEAN-China "10 + 1" summits**

On December 16, 1997, the first ASEAN-China Summit was held in Kuala Lumpur, Malaysia. At the meeting, Chinese President Jiang Zemin delivered a speech entitled "Establish Good-neighborly Partnership of Mutual Trust Oriented to the 21st Century". After the summit, the two sides issued the Joint Declaration of the People's Republic of China and ASEAN Summit, establishing guidelines for their relationship and common policies of good-neighborly partnership of mutual trust oriented to the 21st century.

On December 16, 1998, Chinese Vice President Hu Jintao attended the second ASEAN-China Summit in Hanoi, Vietnam. Leaders of the two sides agreed to maintain friendly exchanges between China and ASEAN countries in various fields, at different levels and through various channels within an all-around dialogue cooperation framework. They also reached consensus on appropriately dealing with differences to boost their partnership.

On November 28, 1999, Chinese Premier Zhu Rongji attended the third ASEAN-China Summit in Manila, the Philippines. He offered China's advice on strengthening the partnership of good-neighborliness and mutual trust with ASEAN in the 21st century. The ASEAN countries praised China's achievements in its development, and spoke highly of its support and assistance to them in the Asian Financial Crisis.

On November 25, 2000, the fourth ASEAN-China Summit was held in Singapore. At the meeting, Chinese Premier Zhu Rongji spoke highly of the relationship between China and ASEAN, and offered advice on cooperation between the two sides in politics, human resource development, the construction of infrastructure projects on the Mekong River[3], advanced technology, agriculture, trade and investment.

On November 6, 2001, Chinese Premier Zhu Rongji attended the fifth ASEAN-China Summit in Bandar Seri Begawan, Brunei. The two sides agreed on the establishment of the China-ASEAN Free Trade Zone over the following 10 years, and senior officials were authorized to begin negotiations on relevant agreements as soon as possible.

On November 4, 2002, the sixth ASEAN-China Summit was held in Phnom Penh, Cambodia. Chinese Premier Zhu Rongji and ASEAN leaders signed the Framework Agreement on China-ASEAN Comprehensive Economic Cooperation, deciding to establish the China-ASEAN free trade zone by 2010. They delivered the Joint Declaration of ASEAN and China on Cooperation in the Field of Non-traditional Security Issues. At the same time, some substantial progress has been achieved in China-ASEAN cooperation. China and ASEAN have reached a consensus and further signed the Ultimate Agreement on Declaration on the Code of Conduct of Parties in the South China Sea.

On October 8, 2003, Chinese Premier Wen Jiabao attended the seventh ASEAN-China Summit in the Indonesian resort island of Bali. During the summit, ASEAN and China agreed to establish "a strategic partnership for peace and prosperity". China acceded to the Treaty of Amity and Cooperation in Southeast Asia. They signed a Joint Declaration of the Heads of State/Government of the Member States of ASEAN and the People's Republic of China on Strategic Partnership for Peace and Prosperity and Protocol to Amend the Framework Agreement on Comprehensive Economic Cooperation Between the Association of Southeast Asian Nations and the People's Republic of China.

On November 29, 2004, Chinese Premier Wen Jiabao attended the eighth ASEAN-China Summit in Vientiane, Laos. At the summit, Premier Wen delivered a speech on the appraisal of China-ASEAN cooperation, China's policy toward ASEAN countries, principles for cooperation and proposals for further cooperation. During the meeting, the leaders adopted the Plan of Action to Implement the Joint Declaration of the Heads of State/Government of ASEAN and China on Strategic Partnership for Peace and Prosperity, and singed the Agreement on Trade in Goods of the Framework Agreement on Comprehensive Economic Cooperation Between the Association of Southeast Asian Nations and the People's Republic of China and Agreement on Dispute Settlement Mechanism by the ASEAN-China economic ministers as part of the implementation of the Framework Agreement on Comprehensive Economic Cooperation.

On December 12, 2005, the ninth ASEAN-China Summit was held in Kuala Lumpur. Five new priority areas of cooperation, namely energy, transport, culture, public health and tourism, were endorsed by the leaders of ASEAN and Chinese Premier Wen Jiabao. They agreed to commemorate the 15th anniversary of ASEAN-China dialogue relations in 2006 and call 2006 as the "Year of Friendship and Cooperation Between ASEAN and China".

On October 30, 2006, in the Year of Friendship and Cooperation Between ASEAN and China, the leaders of ASEAN and China gathered in Nanning, China, to commemorate the fifteenth anniversary of the ASEAN-China dialogue relation. They reviewed the progress in ASEAN-China dialogue relations, expressed the satisfaction that this cooperation had been comprehensive and deepening in many areas, and agreed to further enhance mutual trust and understanding with the objective of their strategic partnership. They signed the Joint Statement of ASEAN-China Commemorative Summit Towards an Enhanced ASEAN-China Strategic Partnership.

On January 14, 2007, the tenth ASENA-China Summit was held in Cebu, the Philippines. The leaders of ASEAN and Chinese Premier Wen Jiabao recalled the successful ASEAN-China Commemorative Summit held on October 30, 2006 in Nanning, Guangxi in China, to mark the 15th anniversary of ASEAN-China relations. Premier Wen put forward a five-point proposal of "strengthening political mutual trust, bringing ASEAN-China economic relations and trade to a new level, carrying out cooperation in non-traditional security fields, actively supporting ASEAN community building and integration, and expanding social, cultural and people-to-people exchanges". They signed the ASEAN-China Agreement on Trade in Services (TIS), the Plan of Action to Implement the Beijing Declaration on ASEAN-ICT Cooperative Partnership for Common Development, and the Memorandum of Understanding Between the ASEAN Secretariat and the Ministry of Agriculture of the People's Republic of China on Agricultural Cooperation. Meanwhile, Premier Wen made a proposal on exploring the feasibility of Pan-Beibu Gulf economic cooperation.

On November 20, 2007, the eleventh ASENA-China Summit was held in Singapore. The heads of member countries of ASEAN and China had a substantive meeting. They noted progress in the implementation of the joint statement issued at the ASEAN-China Commemorative Summit, to mark the 15th anniversary of ASEAN-China relations. They acknowledged the important role that China had been playing in regional and global affairs.

The 16th ASEAN-China Summit was held on October 9, 2013 in Bandar SeriBegawan, Brunei. The Summit was attended by all Heads of State/Government of the Member States and Li Keqiang, Premier of the State Council of the People's Republic of China. The summit reaffirmed the strong commitment in further strengthening the ASEAN-China Strategic Partnership particularly in the eleven priority areas, namely agriculture, information and communication technology, human resource development, investment, Mekong Basin Development, transportation, energy, culture, tourism, public health and environment.

(2) **ASEAN-China cooperation under the "10 + 1" framework**

Under the framework of "10 + 1", ASEAN and China has been strengthening the cooperation in various fields, including political and security cooperation, economic cooperation and functional cooperation, regional and international cooperation.

① Political and security cooperation

China has entered into a number of agreements with ASEAN in the area of political and security cooperation. It was the first dialogue partner to accede to the Treaty of Amity and Cooperation (TAC) in Southeast Asia at the ASEAN-China Summit in October 2003 in Bali, Indonesia. In security, ASEAN and China have worked to actively implement the concept of enhancing mutual trust through dialogue, resolving disputes peacefully through negotiations and realizing regional security through cooperation. The two sides signed the Joint Declaration of ASEAN and China on Cooperation in the Field of Non-traditional Security Issues and the Declaration on the Conduct (DOC) of Parties in the South China Sea, concluded at the ASEAN-China Summit in Phnom Penh, Cambodia in 2002. The signing of the Joint Declaration on Strategic Partnership for Peace and Prosperity in Bali in 2003, and the adoption of the ASEAN-China Plan of Action in Vientiane in 2004 were highly appreciated by the leaders from two sides for strengthening political and security cooperation. China has expressed its willingness to work with ASEAN for its early accession to the Protocol to the Treaty on Southeast Asia Nuclear Weapons-Free Zone

(SEANWFZ). In the field of non-traditional security issues, ASEAN and China signed a Memorandum of Understanding (MOU) on Cooperation in the Field of Non-Traditional Security Issues in Bangkok in January 2004 to implement the Joint Declaration in the Field of Non-Traditional Security Issues. In 2007, the ministers of ASEAN member countries and China responsible for cooperation in combating transnational crime convened an Informal ASEAN Ministerial Meeting on Transnational Crime (AMMTC) Plus China Consultation in Bandar Seri Begawan, Brunei.

② Economic cooperation

Over the years, economic and trade cooperation between ASEAN and China has grown rapidly. The trade volume between China and ASEAN increased from US$105.9 billion in 2004 to US$202.5 billion in 2007. China and ASEAN became each other's fourth largest trading partner.

In November, 2002, the leaders of ASEAN member countries and China signed the Framework Agreement on Comprehensive Economic Cooperation, which provided for an ASEAN-China Free Trade Area by the year 2010 for Brunei, China, Indonesia, Malaysia, the Philippines, Singapore and Thailand, and by 2015 for the newer ASEAN member countries, Cambodia, Laos, Myanmar and Vietnam. In Vientiane in November, 2004, ASEAN and China signed the Trade in Goods Agreement and the Dispute Settlement Mechanism Agreement at the ASEAN-China Summit. In 2004, the 1st China-ASEAN Expo and the 1st China-ASEAN Business and Investment Summit, which were successfully held in Nanning, China, meant that a further step had been made for promoting the building of China-ASEAN Free Trade Area. In July, 2005, the tariff reduction process under the FTA was initiated on a full scale. In January, 2007, the two sides entered into the "Agreement on Trade in Services" under the FTA. During the 3rd China-ASEAN Business and Investment Summit and the 10th China-ASEAN Leaders Summit, Premier Wen Jiabao raised two similar proposals on exploring the feasibility of Pan-Beibu Gulf economic cooperation. In addition, sub-regional economic cooperation initiatives such as the Great Mekong River and ASEAN-East China Growth Region are also moving forward steadily along sound momentums.

③ Functional cooperation

At the ASEAN-China Summit on November 6, 2001 in Brunei, ASEAN and China agreed to focus their cooperation on five priority areas in the early part of the 21st century, namely agriculture, information and communications technology (ICT), human resource development (HRD), Mekong River Basin development, and two-way investment.

In order to strengthen the cooperation in the five agreed priority areas, ASEAN and China signed an MOU on Medium- and Long-Term Plan of Agricultural Cooperation between the Ministry of Agriculture of the People's Republic of China and the ministries of agriculture of the ten ASEAN member countries on November 2, 2002 in Phnom Penh and an MOU on Cooperation in Information and Communications Technology (ICT) on October 8, 2003 at the Bali Summit. The first China-ASEAN Forum on Social Development and Poverty Reduction strengthened their cooperation for balancing the development against poverty. In November 2008, the second forum approved a Nanning Output for building up a domestic food security and natural disaster management system, and regional cooperation mechanism to cushion the impact of price increases and natural disasters.

ASEAN and China are working closely in implementing the Mekong Basin development programs and projects within various frameworks such as Greater Mekong Sub-region (GMS), ASEAN Mekong Basin Development Cooperation (AMBDC) and the Mekong River Commission (MRC).

In the area of public health, leaders from China and ASEAN convened the Special Conference on SARS in April 2003 in Bangkok, whereby Special Conference Joint Declaration was delivered calling for the concerted efforts to combat the SARS through mutual exchange and cooperation.

In the area of culture, ASEAN and China have achieved a milestone in cooperation with the signing of a Memorandum of Understanding on cultural cooperation on August 3, 2005, aiming to promote culture cooperation through artistic collaboration and exchange, joint research and study, exchange of information and people-to-people exchange and interaction.

In the area of labor and human resources, ASEAN's work has been guided by the ASEAN Labour Ministers (ALM) Work Programme. Total employment in ASEAN increased by 11.8% between 2000 and 2006. In September 2007, the China-ASEAN High-Level Seminar on Human Resource Development was held in Kunming, China sought to establish a "China-ASEAN Information Exchange on Human Resource Development" as a platform for future collaboration.

In the area of youth, ASEAN and China established the Senior Officials Consultation Meeting on Youth in May 2004 and the ASEAN-China Ministers for Youth Affairs Meeting in September 2004. The assignment of Nanning Declaration of the China-ASEAN Young Entrepreneurs Forum on October 21, 2008, strengthened the cooperation in the priority areas of youth development as identified in the 2000 UN Millennium Summit Declaration, the 1995 World Programme of Action for Youth and the 2004 Beijing Declaration of the Ministers Responsible for Youth of the ASEAN and China on ASEAN-China Cooperation on Youth.

In June 2007, at the third conference on China-ASEAN People-to-People Friendship Organizations held in Jakarta, the 2008-2009 China-ASEAN People-to-People Friendship Organizations Cooperation Plan was approved and five working groups in charge of detailing and implementing the cooperation plan, namely, the economic, cultural, educational, health and sports working groups were set up.

Cooperation in tourism with China is conducted through meetings of ASEAN + 3 National Tourism Organizations and ASEAN +3 Tourism Ministers. The possible ASEAN +3 cooperation activities under the ASEAN + 3 framework include research on tourism and information technology, seminars on hospitality and tourism, issuing tourism publications, establishing tourism networks, and setting up a Centre for Tourism Resource Management. Cooperation in information and media has been promoted by the assignment of Memorandum of Understanding on Information and Media Cooperation in Nanning 2008.

④ Regional and international cooperation

The regional and international cooperation between ASEAN and China has been strengthened with fruitful work. Both sides consult closely on sub-regional, regional and international issues and promote cooperation in sub-regional, regional and international fora. Both sides affirm the establishment of the East Asia community as a long-term goal. China supports ASEAN's role as the driving force in regional processes, such as the ASEAN Regional Forum, ASEAN Plus Three and East Asia Summit. ASEAN believes that a stable, developing and prosperous China will contribute to peace, stability and sustainable growth for the development of the region and reaffirms its One-China Policy.

Notes

[1] ASEAN Declaration or Bangkok Declaration is the founding document of ASEAN. It was signed in Bangkok on August 8, 1967 by the five ASEAN founding members—Indonesia, Singapore, the Philippines, Malaysia and Thailand as a display of solidarity against Communist expansion in Vietnam and communist insurgency within their own borders. It states the basic principles of ASEAN such as cooperation, amity and non-interference.

[2] The Chiang Mai Initiative (CMI) is an initiative under the ASEAN +3 framework which aims for creation of a network of Bilateral Swap Arrangements (BSAs) among ASEAN +3 countries. After 1997 Asian Financial Crisis, member countries started this initiative to manage regional short-term liquidity problems and to facilitate the work of other international financial arrangements and organizations like IMF.

[3] The Mekong River is one of the world's major rivers. It is the world's 10th longest river and the 7th longest in Asia. From the Tibetan Plateau, this river runs through China's Yunnan Province, Myanmar, Thailand, Laos, Cambodia and Vietnam. All these areas except China and Myanmar belong to the Mekong River Commission.

Exercises

1. **Explain the following in English.**
   (1) ASEAN Community
   (2) ASEAN Summit
   (3) ASEAN Plus Three Cooperation (10 +3)
   (4) ASEAN Free Trade Area (AFTA)

2. **Fill in the blanks.**
   (1) The administrative body of ASEAN is _____, based in Jakarta, the capital city of _____.
   (2) The purpose of founding ASEAN is to promote _____ and _____.
   (3) The signing of _____ and _____ at the first ASEAN Summit in 1976 reaffirmed the ASEAN objectives and principles.
   (4) _____ is a constitution for ASEAN, which adopted at the 13th ASEAN Summit in November, 2007.
   (5) With the intent to foster dialogue and consultation, and promote confidence-building and preventive diplomacy in the region, _____ was established in Bangkok in 1994.
   (6) ASEAN Plus One Summits are three ASEAN +3 summits that ASEAN respectively meets with _____, _____, _____. In 2003, the _____ Summit was added to the fourth ASEAN +1 Summit.
   (7) In November, 2001, the heads of ASEAN member states issued _____ to strengthen national mechanisms to combat terrorism.
   (8) ASEAN has a positive progress in _____ cooperation, especially in prevention and control of HIV/AIDS and drug abuse, environment protection, health and so on.
   (9) In the field of external relations, ASEAN pursues _____ and speaking in _____, and put forward an object of building _____, _____ and

_____.

(10) On December 16, _____, the first ASEAN-China summit was held in Kuala Lumpur. The year 2006 was called the "Year of _____ and _____ Between ASEAN and China".

3. **Answer the following questions.**

   (1) What are the major achievements in regional cooperation in security?

   (2) Give a brief description of constant progress in ASEAN economic integration.

   (3) Which areas have been intensified in current ASEAN science and technology cooperation?

   (4) Under the frame of ASEAN +3 Cooperation, what measures were taken in tourism after the SARS epidemic?

   (5) What do you think of ASEAN-China "10 +1"? What can you benefit from it?

4. **Discussion.**

   (1) Discuss the significance of the establishment of ASEAN.

   (2) The initial purpose of founding ASEAN is for the regional security. Is it still carried out in recent years? In what way?

   (3) What are the advantages of ASEAN integration?

CHAPTER 13

ASEAN Free Trade Area

AFTA is a short form of the Association of Southeast Asian Nations Free Trade Area, which was proposed to be set up in 1992. It includes the six former members (Indonesia, Thailand, the Philippines, Singapore, Malaysia and Brunei) and the four new members (Vietnam, Laos, Myanmar and Cambodia) of ASEAN. The total ground area in AFTA covers about 4.44 million square kilometers (the Exclusive Economic Zone of Indonesia and Timor-Leste are excluded) with a total population of 618 million (2014). Through 10 years of efforts, the six former ASEAN members started officially to establish AFTA in 2002; the other new Members of ASEAN promised to quicken their speed to reduce the tariff within the time required.

13.1 Birth of AFTA

In the early 1990s, the ASEAN countries were eager to enlarge further economic cooperation with one another as well as their political cooperation. At the 4th ASEAN Summit held in Singapore in January, 1992, the representatives attending the meeting made a positive response to the idea of establishing an ASEAN Free Trade Area proposed by Thailand in September, 1991 and made a decision to establish AFTA within 15 years from 1993 on.

The main purposes of establishing AFTA are the following: To promote ASEAN to become a competitive base so as to attract foreign investment; to eliminate tariff and non-tariff among the ASEAN countries so as to enhance regional trade-liberalization; to extend the scope for reciprocal preference in trade among the ASEAN countries in order to promote regional trade; and to set up the internal market within AFTA.

In October, 1992 at the Conference of Economic Ministers of ASEAN, the agreement of Commonly Effective Preferential Tariff (CEPT) was adopted. The conference decided to implement the agreement in the next year, whose core was to reduce gradually the tariff within the ASEAN member states. The tariff within ASEAN should be reduced to below

5% by 2008, and in addition, all of the non-tariff barriers among the ASEAN members should be totally eliminated by 2008. For this purpose, ASAEN set up the especial Council of AFTA, which was responsible for the supervision and coordination of the implementation of the Agreement.

In September, 1994, the Conference of Economic Ministers of ASEAN decided to advance 5 years to realize AFTA instead of 15 years, that is, to advance from 2008 to 2003. The economy in many of the ASEAN countries went into a decline during the Asian Financial Crisis in 1997, so there was an urgent need to strengthen their economic cooperation within ASEAN. In December 1998, the ASEAN Summit made a decision to advance one year again from 2003 to realize AFTA. Later on, ASEAN made a new decision that the ASEAN members should reduce their tariff to below 5% by 2002. Considering the differences among the new members of ASEAN, the new members could postpone the deadline for tariff-reduction to 2006.

All of the ASEAN members are determined that the final aim for the establishment of AFTA was to reduce the tariff within the association to zero at the 13th Council Meeting of ASEAN held in September 1999. The deadline for the six old members to realize the zero-tariff within AFTA was set in 2015 while the deadline for the four new members to realize zero-tariff was set in 2018. As an interim measure, all of the ASEAN members should reduce 60% of their tariff to zero before 2003. The deadline for the six old members to realize the zero-tariff had been advanced again from 2015 to 2010 and the deadline for the new members to realize the zero-tariff was also advanced from 2018 to 2015 at the 3rd Non-Official Meeting of ASEAN held in kuala Lumpur in November of the same year. The six old members of ASEAN advanced first to set up AFTA in 2010.

13.2 The Framework and Contents of AFTA

Framework: Progress and Timetable of AFTA

The proposal of setting up AFTA within 15 years from January 1,1993, was adopted at the 4th ASEAN Summit held in Singapore in January, 1992. The main mechanism of setting up AFTA was CEPT, which was prescribed to be implemented by stages. The tariff of industrial manufactured products for trade within the area would be reduced to below 5%. The Conference of Economic Ministers held in September 1994 decided to shorten the time for establishing AFTA within 10 years instead of 15 years; that is, the tariff levied within the internal trade of ASEAN before January 1, 2003, ought to be reduced to 5%. In accordance with the different levels of economic development of the four new members, ASEAN agreed that Vietnam could postpone the time for tariff-reduction to 2006 and Laos, Cambodia and Myanmar could postpone the time for tariff-reduction to 2008.

The 30th Conference of Economic Ministers of ASEAN held in October 1998 decided to set up AFTA in 2010. The Hanoi Declaration, Hanoi Action Project and Declaration of Bold Measures adopted at the 6th ASEAN Summit in Hanoi in December 1998 proposed to advance one year for the six former members to start to establish AFTA, namely, advance from January 1, 2003 to January 1, 2002.

The six former members agreed to reduce the tariff of 60% of their products in the tariff-list prescribed in CEPT to zero. The products which were excluded in Tariff-Reduction Plan should soon be included in the list of tariff-reductions. The four new members also agreed that they would try to extend the categories and quantities of the tariff-products listed from 0% to 5% and categories and quantities of zero-tariff products. Vietnam would reduce the tariff prescribed in CEPT to 0%–5% in 2003, and Laos and Myanmar would reduce the tariff prescribed in CEPT to 0%–5% in 2005. Vietnam tried to increase the categories of commodities of zero-tariff in 2006, and Laos and Myanmar were to increase the categories of commodities of zero-tariff in 2008.

Economic ministers of ASEAN approved a new solution that AFTA would be established in 2002 at the Conference of Economic Higher Officials held in Singapore on September 27 – 28, 1999, and agreed that the time for the new member of ASEAN, Cambodia, to reduce the tariff to 0%–5% was in 2010. At the 3rd ASEAN Summit Non-Official Meeting held in Manila in November, 1999, the ASEAN leaders agreed to advance the time for the six old members to realize the zero-tariff from 2015 to 2010 and the time for the four new members to realize the zero-tariff from 2018 to 2015.

At the Economic Higher Officials Meeting held in Hanoi on September 7 – 8, 2001 and at the Conference of the 15th AFTA Council on September 14, 2001, the economic ministers of ASEAN welcomed the six former members of ASEAN to start AFTA officially.

Contents of AFTA

① five parts in the Tariff-Reduction Project:
　Fast tariff-reduction;
　Normal tariff-reduction;
　List of the general exceptions;
　List of the sensitive products;
　List of the interim exceptions.
② Most-Favored-Nation Treatment
③ Elimination of Restriction in Quantity and Non-Tariff Barriers

④ Rules of Origin

⑤ Open to Trade of Service

⑥ Establishment of AIA (ASEAN Investment Area); Realization of Investment-Liberalization

⑦ AICO(ASEAN Industrial Cooperation Object)

⑧ AISP(ASEAN Integration System of Preference)

⑨ ASEAN Facilitation of Transport

⑩ Unification of Measures of Standard and Quality

⑪ E-ASEAN and Trade-Liberalization of Products of Information and Communication

The core of AFTA is CEPT, which demands that the ASEAN countries reduce tariff and eliminate all of the non-tariff barriers in 15 years beginning from 1993 and reach the average level of tariff below 5% by 2008. By then all the member states of ASEAN would benefit from CEPT. Trade policies of the member states of ASEAN for the states outside of ASEAN, however, will still be decided by each member state on their own.

CEPT consists of all of the industrial manufactured products and capital goods and processing of agricultural products. They are included respectively in the Incision List (IL), Temporary Exclusive List (EL) and Sensitive List(SL). The different categories of products are arranged in different schedules. For the products listed in IL, its tariff-reduction can also be divided into two plans: Fast Track Program and Normal Track Program.

Fast Track Program includes 15 commodities: vegetable oil, cement, chemical products and chemical fertilizer, rubber goods, paper and paper-pulp, wooden and rattan furniture, precious stone and jewels, medicinal material, plastics, leather goods, textile, pottery and porcelain, glasswork, copper line, and electronic products. The tariff on commodities above 20% within ASEAN would be reduced to 0%–5% by January 1, 2003 (the deadline). The tariff on commodities equal to or less than 20% within ASEAN would be reduced to 0%–5% by January 1, 2000 (the deadline).

Normal Track Program: Two steps are divided to cut the tariffs which are more than 20% for the commodities. At first, the tariffs on commodities would be reduced to 20% by no later than January 1, 2000, and then to 0%–5% by no later than January 1, 2008. Second, for the commodities whose tariffs are equal to or less than 20%, the tariffs would be reduced to 0%–5% by no later than 2003.

There are three categories of commodities listed in EL:

① The commodities concerning of the national security and some social factors are free from tariff-reduction, which conforms to Article 10 of GATT.

② The commodities with tariff-exemption license (TEL) because of the different levels of each national economic development. Such commodities need interim protection and cannot be given the tariff preferences provided by CEPT in the other states of the region.

③ The sensitive commodities characterized by processing of the agricultural products, which are also exempt from tariff-reduction temporarily.

In order to promote the trade-liberalization of ASEAN, the member states of ASEAN agreed to strengthen cooperation in the other aspects under the frame of CEPT, including unification of the standards, mutual recognition of the inspection and certificates of the products, elimination of barriers to foreign investment, macro-economic consultation, and principles of just competition and promotion of venture investment.

The key point for ASEAN to do at present is to strengthen the enforcement of the customs law and to eliminate barriers to trade so as to simplify and unify the customs proceedings for all the member states of ASEAN, especially in terms of customs terminology and implementation of WTO Valuation Agreement (WVA). As scheduled, ASEAN would complete the drawing up of the unified terminology on tariff and implement them from 2002. Most of the ASEAN countries would implement WVA by 2000. In addition, ASEAN has laid down an overall working plan for execution of policy so as to make the administrative supervision of the customs in the region more effective and contemporary, including friendly cooperation with business circles, office automation, improvement of transparency, sequence of goods and strict supervision.

ASEAN will draw up a Mutual Recognition Agreement (MRA), for the standard products so that the standards and regulations related to the products will not become technical barriers to trade. The products include cosmetics, medicinal material, electronic products and communication equipment. All member states of ASEAN agree to connect each national standard to the international standard. By 2000, the 20 most frequently-used commodities of the regional trade, such as radio, televisions, air-conditioners, and telephones, would adopt the internationally-recognized standard, for example, the standard of ISO, International Electric Committee (IEC), and International Technological Union (ITU).

The Blueprint of Economic Community of ASEAN was adopted at the 13th ASEAN Summit held in Singapore on November 20, 2007. The Blueprint is an overall project of ASEAN economic integration construction and as well as a guiding document. The main contents are as follows:

Aim: The unified market and productive base will be established by 2015, under the frame of which the free movement of goods, service, investment and technical workers within ASEAN will have been realized, and, at the same time, a balanced development of the economy, elimination of poverty, and the differences of society and economy within ASEAN will have been ensured.

Pillars: ASEAN Economic Community is composed of 4 pillars: a unified market and productive base, a competitive economic area, an economic area with balanced development, an area which keeps pace with the world economy.

Setting up a unified market and productive base is an important tasks for ASEAN to complete for the present. ASEAN has made much progress in tariff-reduction since 1992. The Blueprint prescribed that the main measures would be focused on logistics, elimination of non-tariff barriers, and improvement of customs systems within ASEAN.

Trade of Service: All the restrictions on trade of service within the ASEAN district will be lifted before 2015, including elimination of restrictions on market access, equal treatment between local and foreign investors and service suppliers, and promotion of foreign businesses' equal participation in the service industry. The purpose of the measures above is to provide more convenience and opportunity for ASEAN enterprises to enter each of the other AEASN member states' markets.

Investment: All of the ASEAN agreements concerning investment are to be improved, and an overall agreement covering all of the aspects is to be achieved, including the aspects of opening to the outside, and protection and promotion of investment. The revised agreement is expected to involve all of the foreign investors who are based in ASEAN, not only for the local businesses of ASEAN.

Timetable: ASEAN will realize the integration in the different economic aspects between 2009 and 2015.

13.3 Characteristics of AFTA

AFTA, which has been basically set up within the six old member states of ASEAN since 2003, presents these four characteristics: practical system and measures, loose organizational structure, flexible operational mechanism and internal integration, and open to the outside.

Practical System and Measures

(1) Basic legal documents

The basic legal documents of AFTA can be divided into two categories: fundamental and specific documents.

Singapore Declaration and Enhancement of Frame Agreement on Economic Cooperation of ASEAN as the fundamental documents for the establishment of AFTA was adopted at the 4th ASEAN Summit in January 1992. At the same time, CEPT, as a main measure to set up AFTA, was also adopted. These documents, together with Declaration of Assumption of Establishing Southeast Asian Community with the Ten Countries constitute the programmatic or fundamental documents for AFTA.

In accordance with CEPT, all of the member states of ASEAN should make quick, normal tariff-reduction respectively for the products listed within the scope of CEPT so as to realize the goal of tariff-reduction before 2008. Through many years of hard efforts, especially with the two times of acceleration of tariff-reduction, AFTA was basically set up among the six old member states of ASEAN in 2003. Up to the present, AFTA has made smooth progress in tariff-reduction and has been striving for reaching the final goal of zero-tariff within the Area. As to the tariff of non-ASEAN member states, it will be left to each of the member states of ASEAN to decide.

(2) **The specific legal documents**

Trade and investment have continually been the important parts in economic communication among the member states of ASEAN. ASEAN members have stressed foreign investment in their economic development. In December 1987, the six old ASEAN members signed the Agreement on Promotion and Protection of Investment, which applies to the direct investment among the ASEAN member states. In October, 1998, the nine ASEAN member states signed the Frame Agreement on ASEAN investment area to encourage the investment in the area for both ASEAN member states and non-ASEAN states. In the light of the agreement, ASEAN would establish a competitive Investment Area by 2010. All trades would be opened freely to the investors who invest in ASEAN by 2010, and to all of the investors by 2020 through liberalization, facilitation, and transparency of investment. All of the investors who invest in ASEAN would be given MFN by 2010 and all of the investors will be given MFN by 2020 with the exception of a few sensitive departments and the interim exclusive departments. For the sake of acceleration of building in the investment area, the ten ASEAN member states revised the Frame Agreement on ASEAN Investment Area in 2001 for the interim exclusive departments. In sum, ASEAN is trying to reach the goal of investment-liberalization in AFTA by 2020.

Except for the two basic regulatory documents, such as CEPT and FAIA, in order to offer more trade preferences and lower tariff to the member states than the non-member states in ASEAN, the Rules of Origin was signed in 1992 based on the Agreement of Arrangement for Trade of Special Preferences of ASEAN 1977. In order to open trade of service, the Frame Agreement on Trade of Service was signed in 1995. With a view to enhancement of industrial cooperation, the Agreement on Planning of Industrial Cooperation was signed in 1996. For setting up the transport system with high speed and integration, the Frame Agreement on Promotion of Facilitation of Cargo Transportation was signed in 1998. In the light of unification of standard, the Frame Agreement on

Arrangement of Standard Terminology and Mutual Attestation of ASEAN was signed in 1998 so as to examine the regional products for attestation. For keeping pace with the times of information and promotion of e-commerce, the Frame Agreement on Electronic ASEAN was signed in 2000.

(3) "ASEAN Law" and the National Laws of ASEAN

All of the treaties, conventions and agreements prescribed by ASEAN and AFTA can be called "ASEAN Law", which shows the different relationships with the laws in each of the member states in ASEAN.

First, ASEAN Law applies in priority; that is, ASEAN Law is superior to the domestic laws of each member state of ASEAN in application and it can be applied directly in all of the member states (There is no need for the member states to transfer it to the domestic laws). This is the international principle. ASEAN Law has no legal force for the time being for each member state who has not signed the ASEAN Law. This is the principle of sovereignty.

Second, reservation may not be made on application of ASEAN Law. That is, ASEAN Law doesn't impede any individual member state of ASEAN to take or implement the necessary measures on protection of the national security, the relics possessing value of art, history and archaeology or on maintenance of public morality or on protection of life and health of human beings and animals or plants.

Third, the principle of exceptions is applied in ASEAN Law. That is, ASEAN Law doesn't impede any individual member state of ASEAN to reach bilateral or multilateral agreements with the other ASEAN member states and non-ASEAN countries in trade of goods, trade of service, investment and other economic cooperation. The uniform rules set by ASEAM Law do not apply to the special stipulations made in the bilateral and multilateral agreements.

Loose Organizational Structure

(1) Decision-making institutions

ASEAN has not formed a super-national decision-making institution because of the history, ethnic characteristics and the states' interest. In the organizational structure, four organizations play the role of decision-making: The first is ASEAN Summit which decides the important issues and guides the development of ASEAN. The second is the conference of foreign ministers which is to be held in turns in each state in ASEAN and is responsible for making the basic policy of ASEAN; in addition, the foreign minister who is on duty in turns to be Chairman of the year will act as Chairman of the standing committee of ASEAN, the ambassadors (or the higher-rank officials) of other states to the chairman state will act as commissioners of the standing committee. The committee holds unscheduled meetings every year, dealing with the routine affairs of ASEAN and preparation for conference of foreign ministers, executing resolutions made by the Conference and making a declaration of the Chairman on behalf of ASEAN. The third is the conference of economic ministers which is responsible for stipulating the policy of the economic cooperation within ASEAN and plays a leading role in cooperation of the regional economic integration. The fourth is the other conferences of ministers, such as Conference of Labor, Conference of Social Welfare, Conference of Science, Education, Culture and Health, and Conference of Environmental Protection.

(2) **Executive institutions**

The secretariat, as the administrative headquarters of AFTA, has been set up. As required by the work, several special committees have been set up.

AFTA Council was set up in September 1992 in order to assist the conference of economic ministers to promote and coordinate the affairs concerning AFTA. A special high-ranking official meeting has been set up under the supervision of the council. A council has also been set up in the ASEAN Investment Area. Hence a system of organizational leadership of AFTA has been formed: Summit→Conference of Economic Ministers→AFTA Council→Economic Conference of Higher Ranks. It can be even considered that ASEAN is in reality the same institution as AFTA.

Flexible Operational Mechanism

(1) **Principles and proceedings of decision-making**

The general principle of decision-making for ASEAN is that each member state of ASEAN, big or small, strong or weak, is given equal status in decision-making. The detailed descriptions are as follows:

① Non-interference in each other's internal affairs

② Unanimity through consultation

No bills can be adopted and announced in public or no actions are taken on behalf of ASEAN until all of the member states show no objection to them or obtain common understanding of them. So long as one member state presents a different opinion about the bills, the bills will be reserved. ASEAN takes the principle of "consensus" rather than "the minority should be subordinate to the majority".

③ Non-official consultation

This is also called the consultation before conference. Before decision-making, all of the member states reach an agreement step by step through the bilateral or multilateral contacts and make full preparation for the decision-making.

④ "N-X" principle

Namely, if the minority of the member states do not take part in a vote for a certain bill, whereas they don't reject it, then the bill can be adopted. The postponement of the minority of the member states to vote the bill is allowed. This principle is used as a supplement and development of the principle of "consensus". For example, Conference of Foreign Ministers of ASEAN accepted the principle of "Six Minus X" in 1987, which was only applied in the certain cooperative planning and it shows no influence on the principle of consensus when decision-making is made.

(2) **Operational methods**

① Non-official dialogues, discussions and consultations before meetings instead of face-to-face negotiations for all issues.

② Some member states mediate the specific disputes and conflicts among the other member states and try to solve the problems by means of non-antagonism.

③ The aim for all-inclusiveness and consensus is reached by way of tackling the easy before the difficult and making a progressive push.

④ Common resolutions adopted before common actions taken.

The model of decision-making and operation which shows equality and non-core country with high efficiency is called the "ASEAN Model".

Tendency for Internal Integration and Openness to the Outside World

(1) **Aim for economic integration in ASEAN**

From 1967 to 1991, though the internal economic cooperation within ASEAN had been well-developed, it was very slow and could not satisfy the need of reality. This situation aroused a great dissatisfaction among the persons of noble aspirations in ASEAN, which led to the decision of the establishment of AFTA in 1992 and the new plan for the economic cooperation of ASEAN. Later on, ASEAN made quicker development in economic cooperation in over 10 years of efforts. Facing the heavy challenge of economic globalization, ASEAN determined to "scale new heights" and issued the document concerning "AEC" (ASEAN Economic Community) in October 2003, emphasizing that a unitary market and productive base in ASEAN would be set up by 2020. This market would be characterized by the freer movement of commodities, service, investment and capital so as to realize the final aim of the economic integration determined in Assumption of ASEAN 2020. By then ASEAN will become the most energetic and powerful participant in the supply-chain of the globalization.

ASEAN countries have not only made declarations, but also have taken actions in their process of integration. In order to narrow down the differences in development among the ASEAN member states, the first projects with 54 items of ASEAN integration have been going on smoothly since their start in 2002. The internal economic integration within ASEAN has been put into operation. ASEAN plans to establish special institutions to study the influence on agriculture and agricultural products of ASEAN member states due to the unfair terms of trade in the current world so as to seek common way to solve them for ASEAN.

(2) **Relationship between ASEAN Law and WTO rules**

Free Trade Area (FTA) is allowed by the WTO rules. Paragraph 5 under Article 24 of GATT (General Agreement on Tariffs and Trade), 1947 indicates that "The provision of this agreement shall not prevent, as between the territories of contracting parties, the formation of a customs union or of a free-trade area or the adoption of an interim agreement necessary for the formation of a customs union or of a free-trade area." At the same time, some restrictive conditions are also provided. WTO Secretariat points out that generally speaking, setting up a customs union or free-trade area breaks the principle of the WTO, in which all the trade partners are equally treated (MFN principle). But, as a special exception, Article 24 of the Agreement allows the establishment of regional-trade arrangements, which, nevertheless, should conform to some strict standards. Most important of them is that these arrangements should spur the free movement of trade within the member states of the group and should not increase the barriers to trade for the countries outside of the group. In other words, the regional integration should be supplementary to the multilateral trade system other than a threat to it. WTO Secretariat differentiates especially the customs union from free trade area, and points out that "Customs Union: All member states in the Customs Union should impose the same tariff on the import products from the non-member states. The EU is the customs union. Free Trade Area: Trade within the region is tariff-free, but each member state can set tariff-rate and impose tariff on import products coming from the non-member states of FTA at its disposal, such as North American Free Trade Area and ASEANFTA."

First, the rules for FTA should agree with those of the WTO. Rights and obligations among the member states prescribed by the WTO rules should be applied in priority as long as they are concerned with FTA. FTA must be established within the framework of the WTO.

Second, generally speaking, within the scope of the FTA, the FTA rules may exceed the WTO rules in contents and should be applied first.

Third, for the rights and obligations between the WTO member states and the non-WTO member states within the FTA, the FTA may stipulate that the non-WTO member states may be given the MFNT conforming to the WTO rules, such as the same treatment under the General Agreement of Trade of Service of the WTO.

(3) **Relationship between ASEAN and the countries (districts) beyond ASEAN**

Southeast Asian countries lay stress on openness to the outside world. For more than 40 years, ASEAN's has made great progress in opening to the outside by dealing with foreign trade, investment and other economic co-operations. ASEAN's opening to the world can be divided into two categories: one is an individual country's opening to the world, the other is ASEAN's opening to the world as a whole. Treaties and agreements stemming from the two categories of opening result in the relationships between ASEAN Law, national laws of each member state of ASEAN, and foreign laws and international laws.

All the ten ASEAN countries are members of the WTO. Brunei, the Philippines, Singapore, Thailand, Indonesia, Malaysia and Vietnam are members of the APEC. Therefore, the WTO rules and APEC rules have great influence on the ASEAN countries.

Up to the present, nine of ASEAN countries have signed the bilateral agreements on investment except Myanmar. ASEAN and China decided officially to set up China-AFTA within 10 years in November, 2001. Later, they also signed the Frame Agreement on Overall Economic Cooperation, that is, the "10 + 1" Cooperation System, which has aroused the great attention of the world. China is the first big country to enter into the Treaty of Friendship and Cooperation of Southeast Asia beyond the Southeast Asian countries. China and ASEAN are taking active steps to ensure the establishment of China-ASEAN Free Trade Area as scheduled.

Up to now, ASEAN as a whole or an individual member state of ASEAN has made extensive economic cooperation with many countries and districts in the world, such as China, the United States, the EU, Japan, the Republic of Korea, Australia, New Zealand, Canada and Russia.

What is worth mentioning here is that the ten ASEAN countries and the three countries in Northeast Asia (China, Japan and the Republic of Korea) are cooperating hand in hand and striving for the establishment of East Asian FTA, which is the "10 +3" Cooperation Mechanism. The realization of the "10 + 3" Cooperation Mechanism, however, is more difficult at present. If "10 +3" could be divided into three "10 +1"s and pushed forward step by step and stage by stage, the final realization of "10 +3" would be considered as a feasible and practical policy. China and ASEAN "10 +1" play an active and leading role in the cooperation of East Asia. China-ASEAN FTA and AFTA will be merged in 2010, an event which will push forward the construction of East Asian FTA. China makes clear that China continues to support ASEAN's leading status and role in cooperation with East Asia and claims that China, Japan and the Republic of Korea will try their best to develop their advantages and roles respectively in the cooperation.

13.4 Significance of AFTA

The establishment of AFTA in 2010 is of historic and far-reaching importance to both ASEAN and China. Establishment of China-ASEAN FTA in 2010 has a tremendous influence on the Asian economic development as well as the world economic development.

Political Significance

(1) **Relationship between China and ASEAN**

In terms of the relationship between ASEAN and China, the establishment of AFTA and China-ASEAN FTA would be good to clear the ASEAN members' minds of doubt about China and could be helpful in developing the friendly relationship between China and ASEAN.

For centuries, the relationship between China and ASEAN countries has been very delicate. Most of the ASEAN member states have maintained good and neighboring contact with China, considering their political and economic interests. However, hence having kept a wary and worried eye on China or even stayed at a respectful distance from China in the past. After the establishment of China-ASEAN FTA, China and ASEAN signed the Norms of Behavior of the South China Sea. China is the first country outside ASEAN to join in the treaty of Friendship and Cooperation of Southeast Asia as a positive response to the will of ASEAN to form strategic partnership with ASEAN. China's accession to the treaty is of active significance not only for strengthening the harmonious relationship with China's neighboring countries but also for the maintenance of peace and stability in East Asia and the Asia-Pacific districts. Chinese action to join the treaty will results in a domino effect and take a leading role for the other Asia-Pacific countries, especially for the big powers.

(2) **International new system**

In terms of the establishment of the international new system, the setting up of AFTA is conducive to the unity and cooperation among the developing countries. Although the ASEAN member states have different levels of development in economy and different social systems, they are developing countries and mutually face the opportunities and challenges of the increasingly changing world. If all of the member states of AFTA can form an effective and supplementary mechanism by establishing FTA, the ability for each member state of ASEAN to resist the external risk of the regional economy will be raised respectively. This will lighten the excessive dependence on markets of the developed countries and create a new model for the common cooperation of developing countries. During the process of the setting up of the AFTA, the ASEAN member states have negotiated in line with equal status for each country, big or small, and the principle of mutual benefits and preferences. The different levels of economic development within ASEAN and the less developed countries are taken fully into account. The ASEAN people are eager to build a just, reasonable international new system and realize the economic globalization by way of equality, common benefits, coexistence and double-wins.

(3) **National security**

In terms of national security, the establishment of both AFTA and China-ASEAN FTA in 2010 is beneficial to ensure the unblocking of both China and ASEAN marine transport and the development of sea space in ASEAN. The Western powers have long set up many marine military bases historically and presently. Therefore, Southeast Asian district constitutes the most important part in the Chinese marine geographic line and is the strategic border in the southeast of China.

(4) **International status**

In terms of enhancement of the international status of ASEAN, the setting up of AFTA is beneficial to the more active role played by ASEAN in the international affairs. The significance of setting up of the two FTAs is obvious: First, the external world will develop more confidence in ASEAN and more capital will be invested in ASEAN. Second, the United States, Japan, Russia and India will develop new political and economic relationships with ASEAN one after another. Third, the cohesive force of ASEAN is strengthened. "China's setting up of FTA with ASEAN", as Bolkiah, Brunei Sudan described, "is a decision which is of historic significance for the ASEAN countries". Nowadays, the international position of ASEAN is increasing, and the independence and stability of East Asian countries are enhanced.

(5) **Smash of dreaming of "Taiwan independence"**

In terms of smashing of dreaming of "Taiwan independence", the setting up of AFTA is positive for China to resolve the Taiwan problem. ASEAN has had wide economic and trade relations with Taiwan for a long time because of its closeness to Taiwan in geography. "Taiwan independence" advocates have been trying to develop the so-called "international space" in ASEAN and hoping to divide Taiwan from the motherland. Taiwan authorities encourages Taiwan enterprises to increase their investment in Southeast Asia in order to stop their development of business in the motherland and attempt to realize the purpose of their political relations by strengthening economic relationships with some ASEAN countries. The setting up of FTA between China and ASEAN, together with the establishment of China's strategic partnership with ASEAN has made the Southeast Asian countries and China become closer in economy. ASEAN's economic and trade relationship with China has been much stressed than before and its relationship with Taiwan is put in the second and subordinate position, which plays an obvious role in restraint of Taiwan's "Southward Strategy" and is no doubt a heavy blow to the political force of "Taiwan independence". AFTA and China-ASEAN FTA will have a profound and active influence on the merge and unification of Taiwan and China's mainland.

Action Program of Joint Declaration for Implementation of Strategic Partnership with Peace and Prosperity, signed by China and ASEAN at the 8th Chinese and ASEAN Top

Meeting on November 29, 2004, planned complete cooperation in various aspects between China and ASEAN in the next five years. This program has taken another important step in the process of development in the China-ASEAN relationship and has been a sign which marks the bilateral relationship more comprehensive, systematic and practical.

Economic Significance

The setting up of AFTA and China-ASEAN FTA will not only consolidate and strengthen China's good and friendly relationship with ASEAN, but also because of the convenience of their geographic location, promote the economic development of both China and ASEAN respectively and enlarge the scope of cooperation and trade between the two countries, and in addition, it will increase each other's competitive power and realize mutual supplementary advantages, and improve the regional integral competitive ability. The two FTAs will promote the movement of talent, logistics, capital and information, and the development of the regional markets within the two FTAs will create more wealth and benefit more people of the two FTAs.

(1) **Promotion of Chinese economic development**

Setting up of China-ASEAN FTA is of positive sense for Chinese economic development.

① Be beneficial to the enhancement of Chinese economic power and optimization and upgrading of the product structure;

② Be beneficial to winning the trust and support of the neighboring countries and lessening of resistance and clash in China's economic development;

③ Be beneficial to the adaptation of China's economic system to the requirements of the development of economic globalization;

④ Be beneficial to China's involvement in the international affairs and to her overall integration into the international economy in trade, investment and market access;

⑤ Be beneficial to the implementation of the strategy of "Going Overseas" for Chinese enterprises in order to obtain the new space in the overseas markets;

⑥ Be beneficial to China's need for the natural resources and energy of ASEAN caused by the rapid economic development of China;

⑦ Be beneficial to the enhancement of China's ability to deal with the unexpected incidents which may occur in economic globalization.

(2) **Promotion of development of ASEAN**

① Going in advance into China's huge market

It is beneficial for ASEAN enterprises to go in advance into the huge market in China because of the establishment of the two FTAs. For ASEAN, China is not only a huge and real market, but also a huge and potential market. China has a population of 1.3 billion and has great demand for various products. As the Chinese people's income increases and the China's open economy matures, China's imports from ASEAN will rocket year by year. So boundless commercial opportunities are provided for the ASEAN countries.

② Attraction of foreign investment

It is beneficial for ASEAN to attract foreign investment. A report made by the UN Trade and Development Conference in October 2013 pointed out that Southeast Asia, in which the Financial Crisis took place six years before, except for a few countries which were unstable in politics, attracted more foreign direct investment in 2003 (US $ 215 billion in 2012).

③ Acceleration of ASEAN integration

It is beneficial for ASEAN to hasten the process of ASEAN integration. The ministers of finance of ASEAN reached a common understanding that the unitary market similar to that of EU would be established among ASEAN countries in Djakarta, Indonesia on September 5, 2004. The free trade agreement reduced tariffs on 7,881 product categories, or 90% of imported goods, to zero. This reduction took effect in China and the six original members of ASEAN: Brunei, Indonesia, Malaysia, the Philippines, Singapore and Thailand. The remaining four countries will follow suit in 2015. The average tariff rate on Chinese goods sold in ASEAN countries decreased from 12.8% to 0.6% on January 1, 2010, pending implementation of the free trade area by the remaining ASEAN members. Meanwhile, the average tariff rate on ASEAN goods sold in China decreased from 9.8% to 0.1%.

④ Close economic relationships with foreign countries

It is beneficial for ASEAN to establish close economic and trade relationship with foreign countries. Recently, ASEAN has had numerous bilateral and multilateral meetings with the main trade partners in the world, including China, Japan, the Republic of Korea, India, Australia, and the EU. ASEAN signed the Agreements of FTA with Australia and New Zealand on February 27, 2009. ASEAN signed the Agreement of FTA with Japan on August 25, 2007. Since 2001, ASEAN has signed bilateral agreements concerning of setting up of FTAs with India, the Republic of Korea and Canada.

Promotion of Process of Asian Integration

(1) **Desire for Japan and the Republic of Korea to establish East Asia FTA**

The desire of Japan and the Republic of Korea to establish EAFTA was aroused after the setting up of AFTA and China-ASEAN FTA.

As early as in the 1990s, at the 1st Esat Asian Summit held in Kuala Lumpur, Malaysia, the former Premier Mahadile presented the idea of " EAEC" (Esat Asian

Economic Conference) and initiated a desire to establish gradually an East Asia Economic Community by first organizing the East Asia Economic Forum in order to hasten the economic cooperation with East Asia. Ten years from then on, this important idea hadn't come true for many reasons, including the concern by the United States, the ambiguous attitude of Japan, and the financial crisis of Southeast Asia. Thirteen years have passed since then, the former EEC has evolved into the EU in both connotation and denotation. North American FTA has been formed. On the way to regional integration, East Asia has lagged behind. By the end of 2004, East Asia had not had its own Summit Meeting. East Asian cooperation is made mainly through the mechanism of "10 +3".

The East Asian economy includes the Northeast Asian economy and the Southeast Asian economy. Among them, the economy of East Asia, based on China, Japan and the Republic of Korea, is more predominant than that of Southeast Asia, based on ASEAN. In the Northeast Asian economy, Japan's economy is the strongest. The economic power of the Republic of Korea cannot be ignored either, so the integration of the Northeast Asian economy won't develop without the involvement of Japan and the Republic of Korea. Comparing the regional economic cooperation with the regional integration, the former process is developing faster while the later process is falling far behind, that is, the cooperative system between governments lags far behind the close cooperation between the enterprises in the region. A breaking point must be opted for in order to promote the process of the East Asian integration and form the East Asian FTA step by step.

The establishment of China-ASEAN FTA is greatly beneficial to the enhancement of governmental cooperation in East Asia. China is now ASEAN's largest trading partner, while ASEAN remains the No.3 trading partner of China. Two-way trade in 2010 increased 37.5% to US$292.8 billion, hitting a new high. In the first 10 months of 2011, bilateral trade reached US$295.9 billion, a 25.7% increase over the previous corresponding period. Both have set a target of expanding bilateral trade to US$500 billion in 2015. The establishment of China-ASEAN FTA has greatly stimulated the economies of Japan and the Republic of Korea, a fact which will make them quicken the economic merge with ASEAN. China's joint cooperation with ASEAN is called the herald of New Asianism.

Japan signed the Agreement on Free Trade Area with Singapore in 2002. The Agreement was executed in January, 2003. Japan signed with ASEAN Frame Overall of Economic Cooperation between ASEAN and Japan in 2003. Since 2005, Japan has negotiated with ASEAN about the liberalization of commodities, services and investment. Japan has undertaken the official negotiations with Malaysia, Thailand and the Philippines for the establishment of free trade relationships.

The Republic of Korea does not want to fall behind in cooperation with ASEAN. At the top conference between ASEAN and the Republic of Korea held on November 30,

2004, a negotiation of Agreement of Free Trade between ASEAN and the Republic of Korea in 2005 began. Not only trade of goods, but also trade of service are included in the Agreement. Its aim is that the tariff on no fewer than 80% of the commodities for trade would be reduced to zero between the two parties by 2009, and the categories of the commodities for zero-tariff of the two parties will reach to 96% by 2015.

(2) **Growth of East Asian community**

There are 13 countries in North Asia with a population of nearly 2 billion, equal to one third of the world's population, which is a huge consumer market. GDP of East Asia accounts for nearly 20% of that in the world. The foreign exchange reserve in North Asia constitutes 50% of that in the world. The fast economic development of North Asia has made it clear that it is an important part of the world. AFTA and China-ASEAN FTA are upgrading and promoting the economic integration of East Asia. East Asia's continuous growth in economy leads in the other areas of the world. East Asia has become an important impetus to world's economic development.

Viewed from the present situation, there are at least four options for the road to "East Asian Community (EAC)": First, develop three "10 +1"s and then combine them into EAC. Second, on the basis of cooperation of the ASEAN countries and the cooperation among China, Japan and the Republic of Korea, set up EAC. Third, while developing the three "10 +1"s, promote cooperation among China, Japan and the Republic of Korea. When the conditions mature, set up EAC. Fourth, set up the Economic Community (EC) of Japan, the Republic of Korea and Singapore first, and then enlarge it gradually to EAC. Among the four options, the first option is realistic. In the construction of the three "10 + 1"FTAs, China-ASEAN FTA is moving ahead to take a leading role in the realization of a East Asian Community.

Recently in Asia, the issues of turning of the "10 + 3" system into a East Asian Community and the need for having a top meeting of East Asia have been heatedly discussed. China claims that ASEAN should take the guiding role in promoting regional cooperation. ASEAN should be the base and core in East Asian Cooperation. The ten ASEAN countries have different levels of economic development and differ in political and cultural systems. If the ten countries of ASEAN are not organized and united, it is not easy to sponsor East Asian cooperation. If ASEAN is not taken as the core in East Asian cooperation, the small countries in ASEAN may think that they would be oppressed and controlled by the big countries in Northeast Asian cooperation. In East Asian cooperation, the "10 + 1" mechanism and the three "10 + 1"s mechanism are important and supplementary. If China-Japan relationship improves, it would accelerate greatly the cooperative process of "10 +3" so as to advance the whole regional integration in East Asia.

Notes

[1] The EU: On April 8,1965,France,Germany,Italy,Holland, Belgium and Luxembourg signed the Treaty in Brussels and combined the three Treaties (European Coal and Steel Community, European Economic Community and European Community of Atomic Energy) into one community: the European Community, which took effect on January 1,1967. The heads of EC signed the Treaty of European Union at the Conference of Masstricht on December 11,1991, and established the aim for setting up the European Economic Monetary Unit, and the European Political Union. The Treaty took effect on November 1,1993. From then on, EC has been developed into the European Union. The EU has been enlarged five times since its foundation. There are 26 member states in the EU now.

[2] NAFTA: Implementation of the North American Free Trade Agreement (NAFTA) began on January 1, 1994. This agreement will remove most barriers to trade and investment among the United States, Canada, and Mexico. Under the NAFTA, all non-tariff barriers to agricultural trade between the United States and Mexico were eliminated. In addition, many tariffs were eliminated immediately, with others being phased out over periods of 5 to 15 years. This allowed for an orderly adjustment to free trade with Mexico, with full implementation beginning on January 1, 2008.

Exercises

1. **Explain the following in English.**
   (1) "10 +1" Mechanism
   (2) "10 +3" Cooperation
   (3) The Blueprint of Economic Community of ASEAN
   (4) EAC
   (5) Fast Track Program
   (6) "N-X" Principle

2. Fill in the blanks.

(1) The six old countries of ASEAN are _____, _____, _____, _____, _____, _____.

(2) The total ground space in AFTA is more than _____ square kilometers with a total population of _____.

(3) According to the new decision, the tariff within ASEAN for the old six ASEAN countries would be reduced to below 5% by _____.

(4) The deadline for the old member states of ASEAN to realize the zero-tariff was advanced again to _____ from _____, and the deadline for the new member states to realize the zero-tariff was also advanced to _____ from _____.

(5) The 30th Conference of Economic Ministers of ASEAN held in October 1998 decided to set up AFTA in _____.

(6) ASEAN will realize the integration in different economic fields earlier or later between _____ and _____.

(7) Four organizations play the role of decision-making in AFTA. They are _____, _____, _____, _____.

(8) China-ASEAN FTA will be the first big FTA in the world with a population of _____ and with GDP of US$_____.

(9) East Asian Economy includes _____ and _____.

3. Answer the following questions.

(1) What are the main contents of the Blueprint of Economic Community of ASEAN?

(2) What do you know about the relationship between ASEAN Law and the WTO Rules?

(3) Why is it said that the operational mechanism in ASEAN is flexible?

(4) What are the contents of AFTA?

(5) Why is it considered that setting up of AFTA is of both great political and economic significance?

4. Discussions.

(1) What are the challenges for the establishment of AFTA?

(2) How is the international cooperation and competition dealt with in AFTA?

(3) Why is the integration of East Asia considered beneficial?

(4) Why does China support ASEAN to be the leader in the process of establishing EAC?

CHAPTER 14

China-ASEAN Free Trade Area

14.1 The Emergence of China-ASEAN Free Trade Area

Upon entering the 21st century, the Chinese government made timely diplomatic-strategy readjustments and started to push for better relations with its neighbouring countries, seeking mutual trust politically and co-prosperity economically.

Before the 1990s, there was no official relationship between ASEAN as a grouping and China, although China had official relations with certain individual ASEAN member states on a bilateral basis. From the late 1980s, China intensified its efforts to establish diplomatic relationship with all the remaining ASEAN states as the final step leading to its eventual official relationship with the ASEAN grouping.

Since the 1990s, the integration of regional economies has had strong momentum—a hallmark of accelerated economic globalization. Regional economic organisations such as the European Union (EU) and the North American Free Trade Area (NAFTA) are acquiring increasingly important positions in the world economy. On the other hand, free trade agreements, those signed between developed countries in particular, are posing a serious challenge to both China and ASEAN because the preferential tariff rates granted to each other by free trade agreement members erode the economic and trade advantages enjoyed by developing nations.

China joined the World Trade Organization (WTO) in December, 2001 after more than a decade of painstaking negotiations. As a result, the focus of the country's foreign trade and economic strategy began to shift to regional economic cooperation.

China's WTO membership means that the country's economic development will become increasingly responsive to the world's economy. At the moment, regional economic integration is picking up speed and China would risk being marginalised if it did not join this process. If China failed to embrace regional integration, it would find its global competitiveness significantly diminished. Fortunately, involvement in regional economic cooperation constitutes a new focus of the nation's overseas economic strategy. In the meantime, the economies of the ASEAN members started recovering in 1999 from the ravages of the 1997 Southeast Asian Financial Crisis, which dragged down the once fast-growing economies of the member states. Coincidentally, while ASEAN rose out of economic stagnation, the China's economy entered a phase of high-speed development. Doubtless, Chinese demand helped facilitate their economic growth. In light of that, the nature of ASEAN's economic recovery recommended a strengthening of relations with China. It then became obvious that pursuing a China-ASEAN FTA was a wise strategic option beneficial to both sides.

In his visit to Thailand in November, 1988, Chinese Premier Li Peng announced four principles in establishing, restoring and developing relations with all the ASEAN states. After establishing diplomatic relations with the last ASEAN country—Singapore—in late 1990, China pushed for official ties with the ASEAN grouping. On July 19, 1991, Chinese Foreign Minister Qian Qichen attended the opening session of the 24th ASEAN Ministerial Meeting (AMM) in Kuala Lumpur as a guest of the Malaysian government, where he expressed China's interest in cooperating with ASEAN, particularly in the field of science and technology. The latter responded positively. In September 1993, ASEAN Secretary-General Dato' Ajit Singh visited Beijing and agreed to establish two joint committees, one on cooperation in science and technology, and the other on economic and trade cooperation. An exchange of letters between the ASEAN secretary-general and the Chinese Foreign Minister on July 23, 1994 in Bangkok formalized the establishment of the two committees. At the same time, ASEAN and China agreed to engage in consultations on political and security issues at senior officials level. In July 1996, ASEAN accorded China full Dialogue Partner status at the 29th AMM in Jakarta, moving China from a Consultative Partner, which it had been since 1991. By early 1997, there were already five parallel frameworks for dialogue between China and ASEAN. China participated in a series of consultative meetings with ASEAN. In December 1997, Chinese President Jiang Zemin and all the ASEAN leaders had their first informal summit (ASEAN Plus One) and issued a joint statement to establish a partnership of good neighbourliness and mutual trust oriented towards the 21st century. China-ASEAN trade has expanded rapidly, at an annual growth rate of about 15% since 1995, and it jumped by 31.7% in 2002 to US$54.77 billion. ASEAN is now the fifth largest trade partner of China while China is the sixth of ASEAN.

The idea of an FTA between ASEAN and China first emerged during the third ASEAN-Plus-China Summit in Manila in 1999 when ASEAN was recovering from the Asian Financial Crisis. Realizing its vulnerability to world market fluctuations, ASEAN was expecting China to play a more important role and to have more cooperation with China in the regional economy. In response, Beijing proposed closer cooperation between

China and the forthcoming ASEAN Free Trade Area (AFTA)—a proposal that was immediately accepted by ASEAN.

Due to the existing constraints discussed in the previous section, there are therefore alternative proposals for ASEAN to negotiate on FTAs with three Northeast Asian economies—Japan, China and the Republic of Korea—separately within the framework of the APO[1]. This strategy, it is argued, would not only circumvent some major hurdles that prevent the creation of a region-wide FTA in East Asia through APT, but would gradually create conditions for a true East Asian FTA. It is within this context that ASEAN and China announced in November, 2001 their intention to create an FTA between them within a decade.

As part of the effort, the process of bringing about a China-ASEAN Free Trade Area is being driven ahead. As an arrangement for mutual benefits, the bidding for the FTA is powering the all-round economic cooperation between China and ASEAN that, in turn, works as a stabilizing factor for the region. In the following Singapore Summit of 2000, at the initiative of China, it was agreed that an expert group be created to study the feasibility of an China-ASEAN FTA and the implications of China's WTO membership for ASEAN. After a year of research, the expert group submitted a report to the governments of ASEAN countries and China, in which it concluded that the creation of a China-ASEAN FTA would produce a win-win situation for both sides and suggested a 10-year period for the achievement of this objective. The proposal was endorsed by both ASEAN and Chinese leaders. In the Brunei Summit of November, 2001, the leaders of ASEAN and China officially announced the decision to authorize the start of negotiations on a China-ASEAN FTA at the ministerial level.

In November, 2001, China and the 10-member Association of Southeast Asia Nations began negotiations to set up a free trade area. One year later, a framework agreement for the planned FTA was signed. The FTA, a zero-tariff market of more than 1.7 billion people, has been targeted to come into force in 2010 for the six original ASEAN members (Brunei, Indonesia, Malaysia, the Philippines, Singapore and Thailand) and in 2015 for the other four (Myanmar, Cambodia, Laos and Vietnam). Implementation of the framework agreement would occur in stages. China-ASEAN cooperation has broadened to cover the environment, science and technology, non-traditional security areas and related legal issues. China's relations with ASEAN have reached a new era where the two sides have established an economic, legal and political framework for their comprehensive cooperation.

14.2 The Framework and Agreement of China-ASEAN FTA

The Framework Agreement on ASEAN-China Comprehensive Economic Cooperation between China and ASEAN was signed by ASEAN and China on November 4, 2002 to serve as the structure and mechanism for negotiations to establish a free trade area covering trade in goods, services, and investment, as well as to effect various measures for economic cooperation between China and ASAEN. Subsequently, an Agreement on Trade in Goods of the Framework Agreement on Comprehensive Economic Cooperation between ASEAN and China was successfully negotiated and was signed on November 29, 2004, during the ASEAN+China Summit meeting in Vientiane, Laos.

Liberalization of Trade in Goods

Liberalization of trade in goods is divided into two categories: those under the Early Harvest Program[2] (providing for immediate reduction or elimination of tariffs for certain goods), and goods that will come under the comprehensive reduction or elimination of tariffs.

Tariff Reduction under the Early Harvest Program

Agricultural goods in the customs tariff schedule include live animals, meat and other edible animal parts, fish products, dairy products, fowl eggs, live trees, vegetables and fruit, and edible nuts, as well as specific products agreed upon by two countries (for example, Thailand and China have agreed to accelerate tariff reduction on two addition products, anthracite and coal residue). China and six founding member countries of ASEAN (namely Brunei, Indonesia, Malaysia, the Philippines, Singapore and Thailand) implemented tariff reductions on January 1, 2004, with tariffs to be eliminated completely by January 1, 2006. The timeframe and schedule for elimination of tariffs by the four newer member countries of ASEAN (Laos, Vietnam, Myanmar, and Cambodia) is extended to 2010. Tariff rates of those items under quotas, such as onions and garlic, are to be reduced only within the quota quantities. Because Thailand and China perceived the potential for trade in goods under the customs tariff schedule codes 07 and 08, embracing fruits and vegetables lines of products, the two countries, on June 18, 2003, signed an Agreement Between the Government of the People's Republic of China and the

Government of the Kingdom of Thailand on Accelerated Tariff Elimination under the Early Harvest Programme of the Framework Agreement on Comprehensive Economic Cooperation between ASEAN and China, which eliminated tariffs on all items under these categories as of October 1, 2003. Singapore subsequently signed this agreement as well.

Reduction of Tariff on General Goods

Two tracks have been established for trade in goods, a "normal track" under which tariffs will finally be completely eliminated, and a "sensitive track", which sets a more detailed and long-term schedule of tariff reduction and elimination for goods to be safeguarded.

The Normal Track

The TIG Agreement specifies that duties greater than 20% on goods be reduced to 20% by January 1, 2005, and duties less than 20% on goods be progressively reduced, with duties on all goods under this track to be eliminated completely to 0 within 5 years (by January 1, 2010), with the exception of 150 items for which the timeframe for complete elimination of tariffs is extended to 2012. In addition, the percentage of goods bearing duties of 0%-5% shall be increased from 40% in 2005 to 60% in 2007.

The Sensitive Track

No more than 400 items comprising not more than 10% of the value of all goods imported from China by respective ASEAN countries are to be included in the sensitive list, with a reduction of duties on these goods to 20 % by 2012, and final rates of 0%-5% by 2018. It was also agreed that goods in the highly sensitive list should comprise no more than 100 items or 40% of goods in the sensitive list, with the reduction of tariffs on these items to 50% by 2015.

Goods covered under the ASEAN-China FTA Agreement must adhere to the agreed-upon "Rules of Origins" criteria, with some goods comprised of materials wholly obtained within the producing country, and other products consisting of local content at least 40% of their value. "Local content" here includes the value of materials obtained from all ASEAN member countries. Additionally, ASEAN and China have set Product Specific Rules (PSR) for some products to enjoy the advantages of tariff reduction under ASEAN-China FTA as well.

At the same time, both parties have agreed to undertake measures to safeguard domestic industries in each country from negative impacts of trade liberalization between ASEAN and China, such as a flood of imports that injures domestic products and industry, through an increase in duties on those products to equal the WTO member (MFN) rate in effect at the time. This measure would remain in effect for 5 years following implementation of the reduction or exemption on duties under the Agreement. In addition, ASEAN and China have reached an agreement on dispute settlement mechanism acting as a provision of the Free Trade Agreement.

Liberalization of Trade in Services

On January 14, 2007, in Cebu City, the Philippines, ASEAN and China signed an agreement relating to Trade in Services along with provisions for liberalizing trade in services of Group 1, covering private sector businesses in all areas with the exception of government services and government procurement. A table exhibiting liberalization phases of each country appears in the schedule of commitments and is appended to the agreement. Thailand has offered provisions that are consistent with the current Foreign Business Act that governs the conducting of foreign owned businesses in Thailand; i.e. the permission for individuals from China and ASEAN member countries to hold more than 49% share in business ventures, along with conditions attached to specific professions as designated by the professional associations.

Provision for Liberalization of the Initial Group of Service Activities

The members of ASEAN, including Thailand, have offered liberalization provisions beyond those stipulated under the WTO trade liberalization conventions, but fewer than those granted among the ASEAN group itself. Provisions made by Thailand that offer greater advantages than those under the WTO commitments incorporate service activities in the areas of professions, education, health, tourism, and maritime transportation. China has offered provisions beyond those obligated under the WTO conventions in the areas of computers, realty, land transportation, and other service businesses. ASEAN and China negotiated the second group of service activities, which was completed by the end of 2008.

Negotiations Relating to Investment

Negotiations relating to investment are currently in progress; however, an accord has not yet been reached in a number of issues, and discussions are yet to be concluded.

Economic Cooperation

China and ASEAN, including Thailand, have agreed to undertake economic cooperation in five areas, namely agriculture, information technology, human resource development, and development of the Greater Mekong Sub-region (GMS), as well as cooperation in customs issues, intellectual property protection, establishment of a center for facilitation and promotion of trade and investment, Mutual Recognition Arrangements (MRA), implementation of plans with the framework of the Greater Mekong Sub-region cooperation, and assistance to the newer members of ASEAN.

14.3 The Significance of China-ASEAN FTA

The initial phases of the China-ASEAN Free Trade Agreement (FTA) have brought significant benefits for both parties, helping to absorb external pressures at a time of slowing global growth. On October 22, 2008, Chinese Vice Premier Wang Qishan pointed out at the fifth China-ASEAN Business and Investment Summit that it was paramount for the two partners to accelerate their economic cooperation in the face of weakening global demand. ASEAN officials also stated their wish for deeper economic ties with China, stressing the need to reduce the bloc's exposure to slowing demand from the United States, Europe and Japan.

The Framework Agreement on Comprehensive Economic Cooperation Between China and ASEAN has helped advance bilateral trade, with the China-ASEAN trade volume crossing the threshold of US$100 billion for the first time in 2004 and hitting US$130.37 billion the next year. In addition, the two sides have been cooperating closely in direct investment, services and technology, which has also yielded significant results. From the point of view of regional economic integration, future Asian economic integration should be based on a more extensive and more economically powerful regional cooperative entity, of which the China-ASEAN FTA is a vitally important component. Once founded, the China-ASEAN FTA will be the largest FTA in Asia, the most populous FTA in the world and the biggest FTA in the developing world. The China-ASEAN FTA is expected to accelerate the trend of regional integration in Asia and, in turn, will have positive impacts on the world's economy.

Exceptional Performance

Growth among ASEAN economies, headed up to the 1997 – 1998 Financial Crisis, has since been more moderate. China's economic development, meanwhile, has broken virtually all records. Gross domestic product (GDP) of China and ASEAN was largely comparable in size in the early 1990s. At US$1,910 billion in 2005, however, China's GDP was more than twice that of ASEAN's US$849 billion.

The spillover effects of China's growth have been substantial for the world and regional economies. The prices of many commodities such as gold, mineral oils, copper, iron and steel, rubber, etc., reached record-high levels. China has become the third largest importer (behind the US and the EU) of developing countries' goods. The total import bill was US$1.95 trillion in 2013, compared to US$660 billion in 2005.

Competing Problems

Globalization and the intensified competition for markets and resources inevitably carry risks and tensions, even among friends and partners. China's powerful economic performance, in fact, has given rise to dire predictions of China as a global and regional competitor. Against that backdrop, ASEAN's and Chinese leaders met in November 2000 to consider the regional implications of China's accession to the World Trade Organisation; China became a WTO member in December, 2001. The possibility of establishing a free trade area to foster greater cooperation and integration was also examined.

As part of confidence and trust building, ASEAN and China issued in November, 2002 a joint Declaration on the Conduct of Parties in the South China Sea. China became a full dialogue partner of ASEAN in 1995 but was the first dialogue partner to accede in October, 2003 to the Treaty of Amity and Cooperation in Southeast Asia. This treaty is ASEAN's concrete showpiece for regional security and stability.

Domino Effect

Equally important was the China-ASEAN Framework Agreement on Comprehensive Economic Cooperation of November, 2002. The agreement provides for a China-ASEAN Free Trade Area within a decade, the first FTA between ASEAN and a dialogue partner.

The proposed China-ASEAN FTA has a domino effect. ASEAN subsequently entered into other Framework Agreements, including provisions for FTAs, with the Republic of Korea, Australia and New Zealand, Japan and India. Additional FTAs with other trading partners are also on the cards.

The centrality of ASEAN is thus reaffirmed. So is the imperative of a dynamic and integrated ASEAN economic region as a player at the centre-stage of regional linkages, including the ASEAN Plus Three and the East Asian Summit processes.

Dynamic Trade

China-ASEAN FTA is now a reality. The Early Harvest Programme lowers and eliminates import tariffs on selected agro-products during 2004-2006. Tariff reduction or removal under the China-ASEAN Trade in Goods Agreement started in July 2005 for completion in 2010 by China and ASEAN-6 (Brunei, Indonesia, Malaysia, the Philippines, Singapore and Thailand), and in 2015 by ASEAN-4 (Cambodia, Laos, Myanmar and Vietnam).

Mutual interdependence is obvious. If sustained, this will make China the largest trading partner of ASEAN within a decade, another historic milestone in the two-way partnership. ASEAN trade with China, at US$35.3 billion (equivalent to 4.4% of total ASEAN trade) in 2000, reached US$114.3 billion (or 10.9%) in 2005. China became ASEAN's third largest trading partner (after Japan and the EU) in 2005 and ASEAN China's fifth largest (behind the US, the EU, Japan and China's Hong Kong) Partner.

Changing Composition

ASEAN exports to China increased on average by over 46% a year from 2000 to reach US$52.4 billion in 2005. That was much higher than the annual growth rate of 4.3% in ASEAN exports to all markets outside China.

Production sharing boosted the value of electronics equipment and parts from 35% to 49% of ASEAN exports to China between 2000 and 2005. Meanwhile, slower growth reduced the earlier dominance (in the 1990s) of resources-based exports (such as fuels, edible oils, rubber, and forestry and mineral products) from 32% to 28% in those respective years.

Between 2000 and 2005, a rising share in ASEAN exports to China was recorded by Singapore, from 34% to 38% (worth US$19.8 billion) and by Malaysia, from 16% to 18% (US$9.5 billion). Thailand accounted for a relatively stable export share of just below 18% (US$2.8 billion in 2000 and US$9.2 billion in 2005). Despite higher absolute gains, however, Indonesia's export share fell from 18% in 2000 to 13% (US$6.6 billion) in 2005.

Widening Deficits

Data at the ASEAN Secretariat show a trade surplus in Brunei, Indonesia and the Philippines in recent years. Other countries, however, have a variable but growing trade deficit. The overall deficit in ASEAN trade with China totalled US$3.8 billion in 2000 and US$9.6 billion in 2005.

During 2004-2005, Malaysia accounted for almost one-half of the regional deficit, followed by Thailand and Vietnam (around a quarter each). The trade deficits among the less developed ASEAN members are small in absolute terms but are nevertheless significant relative to their exports to China.

Upgraded Capabilities

Electronics and other high-tech products are subject to constant technological and design improvements. They have also enjoyed the fastest growth in an expanding global and Chinese market. Major firms in China, now the export platform to industrialised countries in the West, account for two-thirds of total research and development (R & D) expenditure. R & D spending in China was to be lifted from 1.34% of GDP in 2004 to 2% in 2010. (R & D outlays in many developed countries are around 2.5% of GDP.)

Product and process innovations in ASEAN are constrained by limited R & D spending, less than 0.5% of GDP except in Singapore. Meanwhile, ongoing upgrades in technological and business training and incubation have become even more pressing in, and challenging to, the less developed regional economies. Typically, their resources-based and labour-intensive exports are subject to stiffer competition in both the global and Chinese markets.

Surging Tourismies

As a major services export of ASEAN, inward tourism can partly compensate for the merchandise trade deficit. In 2005, ASEAN hosted 3 million tourists from China, or just 6% of the total of 51.3 million arrivals. According to the World Tourism Organisation, out-bound tourists from China would reach 100 million by 2020. ASEAN's well-developed and diversified tourism sector should be able to cater to a much larger slice of this huge market. Singapore, Thailand and Vietnam shared almost equally 80% of Chinese tourists in ASEAN in 2005. Malaysia received another 12%. Again, the less developed countries would face a more difficult hurdle in their efforts to attract more Chinese visitors. These made up just 3% – 4% of all the tourists in Cambodia, Laos and Burma in 2005.

Equalizing Investment

China's foreign direct investment (FDI) in ASEAN was modest but trending upward to average US$210 million annually during 2003 – 2004. In comparison, global FDI in ASEAN averaged US $ 31.5 billion a year during 2004 – 2005. ASEAN (especially Singapore) is a net investor in China, with annual FDI of US$300 million during 2002 – 2005. But the investment balance will change. FDI is primarily driven by trade expansion. Besides, China has experienced strong wage pressures and a shortage of experienced workers in several major export industries in the recent years.

Therefore, both ASEAN-6 and ASEAN-4 will likely host much larger FDI from China, for example, in natural resources development, manufacturing for the home and export markets, and tourism-related facilities. Some relocation of export-oriented, labour-intensive manufacturing activities from China to ASEAN can be anticipated as well.

In sum, the broadening and deepening of economic relationships between ASEAN and China will continue to yield plenty of opportunities. These can be charted and nurtured for attractive and sustained commercial returns to both sides. It would be simplistic, however, to assume a two-way development and integration process which is totally smooth sailing. But political goodwill and a forward-looking approach will remain effective in managing mutual problems in trade and investment liberalisation, domestic structural adjustments and upgrading, and competition in home and third-country markets.

The evidence suggests a strong political commitment at the top leadership level to maintain the centrality of ASEAN and the vibrant China-ASEAN partnership as the keystone of regional peace and prosperity. The future is bright with such a common endeavour.

14.4 Challenges of China-ASEAN FTA

While the free trade area will grant ASEAN a breather from foreign investment outflow, China will have to forgo some of the foreign investment it desires for its poorer inland regions. Within the free trade area, some ASEAN members, such as Vietnam, Laos and Cambodia, have cheaper labour costs than China to lure foreign investment. Richer countries like Malaysia could also attract some foreign money away from China.

The free trade area would force China to further reform its regulation and goods circulation system so that it could compete with other members within the area.

Besides foreign investment outflow, challenges of the China-ASEAN FTA for China still lie ahead. ASEAN members may request greater concessions on the Chinese side because they worry the huge economic power of China will threaten them.

The varying economic conditions of ASEAN members will also challenge China. If China gives those poorer ASEAN members, such as Cambodia and Laos, greater concessions, it will face a difficult decision of whether or not to extend such rights to richer countries like Singapore and Malaysia. But the mechanism of the China-ASEAN FTA has been designed to follow the free trade area model within ASEAN, to be finished by 2008.

Because of the wide economic and political gap among ASEAN countries, they have set different processes and requirements on advancing the ASEAN FTA; in this aspect, China could have an example from which to learn and take an adaptive and flexible method to reach the free trade goal.

However, despite their hopes that Chinese demand will help compensate for slowing exports to OECD (Organization for Economic Cooperation and Development) economies, ASEAN leaders have less positive expectations for the relationship than their Chinese counterparts. Political and business leaders are worried about their ability to expand or even retain market access in China. There are several concerns.

Structural Shift

China's economy is moving away from traditional processing and assembly operations, sourcing more components domestically as its industries move up the value chain. Southeast Asia lacks the technology and skills to provide many of the required high-end imports and raw materials. It thus risks the prospect of a shrinking trade surplus with China and greater vulnerability to currency fluctuations.

Third Markets

China is likely to move more aggressively into low-cost markets as import demand slumps in the United States and Western Europe, intensifying competition with ASEAN suppliers. Diplomatic relations have already been strained over China's undercutting of rice, footwear, toys, clothing and textile products. Similar frictions are likely over exports of high technology goods, such as chips and disk drives.

Farm Tensions

Pressure to dismantle tariffs on agricultural goods will become a key issue during the final stage of implementation of the FTA 2010 – 2015, as farm sectors underpin the economies of the less advanced ASEAN members. Although the six advanced countries have gained from an Early Harvest Programme of lower tariffs, Vietnam, Cambodia, Laos and Myanmar fear they will be at a commercial disadvantage.

Investment Outlook

Investment is likely to accelerate in both directions as the FTA takes full effect, but will be influenced by development trends within the respective markets.

Policy Flips

China is becoming more selective with the type of investment it wants as it confronts economic instability resulting from excess capacity and a reliance on FDI rather than domestic consumption. On ASEAN's side, the bloc has been unable to achieve consistent investment policies among its own members due to internal rivalries and self interest, undermining efforts to promote the region as a single, unified market.

Growth Triangles

Inadequate infrastructure is hampering efforts to use the FTA as an investment springboard for less developed regions through special economic zones, such as the Indonesia-Malaysia-Thailand Growth Triangle and China's Beibu Gulf Economic Area. Although communications are being improved under the Greater Mekong Sub-region grouping, investors cite higher costs for a reluctance to support fringe areas. China links its investment priorities closely to foreign policy objectives, with Myanmar, Cambodia and Laos of particular strategic importance.

Notes

[1] APO: The Asian Productivity Organization (APO) was established on May 11, 1961 as a regional intergovernmental organization. Its mission is to contribute to the socioeconomic development of Asia and the Pacific through enhancing productivity. The APO is non-political, non-profit, and non-discriminatory.

[2] "Early Harvest Plan" (EHP): On January 1, 2004 the two parties began implementing what China called an "Early Harvest Plan" or EHP. This plan grants a 3-year duty free entry for ASEAN goods into the Chinese markets. After this, China's manufactured goods will have full free tariff access to Southeast Asian markets. This secures China's access to the region's raw materials and at the same time removes barriers to China's exports. The EHP cut tariffs on more than 500 products as part of the efforts to facilitate the FTA. The China-ASEAN FTA will strengthen China's clout by making it the center of gravity in Asia and surpassing the influence of Japan and the US.

Exercises

1. **Explain the following in English.**
   (1) GDP
   (2) Liberalization of Trade in Services
   (3) Early Harvest Plan

2. **Fill in the blanks.**
   (1) _____, China intensified its efforts to establish diplomatic relationship with all the remaining ASEAN states as the final step leading to its eventual official relationship with the ASEAN grouping.
   (2) China joined the _____ in December 2001 after more than a decade of painstaking negotiations.
   (3) In his visit to Thailand in November 1988, Chinese Premier Li Peng announced _____ in establishing, restoring and developing relations with all the ASEAN states.
   (4) The FTA, _____ of more than 1.7 billion people, has been targeted to come into force in 2010 for the six original ASEAN members (Brunei, Indonesia, Malaysia, the Philippines, Singapore and Thailand) and in 2015 for the other four (Myanmar, Cambodia, Laos and Vietnam).
   (5) The timeframe and schedule for elimination of tariffs by the four newer member countries of ASEAN _____ is extended to 2010.
   (6) As part of confidence and trust building, ASEAN and China issued in November 2002 a joint Declaration on _____ in the South China Sea.

3. **Answer the following questions.**
   (1) What was the background of the emergence of China-ASEAN Free Trade Area?
   (2) What do you know about the economic cooperation between China and ASEAN?
   (3) What is the significance of the establishment of China-ASEAN FTA?
   (4) What are the challenges for China and the ASEAN countries within the free trade area?

CHAPTER 15

China-ASEAN Expo

At the 7th China-ASEAN Summit on October 8, 2003, Wen Jiabao, the Premier of the People's Republic of China, proposed that a China-ASEAN Expo be held annually in Nanning Guangxi, China from the year 2004 onwards. His initiative was welcomed by the ASEAN's leaders and was written into the Chairman's Statement released after the Summit.

The China-ASEAN Expo (CAEXPO), proposed by Premier Wen Jiabao, co-sponsored by China and the 10 ASEAN countries as well as the ASEAN Secretariat, undertaken by the Government of Guangxi Zhuang Autonomous Region, is an international trade fair.[1] It is based on the Framework Agreement on China-ASEAN Comprehensive Economic Cooperation, with the sole objective of promoting to build China-ASEAN Free Trade Area, and striving for mutual benefits and common prosperity.[2] The China-ASEAN Expo focuses on regional economic and trade cooperation and provides opportunities for the business communities and themes on promoting the reciprocal cooperation and common development of China and ASEAN.

Since 2004, the CAEXPO has been successfully staged for five years in a row.

This grand event has greatly promoted the bilateral exchanges and cooperation in different fields between China and ASEAN, which is thus of great significance within the China-ASEAN region.

15.1 Proposal of CAEXPO

The idea of China-ASEAN Free Trade Area was put forward in 2001. At the beginning of 2002 the Research Institute of Southeast Asia of the Academy of Social Sciences of Guangxi undertook two projects: the Study on the Establishment of China-ASEAN FTA in Guangxi entrusted by the Planning Committee of the Guangxi Zhuang Autonomous Region, and Opportunities and Challenges—the Strategies of the Establishment of China-ASEAN FTA in Guangxi. On this basis, the book on China-ASEAN

FTA and Guangxi was published.[3] It concluded in the book that "Guangxi enjoys the unique geographical advantage in Southeast Asia, and we should take this advantage to set up the bridge for the commodity trading, information collecting, talent cultivating, and cultural exchanging between China and ASEAN ", and "We should have fairs or expositions annually together with the forums, cooperation, trades or business specially for Southeast Asian countries so that the businessmen of ASEAN will come to Guangxi every year. It can not only promote the commercial relations between Guangxi, China, and ASEAN, but also can promote the business in Guangxi or abroad".

The first China (Guangxi)-Southeast Asia Economic Cooperation Forum was held in Nanning, which is the capital of Guangxi of China, from November 21 – 22 , 2002. It was launched by the Research Institutes of Southeast Asia of the Academy of Social Sciences of Guangxi, sponsored by the People's Government of the Guangxi Zhuang Autonomous Region, and undertaken by the Academy of Social Sciences of Guangxi. About 400 people attended the forum. They are the officials, senior scholars, the entrepreneurs and the news media reporters from the ASEAN Secretariat, Southeast Asia countries such as Singapore, Thailand, Vietnam, Cambodia, Laos, and other international organizations, and from the provinces of China as Beijing, Shanghai, Guangdong, Guangxi, Fujian, Hainan, Sichuan, Guizhou, Yunnan, Hong Kong, Taiwan and Macao. That is the first international symposium on China-ASEAN FTA undertaken by the Chinese local government since it was decided to establish the China-ASEAN FTA within 10 years at the 5th section of ASEAN and "10 + 1" China-ASEAN Summit in November, 2001. Li Zhaozhuo, the Chairman of Guangxi Zhuang Autonomous Region, attended the conference and made the opening speech. Gao Hucheng, Vice Chairman, made the closing speech. Many experts and scholars in the forum put forward their ideas and suggestions that the CAEXPO or something similar should be established in Guangxi.

In February, 2003, China-ASEAN official meetings and China-ASEAN summit forum were held in Guilin, Guangxi. Many representatives also put forward the similar ideas and suggestions.

Therefore, the Government of Guangxi Zhuang Autonomous Region presented the report of CAEXPO to the Commerce Department of the People's Republic of China after a thorough consideration. On August 9, 2003, the Government of Guangxi Zhuang Autonomous Region got the reply of the Commerce Department about the approval of CAEXPO.[4] On October 8, 2003, proposed by Wen Jiabao, Premier of China, at the 7th China-ASEAN ("10 +1") Leaders' Summit held on Bali Island, Indonesia, CAEXPO becomes an annual event convened in Nanning, Guangxi, China since the year 2004. As a pragmatic endeavor to promote the construction of the China-ASEAN Free Trade Area, this proposal was well received by the heads of state/government of the 10 ASEAN countries and was written into the Chairman's Statement released afterwards.

The annual CAEXPO held in Nanning Guangxi is the great results of the elaborated planning and wholeheartedly bidding by the Party Committee and the People's Government of Guangxi, and of the great concern to Guangxi shown by the Central of Committee of the CPC. No doubt, Guangxi is the best site for CAEXPO. The reasons are as follows.

First, Guangxi located in the center of China-ASEAN FTA has its particular geographical advantages. As it is only 100 more kilometers from Vietnam to Nanning, it is convenient for the gathering and collecting of the personnel, goods and information at the annual exposition. It can save time and money.

Second, Guangxi plays an important role in the China-ASEAN FTA and has become the platform for the economic and cultural exchanges and cooperation between China and ASEAN. It has the significant position as a bridge, gateway, stage and the logistics center for China-ASEAN.

Third, Guangxi has laid a solid foundation in the 50 years' construction of the transportation, communication, and infrastructure, especially during the 30-year economy reform in China. Since the early 1990s, Guangxi has been constructed as the sea channel for the southwest of China. It is very convenient for the transportation with railways, highways, ports, airports at advanced level.

Fourth, Guangxi has a close relationship in humanities with Southeast Asian countries, where a large number of overseas Chinese of Guangxi inhabit. A state-owned training base for the Southeast Asian languages has been set up in the Foreign Language Institute of Guangxi University for Nationalities. It can provide rich resources of human talents, majoring in the languages of Laos, Thailand, Vietnam and so on. They act as the translators and interpreters for businessmen. CAEXPO can get along successfully without the obstacles of languages and customs.

Moreover, Nanning, the capital of Guangxi, with convenient transportation and perfect functions, is the center of the politics, economy, culture, science technology, finance and information, and is the great gateway towards Southeast Asia. It is a most proper permanent site of CAEXPO. In particular, Nanning enjoys the reputation of "the Green City of China" with trees and flowers everywhere. Nanning has possessed the facilities to host the large international exposition through the implementation of the construction projects in recent years. Now roads have been greatly expanded, and the magnificent convention center has been built. Nanning has become a beautiful modern city.

15.2 The Contents and Purpose of CAEXPO

 CAEXPO—High-levelled, Large-scaled Comprehensive International Exposition

On December 17, 2003, it was announced in the press conference in Beijing by the Information Office of the State Council that CAEXPO would be held in November annually in Nanning, the capital of Guangxi, since the year 2004.[5] Lu Bing, Chairman of Guangxi Zhuang Autonomous Region, and An Min, Vice Minister of the Commerce Department of China, made a speech on CAEXPO to the reporters at home and abroad.

CAEXPO is sponsored by the Ministry of Commerce of China and the Economy and Trade Departments of the ASEAN countries and undertaken by the People's Government of Guangxi Zhuang Autonomous Region. It is a high-levelled, large-scaled, integrated international trade fair which themes on goods exhibition and trade negotiation, forums, cultural exchange, etc. and aims at promoting the reciprocal cooperation and common development of China and ASEAN.

At the news conference in Beijing, Lu Bing said that CAEXPO would be a platform for commerce and communication, where we could have goods trading, funding circulation, investments and cooperation, and government officials, experts, scholars and elites could have dialogues, presenting their suggestions for the current and future of China-ASEAN FTA. Moreover, CAEXPO would be a platform for cultural exchanges. The Nanning International Folk Song Festival held simultaneously with CAEXPO would provide a colorful stage for the artists from China and ASEAN and all over the world.[6]

 CAEXPO—Platform for Promoting Exchanges and Cooperation within China-ASEAN Regions

Based on the Framework Agreement on China-ASEAN Comprehensive Economic Cooperation, CAEXPO is subject to the exchanges and cooperations in trade and investment. Its aim is to promote the construction of China-ASEAN FTA, strive for mutual benefits and common prosperity, provide and share opportunities for the business communities within the China-ASEAN regions.

(1) **A platform for exchanges and cooperation**

CAEXPO is a platform for cooperation and development for China-ASEAN regions, which has multi-functions as goods displays, trade negotiation, forums, and cultural exchanges. It provides the opportunities for the government officials, entrepreneurs, experts, scholars, and people from all walks of life to get together annually to have their exchanges and cooperation with their abilities and specialty.

(2) The attraction of trade, investment and tourism within China-ASEAN

On October 7, 2003, Premier Wen Jiabao made a speech at the first China-ASEAN Summit on the commerce and investment held in Bali Island, Indonesia. In his speech titled as the Development of China and the Revitalization of Asia, he pointed out that building up the good relationship with the neighboring ASEAN regions is an important part of the development strategies of China. The friendly, harmonious and wealthy neighboring relationship can promote the regional stability, maintain the regional peace and enhance mutual trust, strengthen the regional and sub-regional cooperation, deepen the regional economic integration, and realize common development of the regional countries. As a result, the neighboring countries can become harmonious and wealthy together.

The annual CAEXPO will greatly increase the mutual understanding between China and ASEAN. The participants can get the firsthand information and opportunities of business and tourism, therefore it can increase the volumes of trade and investment, stimulate the tourism and consumption, and promote mutual friendly cooperation and the economic development greatly.

(3) The promotion of the establishment of China-ASEAN FTA

It is a complementary relationship between China-ASEAN FTA and CAEXPO. The former is the foundation, the latter, in turn, promotes the development of the former. In the annual fair the participants—countries, enterprises and individuals all can get benefits. At the same time, the partners of China-ASEAN FTA can meet in the fair every year, sharing the trade information, solving problems, putting forward the new plan, and reaching a new cooperation agreement.

(4) The stimulation of the development of Guangxi

By hosting CAEXPO, we can set up five platforms, e. g. information, trade, finance, human resources, public affairs to promote the opening-up and development of Guangxi. The fair will attract various kinds of high quality goods and high-tech equipment to Nanning, together with a large number of government officials, entrepreneurs, representatives of the chambers, experts and scholars, and media reporters. They will bring investment projects, with lots of trade information, and will trade, invest and travel in Guangxi. At the same time, cooperation of agriculture, energy, mining, tourism and services between Guangxi and ASEAN will be speeded up, which will make the opening up of Guangxi to a higher level, and push the economy of Guangxi a great leap forward.

CAEXPO will make Nanning into an international metropolis. As we know, modern municipal constructions and exhibition facilities, especially the human resources are needed for the high-level international fair. With the annual CAEXPO, Nanning will become a metropolis in South China and in Asia as well. In the aspects of goods distribution, information communication, talent cultivation and urban construction, transportation, tourism, services, etc., Nanning will strive forward to the world.

15.3 The First China-ASEAN Expo

In recent years, political ties between China and ASEAN nations have been developing and expanding smoothly, while marked progress has been made in bilateral trade, two-way investment, project contracting and labor services. Bilateral trade between China and ASEAN has been growing at an annual rate of 20% since 1990. In 2003, trade volume between China and ASEAN reached US$78.2 billion, a rise of 42.8% over the previous year. ASEAN has become China's fifth largest trading partner in the past 11 consecutive years.

The first China-ASEAN Expo was held from November 3 -6, 2004, in Nanning, with the signing of millions of US dollars contracts. During the four-day Expo, Chinese and foreign companies signed 129 contracts worth nearly US$5 billion, and Chinese domestic investors inked 102 contracts worth 47.5 billion *yuan* (US$5.75 billion) with their domestic partners. The total contractual investment includes US$493 million from Chinese investors to overseas projects, setting up 2,506 booths for 1,505 exhibiting enterprises, attracting 18,000 exhibitors and trade visitors, among whom, 4,000 purchasers came from outbound China. 210 categories of exhibits were showcased, covering 11 sectors, including machinery & equipment, household appliances, ICT (Information and Communication Technology) products, automobile & parts, hardware & mineral products, building materials, agro-based products, medical & healthcare products, chemical raw materials, light industrial products and arts & crafts, garment & textiles, etc. 757 booths were used by enterprises from the 10 ASEAN countries and other countries/regions outside China, taking up 42.9% of the total. A trading volume of US$1.084 billion was concluded, among which, US$875 million was the export volume, US$110 million, the import volume, and the rest US$99 million, the Chinese domestic trading volume. More than 1,500 companies from China, ASEAN member nations and other countries participated in the expo. Among them, 19 companies are from World's Top 500.

During the CAEXPO, 26 promotion conferences on investment projects were held, where 129 international investment cooperation projects were contracted, worth US$4.968 billion, and 102 Chinese domestic cooperation projects were contracted, amounting to 48.54 billion *yuan*. Distinguished guests made their presence at this event. The Expo, along with a China-ASEAN investment summit and promotions, covers sectors such as machinery, electronic home appliance, information technology, automobile, construction material, agricultural products, medicine and textile. The Expo was a "great success" and "paved the way for the building of ASEAN-China free trade area", said Pengiran Mashor Pengiran Ahmad, deputy secretary-general of the ASEAN Secretariat.

China and ASEAN Expo was set to forge free trade area in 2010, which will be the world's third largest FTA with a 1.7-billion population, 2-trillion-US-dollars gross domestic product and US$1.2-trillion trade volume, following the European Union and North American Free Trade Agreement. The China-ASEAN Expo was scheduled to be held in Nanning annually, in a bid to promote the common prosperity of the two sides.

The 1st China-ASEAN Expo was a large-scale regional exposition with 2,506 standard booths, equivalent to 50,000 m^2. 1,505 enterprises and over 8,000 exhibitors attended the 1st China-ASEAN Expo, including 516 from outside mainland China, 260 influential branded enterprises, and 19 companies of the World's Top 500.

The 1st China-ASEAN Business & Investment Summit was jointly sponsored by the China Council for the Promotion of International Trade, the Ministry of Commerce of the People's Republic of China and the People's Government of Guangxi Zhuang Autonomous Region. The Summit was successfully held along with the 1st China-ASEAN Expo and was the grandest event of the year in the business and investment fields in China and the ASEAN countries.

From then on, 12 expositions have been held successfully. And the 12th CAEXPO is to be held on September 18 – 20, 2015.

Notes

[1] 中国-东盟博览会是由中国国务院总理温家宝倡议,由中国和东盟10国经贸主管部门及东盟秘书处共同主办,广西壮族自治区人民政府承办的国家级、国际性经贸交流盛会,每年在广西南宁举办。

[2] 中国-东盟博览会基于《中国与东盟全面经济合作框架协议》,以"促进中国-东盟自由贸易区建设、共享合作与发展机遇"为宗旨。

[3] 2002年年初,广西社会科学院东南亚研究所先后承担了广西壮族自治区计划委员会委托的"建立中国-东盟自由贸易区广西对策研究"和广西社会科学院"中国-东盟自由贸易区的建立对广西的机遇和挑战及我们的对策研究"两大课题,并在此基础上出版了《中国-东盟自由贸易区与广西》一书。

[4] 广西壮族自治区人民政府听取各方面的意见,正式向中华人民共和国商务部提出申办中国-东盟博览会的报告。2003年8月9日的《商务部关于同意广西壮族自治区承办中国-东盟博览会的复函》批准同意由广西壮族自治区人民政府承办中国-东盟博览会。

[5] 2003年12月17日,国务院新闻办公室在北京举行了中国-东盟博览会新闻发布会,正式向外界宣布,从2004年起,每年11月在广西首府南宁举办中国-东盟博览会。

[6] 广西是歌仙刘三姐的故乡。与博览会同期举办的南宁国际民歌节,将为来自中国与东盟及世界各国的艺术家提供尽情展示本国文化风采的舞台。

Exercises

1. **Explain the following in English.**
   (1) CAEXPO
   (2) China-ASEAN FTA
   (3) ASEAN
   (4) The 1st China-ASEAN Business & Investment Summit
   (5) CEO

2. **Fill in the blanks.**
   (1) At the 7th _____ on October 8, 2003, Premier Wen Jiabao of the People's Republic of China proposed that a China-ASEAN Expo (CAEXPO) be held _____ Guangxi, China from the year _____.
   (2) The China-ASEAN Expo is _____ by Premier Wen Jiabao, _____ by China and the 10 ASEAN countries as well as the ASEAN Secretariat, _____ by the Government of Guangxi Zhuang Autonomous Region, is an international trade fair.
   (3) It is based on _____ on China-ASEAN Comprehensive Economic Co-operation, with the sole objective of promoting to build _____, and striving for _____ benefits and _____ prosperity.
   (4) Up to 2008, the CAEXPO has been successfully staged for _____ years in a row since _____.
   (5) _____ held simultaneously with _____ would provide a colorful stage for the artists from China and ASEAN and all over the world.

3. **Answer the following questions.**
   (1) Why is Nanning of Guangxi considered as the best site for CASEAN Expo?
   (2) What are the themes and objectives of CASEAN Expo?
   (3) What is the significance to establish the China-ASEAN FTA?
   (4) What are the prominent achievements of the first CASEAN Expo?
   (5) What is the significance of the successful holding of the first CASEAN Expo?

4. Discussion.

(1) How can we speed up the establishment of China-ASEAN FTA?

(2) How can we take the advantages of CASEAN Expo to promote the economy development of Guangxi?

APPENDIX

China-ASEAN Documents

I. ASEAN Important Documents

1. Bangkok Declaration (Bangkok, 8 August, 1967)

The Presidium Minister for Political Affairs/ Minister for Foreign Affairs of Indonesia, the Deputy Prime Minister of Malaysia, the Secretary of Foreign Affairs of the Philippines, the Minister for Foreign Affairs of Singapore and the Minister of Foreign Affairs of Thailand:

MINDFUL of the existence of mutual interests and common problems among countries of South-East Asia and convinced of the need to strengthen further the existing bonds of regional solidarity and cooperation;

DESIRING to establish a firm foundation for common action to promote regional cooperation in South-East Asia in the spirit of equality and partnership and thereby contribute towards peace, progress and prosperity in the region;

CONSCIOUS that in an increasingly interdependent world, the cherished ideals of peace, freedom, social justice and economic well-being are best attained by fostering good understanding, good neighbourliness and meaningful cooperation among the countries of the region already bound together by ties of history and culture;

CONSIDERING that the countries of SouthEast Asia share a primary responsibility for strengthening the economic and social stability of the region and ensuring their peacefull and progressive national development, and that they are determined to ensure their stability and security from external interference in any form or manifestation in order to preserve their national identities in accordance with the ideals and aspirations of their peoples;

AFFIRMING that all foreign bases are temporary and remain only with the expressed concurrence of the countries concerned and are not intended to be used directly or indirectly to subvert the national independence and freedom of States in the area or prejudice the orderly processes of their national development;

DO HEREBY DECLARE:

FIRST, the establishment of an Association for Regional Cooperation among the countries of South-East Asia to be known as the Association of South-East Asian Nations (ASEAN).

SECOND, that the aims and purposes of the Association shall be:
(1) To accelerate the economic growth, social progress and cultural development in the region through joint endeavours in the spirit of equality and partnership in order to strengthen the foundation for a prosperous and peaceful community of South-East Asian Nations;
(2) To promote regional peace and stability through abiding respect for justice and the rule of law in the relationship among countries of the region and adherence to the principles of the United Nations Charter;
(3) To promote active collaboration and mutual assistance on matters of common interest in the economic, social, cultural, technical, scientific and administrative fields;
(4) To provide assistance to each other in the form of training and research facilities in the educational, professional, technical and administrative spheres;
(5) To collaborate more effectively for the greater utilization of their agriculture and industries, the expansion of their trade, including the study of the problems of international commodity trade, the improvement of their transportation and communications facilities and the raising of the living standards of their peoples;
(6) To promote South-East Asian studies;
(7) To maintain close and beneficial cooperation with existing international and regional organizations with similar aims and purposes, and explore all avenues for even closer cooperation among themselves.

THIRD, that to carry out these aims and purposes, the following machinery shall be established:
(1) Annual Meeting of Foreign Ministers, which shall be by rotation and referred to as ASEAN Ministerial Meeting. Special Meetings of Foreign Ministers may be convened as required.
(2) A Standing Committee, under the chairmanship of the Foreign Minister of the host country or his representative and having as its members the accredited Ambassadors of the other member countries, to carry on the work of the Association in between Meetings of Foreign Ministers.
(3) Ad-Hoc Committees and Permanent Committees of specialists and officials on specific subjects.
(4) A National Secretariat in each member country to carry out the work of the Association on behalf of that country and to service the Annual or Special Meetings of Foreign Ministers, the Standing Committee and such other committees as may hereafter be established.

FOURTH, that the Association is open for participation to all States in the South-East Asian Region subscribing to the aforementioned aims, principles and purposes.

FIFTH, that the Association represents the collective will of the nations of South-East Asia to bind themselves together in friendship and cooperation and, through joint efforts and sacrifices, secure for their peoples and for posterity the blessings of peace, freedom and prosperity.

DONE in Bangkok on the Eighth Day of August in the Year One Thousand Nine Hundred and Sixty-Seven.

For the Republic of Indonesia

ADAM MALIK
Minister for Political
Minister for Foreign Affairs

For the Republic of Singapore:

S.RAJARATMAN
Minister of Foreign Affairs

For Malaysia

TOM ABDOL RAZAK
Deputy Prime Minister
Minister of Defence and
Minister of National Development

For the Kingdom of Thailand:

THAMAT KHOMAN
Minister of Foreign Affairs

For the Republic of the Philippines:

MARCISO RAMOS
Secretary of Foreign Affairs

2. Treaty of Amity and Cooperation in Southeast Asia (Indonesia, February 24, 1976)

The High Contracting Parties:

CONSCIOUS of the existing ties of history, geography and culture, which have bound their peoples together;

ANXIOUS to promote regional peace and stability through abiding respect for justice and the rule or law and enhancing regional resilience in their relations;

DESIRING to enhance peace, friendship and mutual cooperation on matters affecting Southeast Asia consistent with the spirit and principles of the Charter of the United Nations, the Ten Principles adopted by the Asian-African Conference in Bandung on April 25, 1955, the Declaration of the Association of Southeast Asian Nations signed in Bangkok on August 8, 1967, and the Declaration signed in Kuala Lumpur on November 27, 1971;

CONVINCED that the settlement of differences or disputes between their countries should be regulated by rational, effective and sufficiently flexible procedures, avoiding negative attitudes which might endanger or hinder cooperation;

BELIEVING in the need for cooperation with all peace-loving nations, both within and outside Southeast Asia, in the furtherance of world peace, stability and harmony;

SOLEMNLY AGREE to enter into a Treaty of Amity and Cooperation as follows:

CHAPTER Ⅰ: PURPOSE AND PRINCIPLES

Article 1

The purpose of this Treaty is to promote perpetual peace, everlasting amity and cooperation among their peoples which would contribute to their strength, solidarity and closer relationship.

Article 2

In their relations with one another, the High Contracting Parties shall be guided by the following fundamental principles:

(1) Mutual respect for the independence, sovereignty, equality, territorial integrity and national identity of all nations;

(2) The right of every State to lead its national existence free from external interference, subversion or coercion;

(3) Non-interference in the internal affairs of one another;

(4) Settlement of differences or disputes by peaceful means;

(5) Renunciation of the threat or use of force;

(6) Effective cooperation among themselves.

CHAPTER Ⅱ: AMITY

Article 3

In pursuance of the purpose of this Treaty the High Contracting Parties shall endeavour to develop and strengthen the traditional, cultural and historical ties of friendship, good neighbourliness and cooperation which bind them together and shall fulfill in good faith the obligations assumed under this Treaty. In order to promote closer understanding among them, the High Contracting Parties shall encourage and facilitate contact and intercourse among their peoples.

CHAPTER Ⅲ: COOPERATION

Article 4

The High Contracting Parties shall promote active cooperation in the economic, social, technical, scientific and administrative fields as well as in matters of common ideals and aspirations of international peace and stability in the region and all other matters of common interest.

Article 5

Pursuant to Article 4 the High Contracting Parties shall exert their maximum efforts multilaterally as well as bilaterally on the basis of equality, non-discrimination and mutual benefit.

Article 6

The High Contracting Parties shall collaborate for the acceleration of the economic growth in the region in order to strengthen the foundation for a prosperous and peaceful community of nations in Southeast Asia. To this end, they shall promote the greater utilization of their agriculture and industries, the expansion of their trade and the improvement of their economic infrastructure for the mutual benefit of their peoples. In this regard, they shall continue to explore all avenues for close and beneficial cooperation with other States as well as international and regional organisations outside the region.

Article 7

The High Contracting Parties, in order to achieve social justice and to raise the standards of living of the peoples of the region, shall intensify economic cooperation. For this purpose, they shall adopt appropriate regional strategies for economic development and mutual assistance.

Article 8

The High Contracting Parties shall strive to achieve the closest cooperation on the widest scale and shall seek to provide assistance to one another in the form of training and research facilities in the social, cultural, technical, scientific and administrative fields.

Article 9

The High Contracting Parties shall endeavour to foster cooperation in the furtherance of the cause of peace, harmony, and stability in the region. To this end, the High Contracting Parties shall maintain regular contacts and consultations with one another on international and regional matters with a view to coordinating their views actions and policies.

Article 10

Each High Contracting Party shall not in any manner or form participate in any activity which shall constitute a threat to the political and economic stability, sovereignty, or territorial integrity of another High Contracting Party.

Article 11

The High Contracting Parties shall endeavour to strengthen their respective national resilience in their political, economic, socio-cultural as well as security fields in conformity with their respective ideals and aspirations, free from external interference as well as internal subversive activities in order to preserve their respective national identities.

Article 12

The High Contracting Parties in their efforts to achieve regional prosperity and security, shall endeavour to cooperate in all fields for the promotion of regional resilience, based on the principles of self-confidence, self-reliance, mutual respect, cooperation and solidarity which will constitute the foundation for a strong and viable community of nations in Southeast Asia.

CHAPTER IV: PACIFIC SETTLEMENT OF DISPUTES

Article 13

The High Contracting Parties shall have the determination and good faith to prevent disputes from arising. In case disputes on matters directly affecting them should arise, especially disputes likely to disturb regional peace and harmony, they shall refrain from the threat or use of force and shall at all times settle such disputes among themselves through friendly negotiations.

Article 14

To settle disputes through regional processes, the High Contracting Parties shall constitute, as a continuing body, a High Council comprising a Representative at ministerial level from each of the High Contracting Parties to take cognizance of the existence of disputes or situations likely to disturb regional peace and harmony.

Article 15

In the event no solution is reached through direct negotiations, the High Council shall take cognizance of the dispute or the situation and shall recommend to the parties in dispute appropriate means of settlement such as good offices, mediation, inquiry or conciliation. The High Council may however offer its good offices, or upon agreement of the parties in dispute, constitute itself into a committee of mediation, inquiry or conciliation. When deemed necessary, the High Council shall recommend appropriate measures for the prevention of a deterioration of the dispute or the situation.

Article 16

The foregoing provision of this Chapter shall not apply to a dispute unless all the parties to the dispute agree to their application to that dispute. However, this shall not preclude the other High Contracting Parties not to party the dispute from offering all possible assistance to settle the said dispute. Parties to the dispute should be well disposed towards such offers of assistance.

Article 17

Nothing in this Treaty shall preclude recourse to the modes of peaceful settlement contained in Article 33(1) of the Charter of the United Nations. The High Contracting Parties which are parties to a dispute should be encouraged to take initiatives to solve it by friendly negotiations before resorting to the other procedures provided for in the Charter of the United Nations.

CHAPTER V: GENERAL PROVISION

Article 18

This Treaty shall be signed by the Republic of Indonesia, Malaysia, the Republic of the Philippines, the Republic of Singapore and the Kingdom of Thailand. It shall be ratified in accordance with the constitutional procedures of each signatory State. It shall be open for accession by other States in Southeast Asia.

Article 19

This Treaty shall enter into force on the date of the deposit of the fifth instrument of ratification with the Governments of the signatory States which are designated Depositories of this Treaty and the instruments of ratification or accession.

For the Republic of Indonesia:

SOEHARTO
President

For the Republic of Singapore:

LEE KUAN YEW
Prime Minister

For Malaysia:

DA TUK HUSEIN ONN
Prime Minister

For the Kingdom of Thailand:

KUKRIT PRAMOJ
Prime Minister

For the Republic of the Philippines:

FERDIN AND E. MARCOS

Article 20

This Treaty is drawn up in the official languages of the High Contracting Parties, all of which are equally authoritative. There shall be an agreed common translation of the texts in the English language. Any divergent interpretation of the common text shall be settled by negotiation.

IN FAITH THEREOF the High Contracting Parties have signed the Treaty and have hereto affixed their Seals.

DONE at Denpasar, Bali, this twenty-fourth day of February in the year one thousand nine hundred and seventy-six.

3. Declaration of ASEAN Concord

Declaration of ASEAN Concord

Indonesia, 24 February 1976

The President of the Republic of Indonesia, the Prime Minister of Malaysia, the President of the Republic of the Philippines, the Prime Minister of the Republic of Singapore and the Prime Minister of the Kingdom of Thailand:

REAFFIRM their commitment to the Declarations of Bandung, Bangkok and Kuala Lumpur, and the Charter of the United Nations;

ENDEAVOUR to promote peace, progress, prosperity and the welfare of the peoples of member states;

UNDERTAKE to consolidate the achievements of ASEAN and expand ASEAN cooperation in the economic, social, cultural and political fields;

DO HEREBY DECLARE:

ASEAN cooperation shall take into account, among others, the following objectives and principles in the pursuit of political stability:

(1) The stability of each member state and of the ASEAN region is an essential contribution to international peace and security. Each member state resolves to eliminate threats posed by subversion to its stability, thus strengthening national and ASEAN resilience.

(2) Member states, individually and collectively, shall take active steps for the early establishment of the Zone of Peace, Freedom and Neutrality.

(3) The elimination of poverty, hunger, disease and illiteracy is a primary concern of member states. They shall therefore intensify cooperation in economic and social development, with particular emphasis on the promotion of social justice and on the improvement of the living standards of their peoples.

(4) Natural disasters and other major calamities can retard the pace of development of member states. They shall extend, within their capabilities, assistance for relief of member states in distress.

(5) Member states shall take cooperative action in their national and regional development programmes, utilizing as far as possible the resources available in the ASEAN region to broaden the complementarity of their respective economies.

(6) Member states, in the spirit of ASEAN solidarity, shall rely exclusively on peaceful processes in the settlement of intra-regional differences.

(7) Member states shall strive, individually and collectively, to create conditions conducive to the promotion of peaceful cooperation among the nations of Southeast Asia on the basis of mutual respect and mutual benefit.

(8) Member states shall vigorously develop an awareness of regional identity and exert all efforts to create a strong ASEAN community, respected by all and respecting all nations on the basis of mutually advantageous relationships, and in accordance with the principles of selfdetermination, sovereign equality and non-interference in the internal affairs of nations.

AND DO HEREBY ADOPT

The following programme of action as a framework for ASEAN cooperation.

A. POLITICAL

(1) Meeting of the Heads of Government of the member states as and when necessary.

(2) Signing of the Treaty of Amity and Cooperation in Southeast Asia.

(3) Settlement of intra-regional disputes by peaceful means as soon as possible.

(4) Immediate consideration of initial steps towards recognition of and respect for the Zone of Peace, Freedom and Neutrality wherever possible.

(5) Improvement of ASEAN machinery to strengthen political cooperation.

(6) Study on how to develop judicial cooperation including the possibility of an ASEAN Extradition Treaty.

(7) Strengthening of political solidarity by promoting the harmonization of views, coordinating position and, where possible and desirable, taking common actions.

B. ECONOMIC

(1) Cooperation on Basic Commodities, particularly Food and Energy

　i) Member states shall assist each other by according priority to the supply of the individual country's needs in critical circumstances, and priority to the acquisition of exports from member states, in respect of basic commodities, particularly food and energy.

　ii) Member states shall also intensify cooperation in the production of basic commodities particularly food and energy in the individual member states of the region.

(2) Industrial Cooperation

　i) Member states shall cooperate to establish lae-scale ASEAN industrial plants particularly to meet regional requirements of essential commodities.

　ii) Priority shall be given to projects which utilize the available materials in the member states, contribute to the increase of food production, increase foreign exchange earnings or save foreign exchange and create employment.

(3) Cooperation in Trade

　i) Member states shall cooperate in the fields of trade in order to promote development and growth of new production and trade and to improve the trade structures of individual states and among countries of ASEAN conducive to further development and to safeguard and increase their foreign exchange earnings and reserves.

ii) Member states shall progress towards the establishment of preferential trading arrangements as a long term objective on a basis deemed to be at any particular time appropriate through rounds of negotiations subject to the unanimous agreement of member states.

iii) The expansion of trade among member states shall be facilitated through cooperation on basic commodities, particularly in food and energy and through cooperation in ASEAN industrial projects.

iv) Member states shall accelerate joint efforts to improve access to markets outside ASEAN for their raw material and finished products by seeking the elimination of all trade barriers in those markets, developing new usage for these products and in adopting common approaches and actions in dealing with regional groupings and individual economic powers.

v) Such efforts shall also lead to cooperation in the field of technology and production methods in order to increase the production and to improve the quality of export products, as well as to develop new export products with a view to diversifying exports.

(4) Joint Approach to International Commodity Problems and Other World Economic Problems

i) The principle of ASEAN cooperation on trade shall also be reflected on a priority basis in joint approaches to international commodity problems and other world economic problems such as the reform of international trading system, the reform on international monetary system and transfer of real resources, in the United Nations and other relevant multilateral fora, with a view to contributing to the establishment of the New International Economic Order.

ii) Member states shall give priority to the stabilisation and increase of export earnings of those commodities produced and exported by them through commodity agreements including bufferstock schemes and other means.

(5) Machinery for Economic Cooperation

Ministerial meetings on economic matters shall be held regularly or as deemed necessary in order to:

i) formulate recommendations for the consideration of Governments of member states for the strengthening of ASEAN economic cooperation;

ii) exchange views and consult on national development plans and policies as a step towards harmonizing regional development; and

iii) perform such other relevant functions as agreed upon by the member Governments.

C. SOCIAL

(1) Cooperation in the field of social development, with emphasis on the well-being of the low-income group and of the rural population, through the expansion of opportunities for productive employment with fair remuneration.

(2) Support for the active involvement of all sectors and levels of the ASEAN communities, particularly the women and youth, in development efforts.

(3) Intensification and expansion of existing cooperation in meeting the problems of population growth in the ASEAN region, and where possible, formulation of new strategies in collaboration with appropriate international agencies.

(4) Intensification of cooperation among members states as well as with the relevant international bodies in the prevention and eradication of the abuse of narcotics and the illegal trafficking of drugs.

D. CULTURAL AND INFORMATION

(1) Introduction of the study of ASEAN, its member states and their national languages as part of the curricula of schools and other institutions of learning in the member states.

(2) Support of ASEAN scholars, writers, artists and mass media representatives to enable them to play an active role in fostering a sense of regional identity and fellowship.

(3) Promotion of Southeast Asian studies through closer collaboration among national institutes.

E. SECURITY

Continuation of cooperation on a non-ASEAN basis between the member states in security matters in accordance with their mutual needs and interests.

F. IMPROVEMENT OF ASEAN MACHINERY

(1) Signing of the Agreement on the Establishment of the ASEAN Secretariat.

(2) Regular review of the ASEAN organizational structure with a view to improving its effectiveness.

(3) Study of the desirability of a new constitutional framework for ASEAN.

DONE, at Denpasar, Bali, this twenty-fourth day of February in the year one thousand nine hundred and seventy-six.

For the Republic of Indonesia:

SOEHARTO
President

For Malaysia:

DATUK HUSEIN ONN
Prime Minister

For the Republic of the Philippines:

FERDIN AND E. MARCOS

For the Republic of Singapore:

LEE KUAN YEW
Prime Minister

For the Kingdom of Thailand:

KUKRIT PRAMOJ
Prime Minister

II. China-ASEAN Important Documents

1. Framework Agreement on Comprehensive Economic Cooperation Between China and ASEAN (Phnom Penh, 5 November 2002)

PREAMBLE

WE, the Heads of Government/State of the People's Republic of China ("China"), and Brunei Darussalam, the Kingdom of Cambodia, the Republic of Indonesia, the Lao People's Democratic Republic ("Lao PDR"), Malaysia, the Union of Myanmar, the Republic of the Philippines, the Republic of Singapore, the Kingdom of Thailand and the Socialist Republic of Viet Nam, Member States of the Association of South East Asian Nations (collectively, "ASEAN" or "ASEAN Member States", or individually, "ASEAN Member State"):

RECALLING our decision made at the ASEAN-China Summit held on November 6, 2001 in Bandar Seri Begawan, Brunei Darussalam, regarding a Framework on Economic Co-operation and to establish a China-ASEAN Free Trade Area ("China-ASEAN FTA") within ten years with special and differential treatment and flexibility for the newer ASEAN Member States of Cambodia, Lao PDR, Myanmar and Viet Nam ("the newer ASEAN Member States") and with provision for an early harvest in which the list of products and services will be determined by mutual consultation;

DESIRING to adopt a Framework Agreement on Comprehensive Economic Co-operation ("this Agreement") between China and ASEAN (collectively, "the Parties", or individually referring to an ASEAN Member State or to China as a "Party") that is forward-looking in order to forge closer economic relations in the 21st century;

DESIRING to minimise barriers and deepen economic linkages between the Parties;

lower costs; increase intra-regional trade and investment; increase economic efficiency; create a larger market with greater opportunities and larger economies of scale for the businesses of the Parties; and enhance the attractiveness of the Parties to capital and talent;

BEING confident that the establishment of a China-ASEAN FTA will create a partnership between the Parties, and provide an important mechanism for strengthening co-operation and supporting economic stability in East Asia;

RECOGNISING the important role and contribution of the business sector in enhancing trade and investment between the Parties and the need to further promote and facilitate their co-operation and utilisation of greater business opportunities provided by the China-ASEAN FTA;

RECOGNISING the different stages of economic development among ASEAN Member States and the need for flexibility, in particular the need to facilitate the increasing participation of the newer ASEAN Member States in the China-ASEAN economic co-operation and the expansion of their exports, including, inter alia, through the strengthening of their domestic capacity, efficiency and competitiveness;

REAFFIRMING the rights, obligations and undertakings of the respective parties under the World Trade Organisation (WTO), and other multilateral, regional and bilateral agreements and arrangements;

RECOGNISING the catalytic role that regional trade arrangements can contribute towards accelerating regional and global liberalisation and as building blocks in the framework of the multilateral trading system;

HAVE AGREED AS FOLLOWS:

ARTICLE 1

Objectives

The objectives of this Agreement are to:

(a) strengthen and enhance economic, trade and investment co-operation between the Parties;

(b) progressively liberalise and promote trade in goods and services as well as create a transparent, liberal and facilitative investment regime;

(c) explore new areas and develop appropriate measures for closer economic co-operation between the Parties; and

(d) facilitate the more effective economic integration of the newer ASEAN Member States and bridge the development gap among the Parties.

ARTICLE 2

Measures for Comprehensive Economic Co-operation

The Parties agree to negotiate expeditiously in order to establish a China-ASEAN FTA within 10 years, and to strengthen and enhance economic co-operation through the following:

(a) progressive elimination of tariffs and non-tariff barriers in substantially all trade in goods;
(b) progressive liberalisation of trade in services with substantial sectoral coverage;
(c) establishment of an open and competitive investment regime that facilitates and promotes investment within the China-ASEAN FTA;
(d) provision of special and differential treatment and flexibility to the newer ASEAN Member States;
(e) provision of flexibility to the Parties in the China-ASEAN FTA negotiations to address their sensitive areas in the goods, services and investment sectors with such flexibility to be negotiated and mutually agreed based on the principle of reciprocity and mutual benefits;
(f) establishment of effective trade and investment facilitation measures, including, but not limited to, simplification of customs procedures and development of mutual recognition arrangements;
(g) expansion of economic co-operation in areas as may be mutually agreed between the Parties that will complement the deepening of trade and investment links between the Parties and formulation of action plans and programmes in order to implement the agreed sectors/areas of co-operation; and
(h) establishment of appropriate mechanisms for the purposes of effective implementation of this Agreement.

PART 1

ARTICLE 3

Trade in Goods

(1) In addition to the Early Harvest Programme under Article 6 of this Agreement, and with a view to expediting the expansion of trade in goods, the Parties agree to enter into negotiations in which duties and other restrictive regulations of commerce [except, where necessary, those permitted under Article XXIV (8) (b) of the WTO General Agreement on Tariffs and Trade (GATT)] shall be eliminated on substantially all trade in goods between the Parties.

(2) For the purposes of this Article, the following definitions shall apply unless the context otherwise requires:
　　(a) "ASEAN 6" refers to Brunei, Indonesia, Malaysia, the Philippines, Singapore and Thailand;
　　(b) "applied MFN tariff rates" shall include in-quota rates, and shall:
　　　　i) in the case of ASEAN Member States (which are WTO members as of 1 July 2003) and China, refer to their respective applied rates as of 1 July 2003; and
　　　　ii) in the case of ASEAN Member States (which are non-WTO members as

of 1 July 2003), refer to the rates as applied to China as of 1 July 2003;
(c) "non-tariff measures" shall include non-tariff barriers.
(3) The tariff reduction or elimination programme of the Parties shall require tariffs on listed products to be gradually reduced and where applicable, eliminated, in accordance with this Article.
(4) The products which are subject to the tariff reduction or elimination programme under this Article shall include all products not covered by the Early Harvest Programme under Article 6 of this Agreement, and such products shall be categorised into 2 Tracks as follows:
   (a) Normal Track: Products listed in the Normal Track by a Party on its own accord shall:
      i) have their respective applied MFN tariff rates gradually reduced or eliminated in accordance with specified schedules and rates (to be mutually agreed by the Parties) over a period from 1 January 2005 to 2010 for ASEAN 6 and China, and in the case of the newer ASEAN Member States, the period shall be from 1 January 2005 to 2015 with higher starting tariff rates and different staging; and
      ii) in respect of those tariffs which have been reduced but have not been eliminated under Paragraph 4(a) i) above, they shall be progressively eliminated within timeframes to be mutually agreed between the Parties.
   (b) Sensitive Track: Products listed in the Sensitive Track by a Party on its own accord shall:
      i) have their respective applied MFN tariff rates reduced in accordance with the mutually agreed end rates and end dates; and
      ii) where applicable, have their respective applied MFN tariff rates progressively eliminated within timeframes to be mutually agreed between the Parties.
(5) The number of products listed in the Sensitive Track shall be subject to a maximum ceiling to be mutually agreed among the Parties.
(6) The commitments undertaken by the Parties under this Article and Article 6 of this Agreement shall fulfil the WTO requirements to eliminate tariffs on substantially all the trade between the Parties.
(7) The specified tariff rates to be mutually agreed between the Parties pursuant to this Article shall set out only the limits of the applicable tariff rates or range for the specified year of implementation by the Parties and shall not prevent any Party from accelerating its tariff reduction or elimination if it so wishes to.
(8) The negotiations between the Parties to establish the China-ASEAN FTA covering trade in goods shall also include, but not be limited to the following:

(a) other detailed rules governing the tariff reduction or elimination programme for the Normal Track and the Sensitive Track as well as any other related matters, including principles governing reciprocal commitments, not provided for in the preceding paragraphs of this Article;

(b) Rules of Origin;

(c) treatment of out-of-quota rates;

(d) modification of a Party's commitments under the agreement on trade in goods based on Article XXVIII of the GATT;

(e) non-tariff measures imposed on any products covered under this Article or Article 6 of this Agreement, including, but not limited to quantitative restrictions or prohibition on the importation of any product or on the export or sale for export of any product, as well as scientifically unjustifiable sanitary and phytosanitary measures and technical barriers to trade;

(f) safeguards based on the GATT principles, including, but not limited to the following elements: transparency, coverage, objective criteria for action, including the concept of serious injury or threat thereof, and temporary nature;

(g) disciplines on subsidies and countervailing measures and anti-dumping measures based on the existing GATT disciplines; and

(h) facilitation and promotion of effective and adequate protection of trade-related aspects of intellectual property rights based on existing WTO, World Intellectual Property Organization (WIPO) and other relevant disciplines.

ARTICLE 4

Trade in Services

With a view to expediting the expansion of trade in services, the Parties agree to enter into negotiations to progressively liberalise trade in services with substantial sectoral coverage. Such negotiations shall be directed to:

(a) progressive elimination of substantially all discrimination between or among the Parties and/or prohibition of new or more discriminatory measures with respect to trade in services between the Parties, except for measures permitted under Article V(1)(b) of the WTO General Agreement on Trade in Services (GATS);

(b) expansion in the depth and scope of liberalisation of trade in services beyond those undertaken China and ASEAN Member States under the GATS; and

(c) enhanced co-operation in services between the Parties in order to improve efficiency and competitiveness, as well as to diversify the supply and distribution of services of the respective service suppliers of the Parties.

ARTICLE 5

Investment

To promote investments and to create a liberal, facilitative, transparent and competitive investment regime, the Parties agree to:

(a) enter into negotiations in order to progressively liberalise the investment regime;

(b) strengthen cooperation in investment, facilitate investment and improve transparency of investment rules and regulations; and

(c) provide for the protection of investments.

ARTICLE 6

Early Harvest

(1) With a view to accelerating the implementation of this Agreement, the Parties agree to implement an Early Harvest Programme (which is an integral part of the China-ASEAN FTA) for products covered under Paragraph 3(a) below and which will commence and end in accordance with the timeframes set out in this Article.

(2) For the purposes of this Article, the following definitions shall apply unless the context otherwise requires:

(a) "ASEAN 6" refers to Brunei, Indonesia, Malaysia, the Philippines, Singapore and Thailand;

(b) "applied MFN tariff rates" shall include in-quota rates, and shall:

i) in the case of ASEAN Member States (which are WTO members as of 1 July 2003) and China, refer to their respective applied rates as of 1 July 2003; and

ii) in the case of ASEAN Member States (which are non-WTO members as of 1 July 2003), refer to the tariff rates as applied to China as of 1 July 2003.

(3) The product coverage, tariff reduction and elimination, implementation timeframes, rules of origin, trade remedies and emergency measures applicable to the Early Harvest Programme shall be as follows:

(a) Product Coverage

i) All products in the following chapters at the 8/9 digit level (HS Code) shall be covered by the Early Harvest Programme, unless otherwise excluded by a Party in its Exclusion List as set out in Annex 1 of this Agreement, in which case these products shall be exempted for that Party:

Chapter Description

01 Live Animals

02 Meat and Edible Meat Offal

03 Fish

04 Dairy Products

05 Other Animals Products

06 Live Trees

07 Edible Vegetables

08 Edible Fruits and Nuts

ii) A Party which has placed products in the Exclusion List may, at any time, amend the Exclusion List to place one or more of these products under the Early Harvest Programme.

iii) The specific products set out in Annex 2 of this Agreement shall be covered by the Early Harvest Programme and the tariff concessions shall apply only to the parties indicated in Annex 2. These parties must have extended the tariff concessions on these products to each other.

iv) For those parties which are unable to complete the appropriate product lists in Annex 1 or Annex 2, the lists may still be drawn up no later than 1 March 2003 by mutual agreement.

(b) Tariff Reduction and Elimination

i) All products covered under the Early Harvest Programme shall be divided into 3 product categories for tariff reduction and elimination as defined and to be implemented in accordance with the timeframes set out in Annex 3 to this Agreement. This paragraph shall not prevent any Party from accelerating its tariff reduction or elimination if it so wishes.

ii) All products where the applied MFN tariff rates are at 0%, shall remain at 0%.

iii) Where the implemented tariff rates are reduced to 0%, they shall remain at 0%.

iv) A Party shall enjoy the tariff concessions of all the other parties for a product covered under Paragraph 3(a) i) above so long as the same product of that Party remains in the Early Harvest Programme under Paragraph 3(a) i) above.

(c) Interim Rules of Origin

The Interim Rules of Origin applicable to the products covered under the Early Harvest Programme shall be negotiated and completed by July 2003. The Interim Rules of Origin shall be superseded and replaced by the Rules of Origin to be negotiated and implemented by the Parties under Article 3(8)(b) of this Agreement.

(d) Application of WTO provisions

The WTO provisions governing modification of commitments, safeguard actions, emergency measures and other trade remedies, including antidumping and subsidies and countervailing measures, shall, in the interim, be applicable to the products covered under the Early Harvest Programme and shall be superseded and replaced by the relevant disciplines negotiated and agreed to by the Parties under Article 3(8) of this Agreement once these disciplines are implemented.

(4) In addition to the Early Harvest Programme for trade in goods as provided for in the preceding paragraphs of this Article, the Parties will explore the feasibility of an early harvest programme for trade in services in early 2003.

(5) With a view to promoting economic co-operation between the Parties, the activities set out in Annex 4 of this Agreement shall be undertaken or implemented on an accelerated basis, as the case may be.

PART 2

ARTICLE 7

Other Areas of Economic Co-operation

(1) The Parties agree to strengthen their cooperation in 5 priority sectors as follows:
   (a) agriculture;
   (b) information and communications technology;
   (c) human resources development;
   (d) investment; and
   (e) Mekong River basin development.

(2) Co-operation shall be extended to other areas, including, but not limited to, banking, finance, tourism, industrial cooperation, transport, telecommunications, intellectual property rights, small and medium enterprises (SMEs), environment, bio-technology, fishery, forestry and forestry products, mining, energy and sub-regional development.

(3) Measures to strengthen cooperation shall include, but shall not be limited to:
   (a) promotion and facilitation of trade in goods and services, and investment, such as:
      i) standards and conformity assessment;
      ii) technical barriers to trade/non-tariff measures; and
      iii) customs cooperation;
   (b) increasing the competitiveness of SMEs;
   (c) promotion of electronic commerce;
   (d) capacity building; and
   (e) technology transfer.

(4) The Parties agree to implement capacity building programmes and technical assistance, particularly for the newer ASEAN Member States, in order to adjust their economic structure and expand their trade and investment with China.

PART 3

ARTICLE 8

Timeframes

(1) For trade in goods, the negotiations on the agreement for tariff reduction or elimination and other matters as set out in Article 3 of this Agreement shall commence in early 2003 and be concluded by 30 June 2004 in order to establish the China-ASEAN FTA covering trade in goods by 2010 for Brunei, China, Indonesia, Malaysia, the Philippines, Singapore and Thailand, and by 2015 for the newer ASEAN Member States.

(2) The negotiations on the Rules of Origin for trade in goods under Article 3 of this Agreement shall be completed no later than December 2003.

(3) For trade in services and investments, the negotiations on the respective agreements shall commence in 2003 and be concluded as expeditiously as possible for implementation in accordance with the timeframes to be mutually agreed: (a) taking into account the sensitive sectors of the Parties; and (b) with special and differential treatment and flexibility for the newer ASEAN Member States.

(4) For other areas of economic cooperation under Part 2 of this Agreement, the Parties shall continue to build upon existing or agreed programmes set out in Article 7 of this Agreement, develop new economic co-operation programmes and conclude agreements on the various areas of economic co-operation. The Parties shall do so expeditiously for early implementation in a manner and at a pace acceptable to all the parties concerned. The agreements shall include timeframes for the implementation of the commitments therein.

ARTICLE 9

Most-Favoured Nation Treatment

China shall accord Most-Favoured Nation (MFN) Treatment consistent with the WTO rules and disciplines to all the non-WTO ASEAN Member States upon the date of signature of this Agreement.

ARTICLE 10

General Exceptions

Subject to the requirement that such measures are not applied in a manner which would constitute a means of arbitrary or unjustifiable discrimination between or among the Parties where the same conditions prevail, or a disguised restriction on trade within the China-ASEAN FTA, nothing in this Agreement shall prevent any Party from taking and adopting measures for the protection of its national security or the protection of articles of artistic, historic and archaeological value, or such other measures which it deems necessary for the protection of public morals, or for the protection of human, animal or plant life and health.

ARTICLE 11

Dispute Settlement Mechanism

(1) The Parties shall, within 1 year after the date of entry into force of this Agreement, establish appropriate formal dispute settlement procedures and mechanism for the purposes of this Agreement.

(2) Pending the establishment of the formal dispute settlement procedures and mechanism under Paragraph 1 above, any disputes concerning the interpretation, implementation or application of this Agreement shall be settled amicably by consultations and/or mediation.

ARTICLE 12

Institutional Arrangements for the Negotiations

(1) The China-ASEAN Trade Negotiation Committee (China-ASEAN TNC) that has been established shall continue to carry out the programme of negotiations set out in this Agreement.

(2) The Parties may establish other bodies as may be necessary to co-ordinate and implement any economic co-operation activities undertaken pursuant to this Agreement.

(3) The China-ASEAN TNC and any aforesaid bodies shall report regularly to the Minister of the Ministry of Foreign Trade and Economic Cooperation (MOFTEC) of China and the ASEAN Economic Ministers (AEM), through the meetings of the MOFTEC and ASEAN Senior Economic Officials (SEOM), on the progress and outcome of its negotiations.

(4) The ASEAN Secretariat and MOFTEC shall jointly provide the necessary secretariat support to the China-ASEAN TNC whenever and wherever negotiations are held.

ARTICLE 13

Miscellaneous Provisions

(1) This Agreement shall include the Annexes and the contents therein, and all future legal instruments agreed pursuant to this Agreement.

(2) Except as otherwise provided in this Agreement, this Agreement or any action taken under it shall not affect or nullify the rights and obligations of a Party under existing agreements to which it is a party.

(3) The Parties shall endeavour to refrain from increasing restrictions or limitations that would affect the application of this Agreement.

ARTICLE 14

Amendments

The provisions of this Agreement may be modified through amendments mutually agreed upon in writing by the Parties.

ARTICLE 15

Depositary

For the ASEAN Member States, this Agreement shall be deposited with the Secretary-General of ASEAN, who shall promptly furnish a certified copy thereof, to each ASEAN Member State.

ARTICLE 16

Entry into Force

(1) This Agreement shall enter into force on 1 July 2003.

(2) The Parties undertake to complete their internal procedures for the entry into force of this Agreement prior to 1 July 2003.

(3) Where a Party is unable to complete its internal procedures for the entry into force of this Agreement by 1 July 2003, the rights and obligations of that Party under this Agreement shall commence on the date of the completion of such internal procedures.

(4) A Party shall upon the completion of its internal procedures for the entry into force of this Agreement notify all the other parties in writing.

IN WITNESS WHEREOF, **WE** have signed this Framework Agreement on Comprehensive Economic Co-operation between the People's Republic of China and the Association of Southeast Asian Nations.

DONE at Phnom Penh, this 4th day of November, 2002 in duplicate copies in the English Language.

For Brunei Darussalam

HAJI HASSANAL BOLKIAH

Sultan of Brunei Darussalam

For the Kingdom of Cambodia

HUN SEN

Prime Minister

For the People's Republic of China

ZHU RONGJI

Premier

For the Republic of Indonesia

MEGAWATI SOEKARNOPUTRI

President

For the Lao People's Democratic Republic

BOUNNHANG VORACHITH

Prime Minister

For Malaysia

MAHATHIR BIN MOHAMAD
Prime Minister
For the Union of Myanmar
SENIOR GENERAL THAN SHWE
Chairman of the State Peace and Development Council and Prime Minister
For the Republic of the Philippines
GLORIA MACAPAGAL-ARROYO
President
For the Republic of Singapore
GOH CHOK TONG
Prime Minister
For the Kingdom of Thailand
pol. lt. col. THAKSIN SHINAWATRA
Prime Minister
For the Socialist Republic of Vietnam
PHAN VAN KHAI
Prime Minister

2. Declaration on the Conduct of Parties in the South China Sea

The Governments of the Member States of ASEAN and the Government of the People's Republic of China,

REAFFIRMING their determination to consolidate and develop the friendship and cooperation existing between their people and governments with the view to promoting a 21st century-oriented partnership of good neighbourliness and mutual trust;

COGNIZANT of the need to promote a peaceful, friendly and harmonious environment in the South China Sea between ASEAN and China for the enhancement of peace, stability, economic growth and prosperity in the region;

COMMITTED to enhancing the principles and objectives of the 1997 Joint Statement of the Meeting of the Heads of State/Government of the Member States of ASEAN and President of the People's Republic of China;

DESIRING to enhance favourable conditions for a peaceful and durable solution of differences and disputes among countries concerned;

HEREBY DECLARE the following:

(1) The Parties reaffirm their commitment to the purposes and principles of the Charter of the United Nations, the 1982 UN Convention on the Law of the Sea, the Treaty of Amity and Cooperation in Southeast Asia, the Five Principles of Peaceful Coexistence, and other universally recognized principles of international law which shall serve as the basic norms governing state-to-state relations;

(2) The Parties are committed to exploring ways for building trust and confidence in accordance with the above-mentioned principles and on the basis of equality and mutual respect;

(3) The Parties reaffirm their respect for and commitment to the freedom of navigation in and overflight above the South China Sea as provided for by the universally recognized principles of international law, including the 1982 UN Convention on the Law of the Sea;

(4) The Parties concerned undertake to resolve their territorial and jurisdictional disputes by peaceful means, without resorting to the threat or use of force, through friendly consultations and negotiations by sovereign states directly concerned, in accordance with universally recognized principles of international law, including the 1982 UN Convention on the Law of the Sea;

(5) The Parties undertake to exercise self-restraint in the conduct of activities that would complicate or escalate disputes and affect peace and stability including, among others, refraining from action of inhabiting on the presently uninhabited islands, reefs, shoals, cays, and other features and to handle their differences in a constructive manner.

Pending the peaceful settlement of territorial and jurisdictional disputes, the Parties concerned undertake to intensify efforts to seek ways, in the spirit of cooperation and understanding, to build trust and confidence between and among them, including:

(a) holding dialogues and exchange of views as appropriate between their defense and military officials;

(b) ensuring just and humane treatment of all persons who are either in danger or in distress;

(c) notifying, on a voluntary basis, other Parties concerned of any impending joint/combined military exercise; and

(d) exchanging, on a voluntary basis, relevant information.

(6) Pending a comprehensive and durable settlement of the disputes, the Parties concerned may explore or undertake cooperative activities. These may include the following:

(a) marine environmental protection;

(b) marine scientific research;

(c) safety of navigation and communication at sea;

(d) search and rescue operation; and

(e) combating transnational crime, including but not limited to trafficking in illicit drugs, piracy and armed robbery at sea, and illegal traffic in arms.

The modalities, scope and locations, in respect of bilateral and multilateral cooperation should be agreed upon by the Parties concerned prior to their actual implementation.

(7) The Parties concerned stand ready to continue their consultations and dialogues concerning relevant issues, through modalities to be agreed by them, including regular consultations on the observance of this Declaration, for the purpose of promoting good neighbourliness and transparency, establishing harmony, mutual understanding and cooperation, and facilitating peaceful resolution of disputes among them;

(8) The Parties undertake to respect the provisions of this Declaration and take actions consistent therewith;

(9) The Parties encourage other countries to respect the principles contained in this Declaration;

(10) The Parties concerned reaffirm that the adoption of a code of conduct in the South China Sea would further promote peace and stability in the region and agree to work, on the basis of consensus, towards the eventual attainment of this objective.

Done on the fourth day of November in the year two thousand and two in Phnom Penh, the Kingdom of Cambodia.

For Brunei Darussaiam

Mohamed Bolkian
Minister of Foreign Affairs

For the People's Republic of China

Wang Yi
Special Envoy and
Vice Minister of Foreign Affairs

For the Kingdom of Cambodia

HOR Namhong
Senior Minister and Minister of
Foreign Affairs and International
Cooperation

For the Union of Myanmar

Win Aung
Minister of Foreign Affairs

For the Republic of Indonesia

Dr. Hassan Wirayuda
Minister of Foreign Affairs

For the Republic of the Philippines

Blas F. Ople
Secretary of Foreign Affairs

For the Lao People's Democratic Republic

Somsavat Lengsavad
Deputy Prime Minister and
Minister of Foreign Affairs

For the Republic of Singapore

Prof. S. Jayakumar
Minister of Foreign Affairs

For Malaysia

Datuk Seri Syed Hamid Albar
Minister of Foreign Affairs

For the Kingdom of Thailand

Dr. Surakiart Sathirathat
Minister of Foreign Affairs

For the Socialist Republic of Vietnam

Nguyen Dy Nien
Minister of Foreign Affairs

3. **Joint Declaration of the Heads of State/Government of the Association of Southeast Asian Nations and the People's Republic of China on Strategic Partnership for Peace and Prosperity**

(1) We, the Heads of State/Government of the Member Countries of ASEAN and the People's Republic of China have reviewed the development of bilateral relationship in recent years. We agree that since the issuance of the Joint Statement of the Meeting of the Heads of State/Government of the Member Countries of ASEAN and the President of the People's Republic of China in 1997, the relationship between ASEAN and China has seen rapid, comprehensive and in-depth growth and ASEAN and China have become important partners of cooperation.

   (a) Politically, our two sides respect each other's sovereignty and territorial integrity and their independent choice of development path. Guided by the spirit of the Joint Statement of the Meeting of the Heads of State/Government of the Member States of ASEAN and the President of the People's Republic of China in 1997, China has signed separately with the ten ASEAN countries political documents aimed at development of bilateral relations in the 21st century. In October 2003, China acceded to the Treaty of Amity and Cooperation in Southeast Asia, which demonstrated that the political trust between the two sides notably enhanced.

   (b) Economically, the two sides have strengthened contacts and exchanges for mutually complementary and beneficial cooperation. Cooperation in the five priority areas: agriculture, information and telecommunications, human resources development, two-way investment and the Mekong River Basin development, has made steady progress. In 2002, the two sides signed the Framework Agreement on Comprehensive Economic Cooperation between ASEAN and China, launched the process towards an ASEAN-China Free Trade Area and moved bilateral economic cooperation towards greater scope and depth.

   (c) In security, ASEAN and China have worked to actively implement the concept of enhancing mutual trust through dialogue, resolving disputes peacefully through negotiations and realizing regional security through cooperation. With a view to securing peace and stability in the South China Sea, the two sides signed the Declaration on the Conduct of Parties in the South China Sea and agreed to work on the basis of consensus towards the eventual attainment of this objective. The two sides have issued the Joint Statement on Cooperation in the Field of Non-Traditional Security Issues, under which active cooperation on transnational issues has been conducted, opening new areas of security cooperation.

(d) In regional and international affairs, ASEAN and China have engaged in productive cooperation. The two sides have joined hands in promoting the sound development of the ASEAN Plus Three cooperation, ASEAN Regional Forum (ARF), Asia Cooperation Dialogue (ACD), Asia-Pacific Economic Cooperation (APEC), Asia-Europe Meeting (ASEM), Forum for East Asia-Latin America Cooperation (FEALAC) and other regional and trans-regional cooperation mechanisms. The two sides have good communication and cooperation on issues of mutual interest and concern and have rendered each other support and cooperation in the United Nations, the World Trade Organization, and other international organizations with mutual understanding.

(2) We are pleased with the depth and scope of the mutually beneficial cooperation between the two sides. We agree that ASEAN-China relations have seen important and positive developments, extensive and substantive cooperation in all areas of mutual interest. We highlight the strategic importance of ASEAN-China relations to peace, development and cooperation in our region and recognize the positive contribution of such relations to world peace and development.

(3) In today's world that is undergoing complex and profound changes, the enhanced cooperation between ASEAN and China, as two important partners in the Asia-Pacific region, will serve the immediate and long-term interests of both sides and is conducive to peace and prosperity in the region. To this end, we agree that ASEAN and China establish a strategic partnership for peace and prosperity.

(4) We declare that the purpose of the establishment of a strategic partnership for peace and prosperity is to foster friendly relations, mutually beneficial cooperation and good neighbourliness between ASEAN and China by deepening and expanding ASEAN-China cooperative relations in a comprehensive manner in the 21st century, thereby contributing further to the region's long-term peace, development and cooperation. This strategic partnership is non-aligned, non-military, and non-exclusive, and does not prevent the participants from developing their all-directional ties of friendship and cooperation with others.

(5) We reiterate that ASEAN-China cooperation will continue to take the UN Charter, the Treaty of Amity and Cooperation in Southeast Asia, the Five Principles of Peaceful Coexistence, and other universally recognized norms governing international relations as its guidance, and the Joint Statement of the Meeting of the Heads of State/Government of the Member States of ASEAN and

the People's Republic of China in 1997 and other cooperation documents the two sides have signed in various fields as its basis.

(6) We agree that ASEAN-China Strategic Partnership for Peace and Prosperity is a comprehensive and forward-looking cooperation focusing on politics, economy, social affairs, security and international and regional affairs.

To this end, we agree to:

(1) Political Cooperation

(a) Strengthen high-level exchanges and contacts, consolidate and deepen understanding and friendship among the peoples of ASEAN and China and give fuller and more effective play to the role of dialogue and consultation mechanism at different levels.

(b) Proceed from the new starting point of China's accession to the Treaty of Amity and Cooperation in Southeast Asia to further enhance mutual trust and lay a solid foundation for bilateral relations.

(c) Continue consultation on China's intention to accede to the Protocol to the Treaty on the Southeast Asia Nuclear Weapon-Free Zone.

(2) Economic Cooperation

(a) Give full play to the respective strength of their markets and maintain the rapidly growing momentum of their economic relations and trade in order to achieve the goal of US$100 billion of two-way annual trade by 2005.

(b) Speed up talks on ASEAN-China FTA, which has become a key pillar in ASEAN-China economic cooperation, so as to ensure its smooth establishment by 2010, and hereby assist ASEAN's new members (CLMV) to effectively participate in and benefit from the ASEAN-China FTA.

(c) Deepen cooperation in key areas, such as agriculture, information and telecommunications, human resources development, two-way investment and the Mekong River Basin development, and earnestly implement long- and medium-term cooperation programmes.

(d) Support each other's endeavour for economic growth and development. China undertakes to strongly support ASEAN's drive in narrowing down the development gap and to assist the new members in the exercise. To this end, China shall increase its input in the Initiative for ASEAN Integration (IAI) and support cooperation at sub-regional level, including the Brunei-Indonesia-Malaysia-Philippines East ASEAN Growth Area (BIMP-EAGA), West-East Corridor (WEC), and the Cambodia, Lao PDR, and Viet Nam Growth Triangle. ASEAN is prepared to participate in China's western region development.

(3) Social Cooperation

(a) Implement the consensus of the Special ASEAN-China Leaders' Meeting on SARS, which was held in April 2003, such as strengthening cooperation in the public health sector. A 10 + 1 special fund for health cooperation will be set up and the 10 + 1 Health Ministers meeting mechanism will be launched.

(b) Further activate exchanges in science and technology, environment, education, and culture as well as personnel exchange, and improve cooperation mechanisms in these areas. Efforts will also be made to enhance tourism cooperation and deepen understanding and friendship between the peoples of their countries.

(c) Attach importance to and strengthen youth exchanges and cooperation and establish a "10 + 1" Youth Ministers meeting mechanism to broaden the base for everlasting friendship.

(4) Security Cooperation

(a) Expedite the implementation of the Joint Statement on Cooperation in the Field of Non-Traditional Security Issues and actively expand and deepen cooperation in such areas.

(b) Hold, when appropriate, ASEAN-China security-related dialogue to enhance mutual understanding and promote peace and security in the region.

(c) Implement the Declaration on the Conduct of Parties in the South China Sea, discuss and plan the way, areas and projects of follow-up actions.

(5) Regional and International Cooperation

(a) Cooperate on major regional and international issues for the maintenance of regional peace and stability, while maintaining the authority and central role of the UN.

(b) Maintain close coordination and cooperation under the framework of ARF and promote its healthy development. China supports ASEAN's role as the primary driving force of the ARF and its commitment to move the overlapping stages of ARF at a pace comfortable to all.

(c) Make the ASEAN Plus Three mechanism as the main channel to move forward cooperation and regional economic integration in East Asia and Asia as a whole so as to promote sustainable development and common prosperity there.

(d) Further promote ACD, APEC, ASEM, FEALAC and other regional and trans-regional cooperation schemes.

(e) Work for free and fair trade worldwide as well as a well-balanced development of economic globalization. China strongly supports an early WTO membership for Lao PDR and Viet Nam.

(f) Respect the diversity in the Asia Pacific, particularly the differences in development path, security concern, values, culture and traditions of the countries in the region. Work jointly to create an environment of tolerance and openness for cooperation and development in the region.

(g) Have a periodic review of the present Joint Declaration when necessary, taking into due consideration the dynamic development in the region and in the world.

Done on the Eighth Day of October in the Year Two Thousand and Three in Bali, Indonesia.

For Brunei Darussalam
HAJI HASSANAL BOLKIAH
Sultan of Brunei Darussalam
Prime Minister

For the People's Republic of China
WEN JIABAO
Premier of the State Council

For the Kingdom of Cambodia
SAMDECH HUN SEN
Prime Minister

For the Republic of Indonesia
MEGAWATI SOEKARNOPUTRI
President

For the Lao People's Democratic Republic
BOUNNHANG VORACHITH
Prime Minister

For Malaysia
DR. MAHATHIR BIN MOHAMAD
Prime Minister

For the Union of Myanmar
GENERAL KHIN NYUNT
Prime Minister

For the Republic of the Philippines
GLORIA MACAPAGAL-ARROYO
President

For the Republic of Singapore
GOH CHOK TONG
Prime Minister

For the Kingdom of Thailand
DR. THAKSIN SHINAWATRA
Prime Minister

For the Socialist Republic of Vietnam
PHAN VAN KHAI
Prime Minister

参考文献

曹云华. 东南亚的区域合作. 广州:华南理工大学出版社,1995.

古小松. 中国-东盟知识读本. 桂林:广西师范大学出版社,2004.

古小松. 东南亚民族 马来西亚 新加坡 印度尼西亚 文莱 菲律宾卷. 南宁:广西民族出版社,2006.

古小松. 中国-东盟自由贸易区与广西. 南宁:广西人民出版社,2002.

谷源洋. 中国缘何建立中国-东盟自由贸易区. 中国网,2002-2-25.

贺圣达,陈明华,马勇,王士录. 走向21世纪的东南亚与中国. 昆明:云南大学出版社,1998.

黄朝翰,陈晓芬. 中国-东盟自由贸易安排:机遇与挑战. www.ecdu.net.cn.

李荣林等. 中国与东盟自由贸易区研究. 天津:天津大学出版社,2007.

赵何曼. 东南亚手册. 南宁:广西人民出版社,2000.

刘底辉,周明伟. 东盟国家经贸指南. 南宁:广西人民出版社,1993.

刘咸岳,黄铮. 东南亚蓝皮书——2001~2002年东南亚发展报告. 南宁:广西人民出版社,2002.

中华人民共和国对外贸易经济合作部. 东盟自由贸易区及其发展动态. www.cofortune.com.cn.

中华人民共和国与东盟国家领导人联合宣言. www.china.com.cn.

新华网:www.xinhuanet.com..cn.

世界知识年鉴(CIA-The World Fact book):https://www.cia.gov.

中国-东盟自由贸易区:http://www.cafta.org.cn.

中国-东盟博览会网:http://www.caexpo.org.

新华网:http://www.xinhuanet.com.

中国日报网:http://www.chinadaily.com.cn.

中国外交部网:http://www.fmprc.gov.cn.

China-ASEAN FTA expected to be new engine to drive world economy. www.chinaview.cn,2007-10-29.

China-ASEAN Expo propels FTA construction. http://english.peopledaily.com.cn,2008-8-28.

Le Tian. China, ASEAN sign trade agreement. www.chinadaily.com.cn,2007-1.

Bangkok Declaration. http://www.aseansec.org/1212.htm.

Treaty of Amity and Cooperation in Southeast Asia. http://www.aseansec.org/1217.htm.

Declaration of ASEAN Concord. http://www.aseansec.org/1216.htm.

Framework Agreement on Comprehensive Economic Cooperation between China and ASEAN. http://www.cafta.org.cn.